THE NEW BODYGUARD
- A PRACTICAL GUIDE TO THE
CLOSE PROTECTION INDUSTRY

PUBLISHED BY:

CLEARWATER PUBLISHING LTD
NETLEY HALL
DORRINGTON
SHREWSBURY
SHROPSHIRE
SY5 7JZ
UNITED KINGDOM

WWW.CLEARWATERPUBLISHING.ORG

CLEARWATER
PUBLISHING

© KEVIN HORAK 2010
SECOND EDITION

ISBN 978-0-9557769-1-5

ALL PHOTOGRAPHS ARE THE COPYRIGHT OF KEVIN HORAK OR PERMISSION HAS BEEN GRANTED FOR THEIR USE.

COVER PHOTOGRAPH OF JENNIFER LOPEZ BY NEELY K VEE

A CATALOGUE RECORD OF THIS BOOK IS AVAILABLE FROM THE BRITISH LIBRARY

The New Bodyguard
A Practical Guide To The Close Protection Industry

By
Kevin Horak

CLEARWATER
PUBLISHING

WWW.CLEARWATERPUBLISHING.ORG

Contents

FOREWORD FROM THE AUTHOR

Close Protection is a craft. A skill that takes years of dedication and constant learning and development. Put simply, there is only so much and so many chapters that I could include within this book.

This book is a training guide and a manual of basic principles and disciplines. It is meant to serve as an introduction to those thinking of entering the industry, as well as a point of reflection for those who are already working within it.

It is not written with high risk assignments and hostile environments in mind.

For those who wish to work in the high risk arena, taking advice and guidance only from a book is not wise and 'top end' assignments can take years of training, perseverance, networking and skills development before the right kind of higher risk challenge is offered to you.

I have also decided not to include physical fitness training, self defence and close quarter battle training within the book – why? Because you cannot learn it from a book. These skills are very important and specialist courses exist and with a little research are not that difficult to find. Knowledge based skills is one thing, practical and physical skills are another.

The same can be said for Medical/First Aid Training. You need to learn it and become qualified in it. For that reason I decided to omit it from this book as there is no substitute for practical learning and qualifications from professional medical personnel.

This book underlines the need for training, 'delivered from qualified' practitioners in Close Protection.

I have also included some photographs of people in the public eye. These VIP's are people that I have worked with, met or been responsible for over the many years I have worked in this business. I believe it to be important to show author credibility, as some Close Protection texts are written without support of the author's credentials and therefore some 'working photographs' need to be shown.

All photography used is taken from assignments or meetings that were in public view or where there has been public record, or permission sought.

Some people in the business will inevitably disagree with this, there is a saying that "those that can, do; those that can't, teach" and so the decision to use some working photography addresses this point.

This book, now in its second edition has been well received by the Professional Close Protection Industry. Even our competitors recognise that there are few professional texts available on this subject written by those who look to promote the industry positively rather than just profit from it: often at the expense of their former Clients.

I and my colleagues are all agreed in developing standards and promoting accurate and necessary training. Whilst we generally don't seek recognition for our work we all know that there is a clear difference between the professionally trained Operator and those that just 'aren't'.

Throughout the book I have used words such as he, him and general references implying the male gender. This is for ease of writing and not a generalised opinion or statement by the author or publisher. Any references to the male gender apply equally to and include the female gender.

I hope that you will enjoy the book as an introduction to the training and disciplines that are necessary to what can become a long lasting, exhilarating and enjoyable career.

"Preparing to board a Clients yacht from a private tender in the South of France"

FOREWORD BY
LIEUTENANT GENERAL SIR JOHN FOLEY
KCB OBE MC DL
(Former Director of the SAS)

"The author with Sir John Foley"

Today the world probably faces the highest ever level of threat to personal security and safety. In recent years, there has been a steady proliferation of terrorism, insurgency, organised crime, extremist movements and others who are prepared to resort to violence against individuals, groups, property and assets of all kinds.

Nobody can safely assume they are immune from the risk of violence whether they are wealthy families or individuals, members of businesses or of the corporate sector, diplomats, royalty, politicians, pop stars or other celebrities or members of a uniformed service. Security and protection has become a serious concern for a wide range of people in any community in any country around the world.

In this security conscious world a "security presence" is now part of everyday life and this development has created a need for specialists in Close Protection. The training of such specialists is nowadays a well regulated business in many but not all countries and there is a recognised and qualification driven career path for its practitioners. Qualified instructors deliver training to the highest standards and training Companies must comply with strict codes of conduct.

Close Protection Companies have operated successfully in recent areas of conflict such as Iraq and Afghanistan carrying out a wide variety of tasks including embassy protection, convoy guarding and of course the protection of high risk individuals. But such high risk environments where there is a clear and present danger form only a part of the general work undertaken by Close Protection Companies around the world every day. The demands of providing an alert, effective and professional 24 hour Close Protection service often in the intense glare of the media places considerable strain on the relationship between the Client and the Operator.

Kevin Horak explores these pressures and explodes many of the myths associated with Close Protection providing a factual account of the real world realities of working in this challenging business.

He has written a comprehensive guide to best practice in the Close Protection business. As an up to date, current manual of basic principles and standard practices it is an essential and invaluable guide for the beginner but will also serve as a useful reference work for the more experienced practitioner and for those who teach at Close Protection centres.

THE NEW BODYGUARD

A PRACTICAL GUIDE TO THE CLOSE PROTECTION INDUSTRY

INTRODUCTION

If there is a single profession that is much misunderstood it is that of the Professional Bodyguard and the Close Protection Industry.

Forget the extravagant lifestyle, befriending celebrities, attending film premieres and driving top of the range vehicles, these perceptions could not be further from the truth.

The Professional Close Protection Operator is in a league of his own. Proud, experienced, intelligent and someone of integrity. Not the stereotypical public image of an oversized man in a suit and sunglasses.

The term "Bodyguard" is clear by definition – one who protects the life of another. However, most professional companies do not use this term, preferring the more appropriate description of Close Protection Operative (CPO) and therefore avoiding any stereotypical viewpoints.

In this industry we are security specialists at the elite end of the security business. This is not a statement of arrogance but a fact. Training can take many years and only the truly dedicated will succeed. To become an expert you will need to acquire a wide knowledge of the security industry in order to be trusted with the protection of someone's life, their family, their business or their assets. Not something to be taken lightly.

Succeeding in this industry is immensely satisfying; however there are some serious sacrifices that you must be aware of right from the start. It will constantly interfere with your family life. The Company, the Client and your career will **always** come first before anything else. Every phone call is different; working in different locations, with different people, even possibly in a different time zone. You can never be prepared enough and will continue to learn every day.

The professional Close Protection Industry is staffed by modest people who generally blend into society and do not brag or try to impress. Those who stand in public places boasting that they are experts in the *'Security and Bodyguarding Industry'* will always gain raised eyebrows and attract the contempt of the true professional.

This business is hard work, a lot of hard work which at times can be thankless, monotonous and dangerous. You will quickly realise if you are cut out for such work. Many professionals thrive on it and you will work in a variety of circumstances where situations can be thrown at you very quickly. Quick thinking, commonsense and confidence are vital ingredients that only experience can teach you – the more you work the more you learn and the better you become.

Your actions as a Close Protection Operative may have to be instantaneous where you have to react to the now in real time and may be judged by others. If you are working with a Principal Client who is in the public eye you may also be judged in a glare of the public media where everyone will have an opinion, including your peers in the Close Protection Industry.

For those who really cut it in this business, a liftime of satisfaction and achievement lies ahead.

It is an unavoidable cliché, but to succeed in this industry you will need to be the best. You will also need to earn the respect of the company you are working for, your team and those who are close to you when it really matters and especially those who will genuinely "watch your back".

"Conducting research in Mexico City with Clearwater Senior Operations Manager, Henry Pattison"

CHAPTER ONE

WHO & WHAT IS THE CLOSE PROTECTION OPERATIVE?

THE CLOSE PROTECTION BUSINESS IS FULL OF DIFFERENT
CHALLENGES IN DIFFERENT ENVIRONMENTS

CHAPTER ONE

WHO & WHAT IS THE CLOSE PROTECTION OPERATIVE?

Those who work in the Close Protection Industry come from a variety of backgrounds, all with different outlooks of what this industry is and what it has to offer them.

Background, experience and various individual disciplines offer different working opportunities. But it is right to state that many views of this business come from the "public image" of this industry and therefore it is important that some of these misconceptions are swept away right from the start.

It is clear that the general public do not appreciate the complexities of this business and often make assumptions visually from what they have seen on the television or on film. This misconception mainly stems from the celebrity protection industry where (historically) the celebrity is often protected by unqualified staff or those of a 'particular look'. This has happened throughout the entertainment industry for many years, especially across the music and film business. These mobile barricades offer no help to the image of this industry in any way.

What "qualifies" someone to work in any facet of this business is often open to interpretation. Background and training are very important and in some countries (such as the UK) there is now mandatory licensing to allow you to work legally. Different countries, different employers and different Principal Clients mean that someone who is qualified for one particular assignment may well not be qualified for another. Working in a designated war zone and undertaking high risk Close Protection duties (often referred to as PSD - Personal Security Detail) is far removed from the red carpet film premier in Los Angeles.

"Advance preparation has it's own complexaties, especially when in another language - in the picture I am talking through a translator in Azerbaijan"

Always do your research and establish exactly what training you need, make sure it is delivered from qualified practitioners of the Close Protection business. Find out if licensing is required for the type of work you want to do and the regulations of that country.

Close Protection for the most part remains 'unseen' with a significant proportion being in operational planning, advance preparation, threat recognition and risk countering. As a consequence the public are not aware of how the 'real' work is done. The celebrity side of the business is the part of the industry that is 'seen' and it is therefore assumed that everyone who works in this industry must be four feet wide and six feet tall as standard, relying on brawn and an ill-fitting suit rather than brains.

Public And Common Misconceptions

High Pay

The subject of money is one of the first questions asked by anyone considering this profession. You need to know *"What is the pay like?"*
It is generally "assumed" that working in the Close Protection industry is highly paid; this is not always true and this business like all others is driven by influencing factors (more to follow).
It must be stated that the Close Protection industry, like all other sectors of the security industry is very competitive. For those seeking employment there are far more "CP" companies around now than ever before. Also other security companies who historically have a background involved in the static patrolling type of business are now "branching out" into this specialist business, often providing inexperienced and unqualified individuals. This has had an adverse effect and has reduced the price of services as competing companies try to undercut each other. It is a fact that some Clients will be price driven as opposed to those who are service driven where they are backed up by a company whose individuals are proven to deliver.

Long standing and successful companies have earned their reputation by providing a very professional service. These companies can command a higher fee as their reputation deserves it. A company with a short trading history may not have this influence and if you are working for a fairly new company you may have to work for a lesser fee.

Be realistic as to what you consider to be an appropriate salary. However, it will not be for you to determine what you get paid. (Unless you are working directly to your own Principal Client). When working for a company, even an established one, the days of dictating your fee and that "I will not work for any less than" are gone. (The exceptions are some Special Forces Operators or those who have served 'their time' in the industry and are highly regarded and trusted).

If you have secured work through your own merits and are not working through a Company (i.e. you have gained your own personal Client, more commonly referred to as a Principal), you will need to consider his standing to determine what you charge for your service.

Before you can make any possible calculation of your professional fees, or if you are considering what a Close Protection company are offering you; you must take into account the following:

- How many hours will I be working?
- How many days a week/month?
- How many days a year?
- What is the risk assessment of this Principal?
- What is the Principal's status?
- What is the Principal's line of business?
- What is the Principal's ability to pay?
- Is the pay commensurate with the risk?

The list can be exhaustive but ultimately you must ask yourself if you can afford to take the job?

Considerations

Careful consideration must be given for accepting the employment as you may earn very good money if looking after a Principal on a good daily rate for four days a month. But what if you have no other means of income between these days? Your overall pay may even fall below the minimum wage over a monthly period, if that is the only work you have.

If working for a Company, pay criteria will be determined by them. Even if you are a very experienced Operator, do not try to negotiate your fee with a Company. If the fee offered to you is not enough, politely decline the assignment.

You also need to consider your Principal's wealth and what is the value of your service? If you were working for a corporate body to protect an asset, your fees should be higher if this asset is worth millions.

There can also be misconceptions when working with celebrities. If you read that a celebrity may earn $20 million per film, it would be a natural assumption that when working for them you will be very well paid – this is not always the case.

Unless you are contracted directly to the celebrity (some do this), the chances are that your service may be engaged by their management where security is just another service provision along with housekeeping. You may also be engaged by the film Production Company, promoters/sponsors or public relations companies. Therefore assumptions about a celebrities wealth being a factor cannot always be taken into account.

Footnote: Never detail names of Clients/Principals in your professional résumé as this can be a breach of confidentiality; it is also viewed by Close Protection employers as unprofessional. Every employer understands that a résumé must show a working background and if you are ever unsure consult with the company you were working with. Generally it is acceptable to detail the company or in the case of celebrities, their Agent. Never detail the person you were protecting.

Generally speaking, what most people earn in a week is roughly what you want to be paid per day and in some cases it should be much more. These figures are all well and good, but if you are only working 2 days per month, then extra employment will need to be considered! At the outset of their career most rookies coming into the CP business will often have to undertake other forms of security related employment.

Although we welcome competition, in this industry it must be stated that competing companies will drive down fees and unless you are a veteran of the industry you may have to consider working for a lesser fee.

I have heard of a company employing people in Europe and paying them minimum wage per day. Rookies are taking this work as they need the experience to develop their résumé. Companies like this regrettably are going to damage this industry as the service will continually decline if a Principal is regularly paying a fee well below standard.

Before accepting an assignment always be sure of the amount of work you are undertaking and whether you can afford to work at that rate.

Travel

Travelling is a necessary part of life for a Close Protection Operative. However the misconception is that this is a glamorous and luxurious lifestyle. Travel will take various forms but in all cases it is very time consuming and most importantly tiring.

If you have never worked abroad before, the thought of flying to an exotic or interesting location will no doubt be 'exciting'. If your sole basis for considering the Close Protection Industry as a career is to travel then you are making a poor choice and should consider the Armed Forces/Military instead. Everyone enjoys travelling the first few times, but you will rapidly discover it to be one of the most tiresome parts of the job.

Travelling is only a means to an end.

Travelling rapidly becomes a formality and your temper will shorten when there are delays. These delays will extend your working hours and will create a mad rush when you arrive at your given destination; this could possibly lead to your Client/Principal becoming irritable and may result in you receiving the backlash of this temper.

One of the most important considerations of travelling is that you will still have to protect your Principal at all times. If you are on a plane, your Principal may take advantage of the in-flight facilities. He may watch a film or enjoy a drink whereas you will have to remain vigilant at all times. When your Principal is relaxing, you are still working and at times if you have been travelling for many hours, the thought of your day's work 'really' starting at the other end can be daunting.

If you know that you are taking a long haul flight with a Principal and that you will have to work when you get off at the other end, a Principal cannot expect you to remain vigilant during a 10 hour flight with a full day at the other end. If you have team members with you, you can take it in turns to get some rest or if working solo do not be afraid to ask to seek clarification of the rules and the Principal's expectations of your service.

Luxury Hotels

Dependant on the exact type of Close Protection you are undertaking and what position you hold in the team, many of your tasks may require you to work from a suitable hotel either directly with the Principal or within the surrounding area.

If your Principal can afford a professional Close Protection service they will certainly expect and demand to stay in a top hotel usually of a five star status or above.

"An example of an executive suite from a London Hotel"

A considerable difference between an experienced professional and an amateur when working and staying in executive hotels is often clear to see. The amateur can be distracted by the whole environment and may lose focus on what they are there to do.

The fact of the matter is that it is rare for you to get any of the benefits of the hotel or its facilities. Depending on how many are in your team, you may obtain some free time to use the gymnasium but rarely anything else.

On bigger teams you may work on a split shift system (usually a 12 hour shift). If you are working a system like this it is not advisable to be seen too much out of working hours, 'Loitering' in the hotel where your Principal is staying is very bad practise and is frowned upon. If you do get down-time it is best to go elsewhere. The hotel is your operating base and a bed for the night and nothing more. You are there by necessity and for no other reason; you must never lose sight of this.

True Case

I was once told of a 'Bodyguard' who loved getting carried away by this lifestyle that he could not personally afford and didn't mind who he told about it. He would happily ring friends from the suite of the hotel he was staying in (using the Principal's phone bill) and he would describe the hotel in every detail as a way of showing off and trying to impress people. This behaviour would become a regular pattern and he would also describe the celebrity Clients he worked with in detail, including their likes and dislikes and any unusual requests they had.

I have heard a rumour that he doesn't work much any more and the industry does not miss him. This sort of behaviour will always be found out. Always remember who you are and why you are there. Be professional at all times. After all, it is a small industry and word of unprofessional Operatives travels.

Executive Cars

Limousines, Bentley's & Rolls Royce are just a few examples of vehicles that belong to the rich and famous. These are the types of vehicles you will be working with. Your mode of transport if you are protecting a wealthy Principal will often be by these means. You need to have a driving licence if you are going to work in the CP industry generally but it is a must if you are intending to work solo. Even in large teams on high risk assignments everyone will be expected to have a driving license.

If you are undertaking a Close Protection training course – fine, but before you invest in any other specialist security training concentrate on obtaining a driving licence.

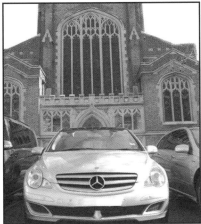

"A classic executive vehicle, a Mercedes AMG R 63"

8

It may be stating the obvious but you do not own the cars; you have no right to the cars and certainly never 'take the car out for a spin'.

You may from time to time be asked by the Principal to use the car to collect a person or property. Always be sure that you are insured to do this. Never drive through the centre of a city in a sports car with the roof down trying to pretend that you are someone you are not (yes, it really does happen!) – It may impress your friends but will not impress the Principal if you are found out or involved in an accident.

Never take any car belonging to the Principal for your own personal use including your shopping, going to the gymnasium or popping round to your friend's house to show off and explain how successful you are these days (yes, this happens as well!).

Of the many things that will anger a Team Leader the most is taking a car off task, (even a pool/team car), without permission.

If you ever feel that a team member is abusing or taking advantage of their position; either from their behaviour in hotels or to the use of the Principal's cars, deal with it. If you can't deal with it yourself, report him to your Team Leader and get him removed. Never forget that a person who behaves like this is a liability and will be endangering you and your Principal. Your team is only as good as the weakest link in that team, the actions of one can get a whole team sacked or killed.

Never take a vehicle off task at any time.

Glamour

For someone who works their whole life in the monotonous drone of a factory from 9 to 5 Monday to Friday their perception of this industry may be that it is glamorous. There are perks to this work and some have already been listed, but glamorous is not a word I would choose to describe it.

Protecting a Principal or a business is a very stressful and demanding career, particularly if you are working alone or in a small team that is under constant pressure. You may enjoy moving from place to place and every time your phone rings never knowing where you will end up. This appeals to most who work in this industry and definitely keeps life and work interesting. Unlike most careers, many who work in this business do not know exactly what or where they will be the following week, let alone the following year.

However, your role may be standing outside of a hotel door all night, when every minute feels like ten. This aspect of Close Protection can be (frankly) soul destroying and you certainly earn your money under these circumstances. Irrespective of who you are and your background, this constant vigilance is more a discipline than a practise.

People interpret glamour in different ways, and living a lifestyle that the average person does not have will always be perceived as "glamorous".

Heroic

People believe that if you undertake this line of work you are a 'tough guy'. This type of person will say 'I am a Bodyguard' when asked what he does for a living. Having a tough mind – yes; this supersedes everything else as mental strength is a true test of 'tough' in this industry.

The true professional in this business seldom looks anything like a 'Bodyguard' or at least what most would expect. The best I have employed or worked with over the years are often termed in the Military as 'Racing Snakes' and wouldn't cause any attention in whatever situation they are in; they most certainly would never answer 'I am a Bodyguard' when asked what they did for a living.

Suits & Glasses

Most of your professional duties, especially public engagements, will require you to dress appropriately and relevant to the event: this will often be a suit and tie.

Your Principal, his agent or your Team Leader should advise you of the dress code as part of the pre-assignment briefing.

You may often see Bodyguards wearing long trench coats. This may be a necessity in the winter or in some cold weather climates; but you may also see these being worn in the summer when someone is trying to convey an image. Trench coats can be very uncomfortable and restrict your movement making you very slow and incredibly hot!

Never wear sunglasses unless you have to and certainly don't wear them to 'look the part'.

Footnote: I have often seen celebrity 'Bodyguards' in magazines wearing sunglasses when attending <u>indoor</u> events which are poorly lit. This type of 'Bodyguard' is useless and in this situation will not be able to see 3 feet in front of his face. His commitment is to his image and his expensive suit and will brag to his friends as he makes the tabloid press with 'did you see me with so and so'. These types of celebrity Bodyguards are a relic of the past and are an embarrassment to a professional industry and profession. – I just wish their Principals realised this.

Away from public engagements the dress code may be very relaxed. Always have clothes to suit the occasion and take spares. Don't show up at the beach in a suit or a business meeting in a pair of shorts. Use your commonsense and you will find that your Principal will appreciate your efforts.

"The public face of the Close Protection Industry?
Suits, glasses and an outstretched hand"

Befriending Celebrities

It is often taken for granted that if you work in the Close Protection Industry you will be working with celebrities. Within this professional industry it may come as a surprise to some but it is often stated that the true professional should avoid such work!

A grade 'A' celebrity may have employed Close Protection for a long time. If this is the case they will understand your role and why you are there and a working relationship may be easier than with someone who is employing Close Protection for the first time.

The public's behaviour can be very strange and quite disconcerting at times where celebrities are concerned. If you are ever in a room with celebrities and you are not working; take the time to sit down and observe what goes on. I have seen top business executives completely embarrass themselves around celebrities from being over servile to comments that are 'far from tactful'. As a psychological exercise it is very interesting and gives you a valuable insight to the way things work; especially with a very manipulative and clever celebrity who will always get what they want. Watch and learn how they do it.

When you work with a celebrity you are there in a professional capacity as a trained security professional. If you ever need to make a point or address a matter of security, do so with respect and courtesy. There are some celebrities who may ignore or disregard your point of view, (like all Clients) and if you show that you are nervous of them, you are now like everyone else – a fan. This is definitely not in your job description. Be firm and professional. The majority of celebrities will respect your point of view and equally respect you if you can speak to them as you would anyone else. By being honest, with no pretence and especially no egotistical or exaggerated behaviour.

True Case

A colleague of mine once told me about someone he had just seen working in his local nightclub. This person had indeed worked with some grade 'A' celebrities; when he was not doing this he worked as a door supervisor. This particular person would tell anyone who was lame enough to listen about the celebrities that he had worked with. My colleague overheard him being introduced as a 'friend of the stars'. This sort of egotistical behaviour is grossly unprofessional. If the Close Protection Company he was working for found out about this he would (or should) be fired instantly.

"Paparazzi pressure can make working with celebrities incredibly difficult"

Satisfying

I have already covered many of the preconceptions that people level at the industry. The realities are much different. – I am not trying to paint a gloomy picture but an accurate one as this job is not meant to be "exciting". When an operation has gone completely to plan and the Principal, team and your employers are happy it can be an exhilarating feeling. Job satisfaction; definitely!!

Physical Presence

It is a common misconception that you have to be a huge man to work in this industry – this is completely untrue.

Admittedly big guys have their uses. They are good for hiding behind.

A few years ago such men specialised in being a barricade against the media. Those days are long gone. Such behaviour would now earn a lawsuit in today's modern claims culture age.

Big people reading this may think that I am being crass. It is true that size may convey confidence and presence and this can be of benefit in some situations but it most definitely does not apply to the professional business executive who is looking for someone more discrete.

Just because someone has a large frame does not give them the automatic right to work in this Industry. To rely on the size of someone or for them to be employed solely for this reason always has the potential to end in disaster.

The most desirable attribute for employment in this industry is the ability to work both as an individual and as a team member. Someone with common sense who is confident (but not arrogant), honest, loyal and experienced.

*" Presence can be demonstrated through professionalism
rather than relying on body size"*

14

CHAPTER TWO

DESIRABLE CHARACTERISTICS

WHERE POSSIBLE; FORMATION DRILLING IN A TOWN CENTRE OFFERS GREAT EXPERIENCE OF PUBLIC INTERACTION

CHAPTER TWO

DESIRABLE CHARACTERISTICS

First impressions are vitally important in the Close Protection business. Your ability to gain sustained employment will often rest on the particular qualities that you display both at interview and operationally on the ground.

Most of the points listed in this chapter sound like common sense, but many Operatives frequently experience the same difficulties, particularly in the early stages of their career.

When you meet a Principal or other employers for the first time – sell yourself and show confidence in everything you do and say. Don't exaggerate or be over confident, just demonstrate your natural abilities, let them feel comfortable and reassured in your presence.

A true skill of a successful Close Protection Operative is someone who can find regular work where he makes the Principal or employer feel safe and secure in their presence irrespective of the situation. If a Principal is suffering from stress because of a threatening situation and you portray an image of confidence, (not dismissive arrogance) you can remove a considerable weight from their mind.

Consider the following points and how they relate to you:

Communication Skills

No Principal will ever seek to employ someone who speaks too loudly, speaks over them, or in some cases does not speak at all. Someone who gives the impression that they know it all very rarely succeeds at the top end of this business where humility and integrity are the best attributes. Generally, speak when you are spoken to.

When asked a question, do not make the mistake of replying "I am sorry sir I don't have an opinion on that". Some training schools and books recommend this response which may, at first, appear the professional answer to give. However, if you continually repeat this answer you become unapproachable, unworkable and ultimately unemployable. In this industry good CPO's are often referred to as "grey men". Someone who blends; they are professional and do not attract unwanted attention to themselves or their Principal. You will need good communication skills as you will from time to time be asked for comment.

Inter-Personal Skills

The majority of assignments within Close Protection generally involve working with others, sometimes as part of a large team with multiple Operators. There may be drivers, personal assistants or managers to name a few. Issuing instructions to those who are not directly part of the security team has to be delivered with tact and (polite) authority. In professional security teams there should always be a chain of command, in other support services this is not always the case. In all scenarios solve problems and try not to create them. Someone who lacks the required communication skills will never last in a team and even more so when working directly to a Principal or his representatives.

Personal Tidiness

When you are on an assignment; even outside of working hours you need to maintain your appearance. A lazy approach to your own appearance suggests a lazy approach to your work and in high risk scenarios this is exactly the signs that a threat may look for.

If you have a generalised guardroom do not leave it in a mess. Make sure you clean up after yourself wherever you can. The guardroom will often be on the Principal's property and as such he could walk in at any time. If you ever use anything of the Principal's, no matter what it is, make sure that you return it or replace it as you found it.

"A professional operations room must be kept tidy at all times"

Personal Hygiene

Embarrassingly you may not be aware if you have a hygiene problem until someone actually tells you! Commonsense should prevail here but it is surprising how often this happens. Look after yourself and present yourself at your best at all times. Male Operatives should shave regularly or trim their beard - facial hair is not always appropriate. Wash your hair and keep it smart.

If you are working in hot temperatures wear suitable clothing as sweat patches and heavy perspiration will look unsightly. If you know that you suffer from the heat try to cover your back and under the arms as best as you can. If you are working in a team and a team member has hygiene problems it is always best to tell them, no matter how difficult you may find this. It is not an exaggeration; if someone has hygiene issues and you are in a car on a warm day it will antagonise the Principal and the whole team can suffer the wrath of this. Do the right thing and tell someone if they have a problem.

Presence

One of the keys to being a successful Close Protection Operative is your personal presence and self-confidence. There will be times where you will need to convey a strong presence and confidence within the assignment. You do not need to be a huge person to have presence. Use your eyes; stand straight and show absolute awareness and vigilance in everything you do. A true professional will always show presence. Presence exudes confidence and will be recognised and appreciated by your Principal.

"Presence is a vital part of successful Close Protection"

18

Appearance

Dress and groom yourself to suit the occasion, never over or under dress or have a hair style that means you have to regularly check yourself in the mirror. Personal appearance should require minimum fuss.

Personality

A good personality will always shine through and some of the points I have already made will only add to this. Having a friendly disposition may make you more 'communicable' but always remember your place.

Ultimately it will be the Principal's decision whether he wishes for you to be communicative with him or not. It may take some time to develop a 'relationship' or understanding between the Principal and the CPO. In any event 'relationships' generally only develop on small teams or when working solo.

Strictly speaking a 'relationship' with the Principal should never happen as overfamiliarity breeds contempt. When working on assignments in a small team or even if you are working solo there is always a potential for a relationship to develop. If a 'relationship' starts to develop, that may generally be interpreted as unprofessional. However, some Principal's genuinely will become used to seeing you and on occasion will want to talk to you about things other than security.

Contrary to what most training and Close Protection texts dictate it is not unprofessional to communicate with a Principal when that is what the Principal wants to do. However a lowering of professional standards and over familiarity can lead to a lack of discipline, which will lead to a loss of effectiveness as a professional CPO.

Education

One person's opinion as to whom or what defines 'educated' is not the same as another's. In this business, life experience far exceeds academic excellence. Having lots of qualifications does not necessarily mean you have any life experience or that your professional opinion as an 'educated' person counts for anything based upon actual fact.

It is not a requirement that you have a University degree but you must give a feeling that you have had some form of balanced education; this will give the Principal confidence. Ignorance to general circumstance and etiquette will have a serious effect on employability at some levels.

A Principal and employer will look for someone who has the ability to communicate at all levels and for some this is not easy.

You are a reflection of the Principal at all times and he must be confident that you do this correctly.

Dedication

Demonstrating commitment to the task in hand and the safety of your Principal should not go unnoticed either by the Principal directly or your employer.

To work in this industry at the top end takes immense dedication as you should be continually creating new goals for yourself to become better and more effective in your career. The most successful Operators in this industry often start with little or no experience at all. It takes time and perseverance to reach the peak of your profession.

Loyalty

You need to display loyalty to your Principal, the task and your employer.

Footnote: Never bite the hand that feeds you. It regularly happens throughout this industry all of the time that an 'employee' may try to take work from the employer. This is a constant problem with freelancers who give their own business card to your Principal or an associate and say "why don't you call me directly next time". This is completely unacceptable and grossly disrespectful to the Principal and the company you are working for. If a freelancer has to give a business card for any other genuine reason he must inform his employer without delay. Generally speaking you should never tout for business. If you do, (And your CP company finds out) you can be fired instantly. Although the majority of CP companies do not work together, they do communicate. All CP companies appreciate being told about those who may try to steal contracts from them and by the method used.

My company 'Clearwater Special Projects' has generalised business cards which we give to team members when on assignment, if they come into contact with someone who asks for a card – they are given a Clearwater one.

Create a Strong C.V.

This can be particularly tough for the beginner who needs experience. At some stage a company or organisation will have to take a gamble on you, and it will be a gamble, so do your best. Keep plugging away and try to stay with a company that you think will give you the opportunity to prove yourself.

Extensive Training

Whenever investing in training make sure you conduct extensive research first. You need to be sure this is the industry for you. Read up on the subject as much as you can to give you an idea of the disciplines that come with this industry. Be honest with yourself and your capabilities to establish what you really need.

I have trained many who, once they got started, realised that the work was not what they thought it would be. Although they finished the course to gain a qualification they don't always seek employment. Training is an absolute necessity and it is helpful for you to develop new skills all of the time.

There are many training companies and many specialist skills to be studied, however the training must be relevant. Make sure that you do not empty your bank account or life savings in doing this and ensure that your training company has your best interests in mind. When you invest in training make sure that it is employable training and practical in its approach. For example there is very little need for counter sniper/counter revolutionary courses in the vast percentage of most professional assignments – so why waste money on them? Such training can also raise questions in some countries.

There are many companies that offer specialist training but always check their reputation and don't just judge them from their website.

All training companies should have good quality literature and be able to send it to you; this will give you an idea of their standards. The statement "all you need to know is on our web site", is not good enough.

"Training must be relevant, how many times will this type of training be beneficial in a general street situation?"

When booking a training course find out whom the company is approved by to deliver the training and what is the exact qualification that you will be gaining.

If it is a specialist course it may not be formally recognised (as a qualification) so you will need to establish what the training company's status is within the industry. This is incredibly important because if it is not a formal qualification you will receive a 'Company' certificate. Prospective employers will want to know that you were trained by a credible organisation.
Try to establish in advance who the instructors are, that they are the right calibre to teach you and that they are qualified to teach!

If you have any uncertainties ask the training company if you can visit them first. Any company that refuses you a visit to their office or training centre should be avoided. If you are investing a lot of money to be professionally taught you have every right to inspect the company and its facilities.

It is bad practice to just show up at a Close Protection company unannounced. You should always arrange an appointment. You may also be asked to provide identification when you arrive.

"A professional Close Protection Company should deliver exactly what you need to know"

Operational Experience

One of the most crucial factors in a well presented résumé is your operational experience. This will determine the rookie Operative from the Professional Operator.

To start in this business you may have to go to some lengths initially to obtain your first assignments, this may include working under the usual pay rate to develop your résumé. If you are someone who wishes to progress in the industry make it known to your employer's right from the start that you wish to take on new opportunities and challenges. Most employers will understand, as this industry is made up of likeminded people.

Over the years I have received résumé's detailing operations that should not have been talked about. To have a Team Leader of another company or Military personnel contact me regarding what I "may have read" is embarrassing, both for the person enquiring and the person who has sent the résumé. If this ever happens I always remember the person who has sent the résumé as this immediately gives the impression that they cannot be trusted. What I look for in a résumé is information I need to know, not what I don't need to see.

Try to gain as much knowledge as you can along the way, as well as suitable references where possible.

The plain fact is that when it comes to being selected for work, you will usually be competing against others. The Close Protection company will always employ the best people that they can – because they can.

Don't be dispirited by this. If you are entering this field as a career consider it as a two year project to become trained and develop a network of contacts. This is a specialist business after all and like all specialist businesses you can't just walk straight into it.

"Clearwater Operatives working under considerable pressure whilst protecting a Grade 'A' celebrity Client"

Sell Yourself (First Impressions)

Try to create the best résumé that you can and store it on a computer so you can update it regularly.

Try to meet the Head of Personnel/Human Resources or the Operations Manager of the Close Protection company you are pursuing. Do not be offended if they initially say no to a meeting or if you are initially greeted by a junior member of staff instead. An Operations Manager has little time to meet prospective employees.

If you cannot get a meeting, send occasional e-mails to say how you are and ask if anything is developing (as they know you and you have permission to do this). That way the personnel manager or someone similar will remember you and hopefully will respond positively.

Do not make constant telephone calls. There is a fine line between being keen and irritating. You may also call at a very bad time. By calling an employer you are taking their time directly, by emailing them they can respond at their leisure.

If you do get to meet the Operations Manager or obtain an interview with the company, always dress appropriately and be confident on your arrival. Try not to look nervous when you meet him and the other members of the team.

Be Well Read

Watching and reading the news and keeping in touch with world affairs is very important, you need to be as well informed as possible. Your opinions may be asked for and depending on the type of Principal you are working with it may be completely relevant to the way you do your job.

Try to have a 'basic' knowledge of politics and religion but never get involved in discussions on these topics.

A Close Protection company will often have Clients of different religions and varying political views. Having an understanding of the current religious and political climate is very helpful when Principal profiling and compiling a threat assessment in the early phases of an operation.

Always try to avoid conversations that could place you in a difficult position and matters of religion and politics will always be deeply personal; use your common sense to avoid such a compromising conversation.

Integrity

Always be honest with your Principal, employers and your co-workers. True integrity always shows and unfortunately is not a virtue that everyone possesses.

Integrity is a major factor in re-employment not just to the company but the Principal as well.

Never lie to an employer in an effort to gain work. This has happened time and time again and even heads of organisations are not always truthful. The most common untruth is someone claiming to be a former Special Forces Operator or from a Government agency. This happens on a regular basis.

Don't forget that most credible Close Protection companies can usually check this with one phone call. Don't ever do it because in this line of business you will always be found out, usually sooner rather than later.

True Case

I remember being approached by someone claiming to be a former British Government Agent from MI6. In fact he duped a whole string of companies and name dropped and bragged as best he could with companies in the UK and the United States. Eventually he name dropped once too often and we received a phone call about him. After investigation it was found that he had worked for the British Government but only as a desk clerk in the Civil Service – Not even remotely the same thing!

Control Your Ego

Never forget who you are, why you are there and the responsibilities you have. Trying to impress your Principal with an over-inflated ego of stories of what you have done in the past does nothing to improve your employability – in fact it's quite the opposite. Be friendly, personable and honest; a valued member of the team; someone who your Principal as well as your colleagues can rely on.

CHAPTER THREE

WHERE DO CLOSE PROTECTION OPERATIVES COME FROM?

THE CLOSE PROTECTION INDUSTRY HAS SUCH A WIDE DEMOGRAPHIC OF CLIENTS, THAT OPERATORS WITH A VARIETY OF BACKGROUNDS WORK IN THIS BUSINESS

CHAPTER THREE

WHERE DO CLOSE PROTECTION OPERATIVES COME FROM?

Civilians

It may surprise some readers with a Military background to learn that most Close Protection Operatives have little or no experience in uniform. They have previously worked with celebrities or in the entertainment industry, have been involved in residential security or the transportation of assets. Their initial background will often be from the static guarding and door supervision/night club security professions.

Well trained civilians can make excellent CP Operatives. However there is a big difference between an Operative and an Operator. Civilians often do not have the working background or meet the criteria for high risk assignments and working in hostile environments. This can also be true of the corporate community as well, where regular trained and proven discipline is required. This may sound like a sweeping generalisation and is definitely not true of all. Civilians are excellent communicators and can be a very good Client liaison especially with Clients who require a 'less formal' approach in lower risk category assignments.

Female Close Protection has been a major growth area of the CP business for some years with many being recruited from a civilian background. From the female business executive to a male Principal who prefers to have a female/s on the team for the protection of his children or wife, there is a diverse and equal range of opportunities.

Female Close Protection is in such demand that there is an industry shortage of qualified and experienced female Operatives. Due to such demand often newly qualified female Operatives can walk straight in at the top end of the industry; something that their male counterparts may have to wait years for.

Former Military Personnel

Definitely the preferred choice of the corporate executive and the high risk arena. The business/corporate end of the Protection industry is completely dominated by former Military personnel. A civilian may struggle in this part of the CP world. However things are changing. Years ago civilians and Military personnel would very rarely work together but with a far more open market place changing so rapidly it is now not so unusual for both communities to come into contact

27

together. Generally speaking, Former Military personnel will always prefer to work together, particularly on advanced assignments where detailed analysis and information gathering is necessary. High-risk environments and the carriage of firearms in the world's 'hotspots' and high risk theatres are not the place for civilians who do not have the experience required for such difficult and skilled tasks.

If you are a civilian entering this industry you must appreciate the special skills possessed by former members of the armed services. They will have probably worked in different environments from you and will have a greater experience of countering difficult situations and thinking on the ground under pressure. Indeed if someone is of a Special Forces background they will often **only** work within their own groups and any civilian will always be seen as the weaker part of any team. It can take years before a civilian gains the respect of Military personnel, especially those from a Special Forces background.

One of the most frequent types of phone calls that my company receives is from potential students from a civilian background who wish to work on the 'world-wide circuit'. They may also refer to firearms as a primary part of what they want to learn but they have no training or experience with them. If this is your goal then pursue it, but remember you are trying to enter a world where you will have to compete against Military people for work. A CP Company and its Clients will very rarely select someone to work in high risk environments (*dependant on regulations of a given country*) where that person has no experience of firearms or professional training. Training on a shoot them/blast them up course for one week or attending a 'Walter Mitty Counter Sniper' course will not hold you in good steed against a Military specialist who has carried firearms for over twenty years.

Former Military Operators make ideal Close Protection specialists due to the training and disciplines they have already received. They are trained to work as a team as well as individually and are self sufficient. They can give and take orders without question which will always make life easier for a Team Leader.

If you are a civilian entering this industry, it is a competitive field and for 'top end' assignments you will certainly be competing against Military Operators. If you have the opportunity to work alongside Military people you should take it, as there is always a different view and tactical approach to be learned.

The Unemployed

Someone who is struggling for work and may have been unemployed for some time may consider this work as a way forward or as a complete career change. We must now be honest; employment in this business can be up and down to say the least, certainly at the outset until you have established your position within a company or worked regularly as a freelance Operator on *"the circuit"*.

Work in this industry is not a quick-fix solution to your current unemployment.

Most CP Companies will seldom consider someone who is unemployed. They will normally be looking for Operatives who have enough security experience to suit the assignment in hand and they will assess this with what the actual requirements of the Principal are. If there is a lack of experience there **must** be a professional qualification or a certificate from a recognised company showing the exact training you have done.

If I am ever speaking to someone who is unemployed and who has no experience of specialist security at all I try to be honest with them. I know this costs us some training business over the years, but if you are considering this career from afresh you must regard it as a minimum two year project and you need to be sure before you invest your savings in this direction.

Operatives must be professionally trained and this costs money which someone who is unemployed can ill afford. My company receives numerous enquiries from people who have paid a lot of money to other firms for training on the promise of substantial employment at its conclusion, only to be met with disappointment.

"Close Protection carries a great deal of responsibility; qualifications from approved companies is a must"

If you are unemployed study and research this industry before undertaking a training course. Be sure that this is right for you and be positive that this is what you want as a career.

You must consider the whole of the security industry for work and you may have to start at the bottom. There is **no excuse** for unemployment in the security industry; jobs are always available in the static guarding sector and you should use this as your training ground. It may not be what you want to do but it will get you on the ladder of progression.

The CP Company that you have trained with should recognise your persistence and see that you are trying everything you can to get work. Try to develop a comprehensive résumé and obtain references where possible.

Some also join the Reserve/part time Forces to obtain Military experience, and in some cases you get paid for it! All of this works in your favour in becoming a more credible employee.

If you are unemployed please take this advice on board and if anyone ever tells you that it will be easy, be wary as this is not how it works in the real world. Not just in Close Protection but any specialist career.

The Bodybuilder

There is a time and a place for bodybuilding but it does not fall within the working hours of a CP Operative.

From my experiences with bodybuilding I can say with all certainty that it is the most dedicated of all sports. I have great respect for the world standard bodybuilders who give their life to their sport. It is exactly for this reason why competitive bodybuilders should not work within the CP industry.

A professional's patience will boil when someone who is a 'big guy' thinks that because of their size they have the automatic right to work in this industry. As already mentioned, this industry needs people who can think and make accurate judgements before the use of muscle or using body size to intimidate others.

Bodybuilders by their sheer weight and muscle density can be slow and their overall size quite simply can take up too much room; this may sound like an obvious statement but in a working scenario a Principal will expect a lot of space and generalised privacy. When travelling in vehicles and general 'moving around' if the size of someone encroaches upon the Principal's private space too much this can lead to anxieties and a restless or ill tempered Principal.

Bodybuilders pre-competition are particularly difficult to work with especially if they are following a very strict diet regime and trying to remove their body fat. This will make them drowsy and irritable and is not practical for the professional environment. Going to the gym once or twice a day is not workable at all and will create more problems than resolutions.

Bodybuilders do however create presence, and are 'more suitable' for the celebrity Protection field where image is important. Big men in suits can look appropriate where status symbols are needed rather than expertise in threat countering.
By the very nature of how a bodybuilder trains, their strength is very powerful in short bursts; however most burn out really quickly and endurance fitness is very unlikely.

In general, bodybuilding within the CP industry does not fit in and any bodybuilders pursuing this field would do better to concentrate on fitness and aerobic exercise rather than anaerobic bodybuilding.

The Door Supervisor – Club/Night Time Security

Door supervision is a commonplace and very visual part of the security industry. A testing and demanding business, it is often unsung from the shear difficulties that face the modern day door supervisor. To secure premises in the face of a few hundred drunken people is never easy and is often testing to say the least. If you look at door supervisors in your local town or city you will see that there is a high turn over of people as few can ever 'cut the mustard' for a long period of time.

Door supervision is a good training ground for future CP Operatives, as you will learn restraint, control and communication skills. We train excellent doormen and doorwomen who move into the Close Protection industry.

However there is the occasional door supervisor who has done their job for a long time and has a 'reputation' at local level. This is the type of person who thrives if a celebrity happens to make a guest appearance at their venue. They may watch over them and then boast to their friends that they have acted as their "Bodyguard" – this is not the same at all, but commonplace nevertheless. Often door supervision companies use these opportunities to promote themselves as 'Bodyguards' and market this as an extra service that their company now offers.

Door supervision is a tough job and I had my share of it in the early days. Door staff, when trained correctly, can have a great future but they must make a choice.

They may face confrontation every night of the week and all it takes is one person to push you too far and your career in the Close Protection industry could be over. You have to make the right choice to suit you as both jobs often **do not** work together.

The Martial Artist

Martial artists show a great desire to work in this industry. This stems from their training, where they have great confidence, ability and dedication in what they do – common traits of the professional CPO.

The very positive attribute to a martial artist working in this industry is that they have been trained in self control, discipline and they have goals which they wish to aspire to. Their training does not need to be done every day and most are very calm and collected people.

Unfortunately there is the occasional rogue who trains because he enjoys the idea of being tough and hurting people. Fortunately these people usually demonstrate their true colours early on if they undertake CP training as this type of person will have an ego and this will always show.

Any martial artist must be realistic about what he is doing; high kicks to the head *(or the Ninja death grip)* are not practical in the street environment.

Close Protection CQB (Close Quarter Battle) training is far different from many styles of martial arts; its techniques are often quick, effective and uncompromising in its approach.

I have a great respect for the martial artist as usually they are following a path of self-development and can make excellent CP Operatives. However the same applies with all; the security industry as a whole must be considered and the fact that someone has numerous black belts and fighting skills does not mean that they have the ability to do this job.

Never forget, if you have to rely on your martial arts skills, you may have made serious mistakes for it to get that far. Martial art skills are a secondary factor, not a primary factor in the Close Protection Industry.

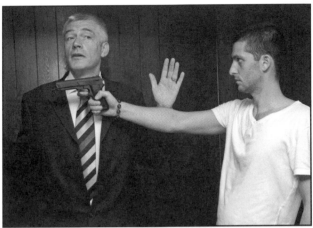

"Close Protection close quarter battle training is far different from any styles of martial arts"

Still Interested?

If you consider that most professional careers take three to five years to become qualified, it may surprise you that to become a fully qualified expert in the Close Protection field may take you up to fifteen years. It is very rare for someone to be a full expert in **all** areas and frankly it is not recommended as life is too short.

Some examples of working roles in the CP field are:

- **Close Protection (Personal Escort Sections)**
- **Residential Security**
- **Advanced Security Teams**
- **Maritime Security**
- **Asset Protection**
- **Working As a Surveillance Specialist**
- **Foreign & Domestic Assignments**
- **Becoming a Professional Investigator**
- **Professional Witness Service – (Acquisition of Evidence for Police and Court processes)**
- **Risk and Threat Analysis**
- **Security Assessors**
- **Being a Safety Trainer**
- **Working as a Research Agent**

No-one knows it all, irrespective of their background. Wherever you go to be trained in this industry always treat instructors with respect because they *(should)* know more than you and are there to help you. That knowledge is what you are paying for.

Make sure you check an organisation before you train with them and ask others in the industry for their opinion of that particular company. Where training and operational companies get unfair press is that they cannot employ everyone. Some people who fail a course will blame the training company. Nothing can be done about this. Close Protection is a specialist skill and the training is tough – and so it should be. With any form of specialist training it is not for everyone and a percentage of people will fail.

If you undertake specialist training consider it as a learning exercise. If you get employment in the future with that company then that is a bonus.

One of the most common questions asked of us is *"do you guarantee work?"* Nobody can do this across a phone line in this industry, as you don't know anything about the person who is enquiring? In every profession or trade, the fact that you may have done some training does not mean that you can walk straight into that career.

A CP Company may have taken years to successfully secure work with some of their Principal Clients. Employee selection should be a thorough process and if any company guarantees work to you over a phone line (as you are a stranger) – keep clear of them.

At the outset consider training as a stepping stone or a rung on the ladder. The fact is, if you want something badly enough you will get it and persistence pays off in this business.

Why Become A CPO?

It may seem that that I have covered a list of negatives which may not sound altogether very encouraging. It is not meant this way, but these are crucial points that need to be covered very early on so any myths or misconceptions are addressed at the outset.

It is important if this industry is to progress that it maintains the right direction of true professionalism. There are many reasons why someone may wish to work in this industry as there are equally many benefits.

To surmise we can consider four main points which the professional will strive towards.

1. **Money**
2. **Job Satisfaction**
3. **Benefits**
4. **Potential for further advancement**

Money

Without trying to contradict some of the opinions already expressed, you can earn good money working in this industry when your career is in full flow.

After your early days of obtaining *'some casual work here and there'* you should be progressing with the company you are working for or may consider working as a self-employed/freelance Operator for multiple companies.

At the outset your network of contacts may be limited and you will have to work with who you know. In the future, as you experience other assignments, your network will develop and you will expect to be paid a comfortable wage commensurate with the nature of the work you are undertaking.

When you are working at the upper end of the market, particularly in business/corporate protection, your wage will increase dramatically. This will of course be dependent on the threat level, location, and the numbers in your team, duration of contract and what responsibilities you have.

There is a fine line between charging your services at a professional rate and scaring a potential Principal away by quoting too much. Generally, cost your services after consideration has been given to the Principal's status, the threat, the country/environment you are working in and exactly what type of role in Close Protection are you taking. Always try to use your network and your personal loop of contacts to find out what people are charging and what is considered reasonable.

The golden rule is never quote too low. Most Principal Clients who are used to CP (especially in the corporate sector) know how much CP costs. Quoting too low is a direct reflection on you and can be interpreted badly as this is how you value the safety of the Principal. Principals used to the service will expect to pay a wage worthy of their status.

If you are unsure always use your loop for guidance on accurate fee quotations.

True Case

On a few occasions we have lost what could be potential new Clients when in their initial opinion we have quoted too high. They have gone to a cheaper firm that has proved unsatisfactory. Most then usually come back to us as they recognise that we provide a professional service. We are not prepared to be flexible with fees unless carried over a long duration of contract. Our fees are based on reputation and quality of personnel.

Work, particularly in the investigations and surveillance side of the business, can often be one-off, and therefore the price is high but relative to the task. Our Principal Clients know and understand this.

Job Satisfaction

It doesn't matter if you are working solo or with a team, if everything goes according to plan there is immense job satisfaction. Never forget that huge responsibility falls upon you. You are there to protect someone, their image, their business or their property. This can never be taken lightly and can weigh heavily on your shoulders. For a Principal to re-employ you and have absolute trust in you is a good feeling. For them to trust you with their family and business affairs is something that cannot be replicated in other forms of employment.

"A professional team should be slick and operational phases should flow"

Benefits

Whilst there are drawbacks to a dedicated career because of the commitments that are required, there are also many benefits. You may travel to destinations or work in environments that may give you immense pleasure and a fascinating and often educated insight into how others live in varying world cultures. You may develop language skills and other work related experience that makes you more employable in the future.

You may also work with an excellent team of people whom you will come to trust and work with again in the future. Good friendships can be made and most people I count on as friends have some association with the industry.

All of these points can be very satisfying and is the drive for a lot of Operators to keep working. Take each assignment as it comes and try to get the best out of it, create a good impression to get re-employed in the future.

Potential for further advancement

Some people are quite happy working in the local factory or for a corporation and dedicating their life to this service or company. Being told what to do 9-5 every week, with each day being the same as the next. The majority of CP Operators would not be content with this, as their outlook often prefers them not to know what they are doing next month, let alone doing the same thing in five years time. Professional Close Protection Operators are very driven people who want to achieve more and experience different environments and do something 'different from the norm' and definitely far different from what the local factory can offer. Whilst this business can be insecure and lacking the guarantee of a regular wage, the perks outweigh this tenfold; not forgetting that a CP working wage per day is often what most would earn per week.

However, it is worth addressing the statement that if someone works as a Bodyguard, *"don't they value their own life?"* On the contrary; you train to live and develop your skills to be the best you can. This may sound full of clichés but it is a reality. After all, we train to live, not to die.

Advancement takes different forms and encompasses all sorts of roles, either to develop new skills, or to move up the rungs in a team or company, progressing to management and team leadership.

This is a very big industry; from being a team member, to working on foreign assignments, investigating espionage, being involved in counter surveillance operations, practising close quarter combat to studying criminology and abnormal psychology. These are just a few of the tasks undertaken within this diverse and skilled profession.

"Clearwater red carpet team, World Music Awards 2006"

CHAPTER FOUR

EMPLOYED/SELF EMPLOYED?

OBTAINING YOUR QUALIFICATION IS JUST
THE START OF YOUR CAREER -
AT THE OUTSET YOU MAY HAVE TO WORK IN OTHER
SECTORS OF THE SECURITY BUSINESS AS WELL

CHAPTER FOUR

EMPLOYED/SELF EMPLOYED?

Work in the CP business is generally self employed, working in a freelance capacity. For those coming out of full time employment or having completed a term of service in the Military or Police this can be a thought provoking and difficult decision.

There will be certain insecurities when a regular wage is taken away. For those from a Military background the lack of resources in civilian life is also worthy of consideration and will certainly be a shock.

After you have undertaken your training and become qualified you will then want to look for employment. When considering employment in CP, approach employers who are known in the industry and have regular contracts. Before any approach, make sure these are the type of assignments you wish to do and that you are honestly capable of completing them.

Generally speaking (and for obvious reasons) it makes sense to select a training provider that is also an employer. Some companies may not have work at that time and when you complete your training you may go onto an approved list. Others who have been with the company for some years will be contacted before you, this is inevitable.

Some companies are training suppliers to other companies that have very big contracts. After you have been trained do not expect your training supplier to do all of the work for you. Employment needs to be sought by you, not your training provider.

An established training organisation will have built up a reputation, especially if they have been training people for several years. A good organisation will provide you with a recognised qualification or a certificate where the name of the training provider 'carries some weight'; or the certificate may relate to an individual specialist skill. Some companies only train people in specialist skills such as counter surveillance or ship security and anti piracy for example. For these reasons some specialist courses are not qualifications and they are there only to teach you new skills, to help you develop your profile and range of talents. For these types of courses the certificate should be a graded certificate, otherwise it is effectively useless as it doesn't give any guidance to you or a potential employer how well you did.

Training courses that are "attended only" are generally worthless as you will receive a piece of paper to say you were there but offer the reader nothing else. From your point of view you may have performed very well on a course and the person next to you may not. Why then should they get exactly the same certificate as you? Courses should always be pass or fail or at least have instructor assessment reports so a training reference can be obtained. References are not always given with certificates and often have to be requested by the applicant.

Ensure that the training course that you are undertaking will genuinely develop your résumé.

Always ensure that you receive the original qualification certificate and not a photocopy. All certificates and references should be personally signed by either the head of training, the instructors or the company CEO and not with a printed company stamp.

All certificates should be attached to your résumé so they can be checked by CP Companies or any potential Clients that you approach directly. If in your country Close Protection licensing is mandatory you should photocopy this and attach it to your résumé as well as clearly stating your licence number.

Be very careful when investing your money in training, especially with companies who "guarantee" work. Those that genuinely guarantee work are usually when you are being trained specifically for hostile environments where that company has genuine contracts and they may be able to offer you employment.

Bear in mind if you invest in the training, do you have enough background and experience to work in a hostile region on your first assignment? Most people do not, and the company may not employ you in any event so the money you have invested may have been wasted. Companies must always be accountable for their actions and selection for employment in hostile environments can be a lengthy and testing process.

Over the years we have received a considerable number of complaints about companies guaranteeing work, only to find that a student will spend a lot of money and then be offered a contract in a country that no one wants to work in or to be offered no work at all!

When you look for work at the outset, research which companies are based in **your** area and at what level they operate at. Sending a new résumé to foreign companies when you are starting out is unlikely to be successful. You must be practical in your approach. Research CP Companies and known security businesses in your area and make contact with them. You never know, you may hit on something.

We receive many résumés from students who have just finished training but have no experience whatsoever. Although we understand that everyone has to start somewhere it would be very unusual for us to employ someone immediately unless he happened to fall lucky and approached us as something came in. If there is an opportunity the applicant needs to be tested and we are more likely to offer casual work to start with; a day here, 3 days there etc. It gives us a good idea of their abilities and how they work before trusting them with more regular contractible work.

"I established the Close Protection Federation to assist those who train with us. This is a mentoring service that we provide completley free of charge to our students. The student in the picture recieves her certificate of membership"

Continue to make yourself known to the companies in your area but never try to push your services too much as there is a fine line between being keen and being irritating.

Hopefully a company will give you an opportunity and try you out on a smaller assignment first. You may also return to your training company and try other courses to expand your knowledge of the industry.
The harsh reality is that it may take you some time to gain work as reputations need to be developed and work at the outset can be unreliable.

It is likely that when you commence your career you will be self employed or often referred to as "freelance".

"A smaller assignment may also mean experience in crowd management; this gives us an excellent indication of how the Operative works individually as well as in a team"

If you are self-employed you pay your own taxes and look after your own finances. To get paid you will have to invoice for your services and state within that invoice when you wish to be paid (in line with whatever agreement you have with that company).

When you are working as a self-employed Operator make sure that you are covered by your own insurance or that of the company you are working for.

Ensure that the employer provides you with a contract or supplies you with a working agreement or Client/working brief. With a contract you should always have your own-signed copy. Be careful of companies who refer to contracts but never offer you a physical contract to sign. It is essential for both you and your employer to have a contract or working agreement.

Many freelancers do not have their own insurance as cover is now incredibly expensive due to recent significant acts of terrorism. Some companies may ask you to sign an agreement that you are responsible for your own insurance. This is far from ideal but it can and does happen.

If I am speaking to a potential employee or freelancer Operator about contracts there may be some apprehension in signing a CP contract. The contract is there to protect **you** as well as the company and should clarify nearly everything you need to know about the task or what is expected from you.

Never ever sign anything unless you are completely sure!

Contracts and working briefs should be accurate at the time of writing and should be provided in good faith. However, by the very nature of this business things change by the day and agreements need to be updated.

The providing of contracts sounds like an ideal situation but the realities in the business are often quite different. A lot of short term work is often managed by phone calls. Situations can change in minutes. For short duration work you may get an instruction brief or assessment overview but no contract. For very quick response work you may not get anything at all other than a phone call asking you to be somewhere. That is a reality of this industry that has to react to events in real time. Paperwork, as important as it is, sometimes has to take second place to actually *doing the real work and getting out on the ground!'*

After you have worked on a few assignments with one company you may seek a full time contractual position or more varieties of assignment. If you cannot obtain more work from the current company you are working for, you may then decide to approach other employers. Most employers in this business will understand. After all, if contracts can't be offered it is a freelancers market.

When you are freelance you don't 'belong' to anyone and freelancers often work and network with multiple companies. A big consideration for employers engaging freelancers is loyalty and trust. Employers will want to be sure that you are trusted to work on assignments and that there is not a clash of interests with other companies that you may work for. Do not be offended if an employer asks you to sign a confidentiality agreement as well as a non-competition agreement. This is standard business practice. If a CP business cannot protect itself then they will never succeed in protecting people and assets.

Employers will do this so that you don't discuss contracts with other CPO's or companies. It is not just to ensure the safety and privacy of the Principal but to stop the clash of interests between competing companies and is therefore necessary. In fact, if a company does not ask you to sign confidentiality or non-competition agreements I would question their business acumen.

After you have worked on the circuit for a few years you may get *'itchy feet'* and want to establish your own company. If you do this you will now become a competitor with your former colleagues or employers. *Now you will understand why they made you sign non-competition agreements!*

Running your own CP organisation is a serious commitment and not recommended unless you are absolutely confident of your personal abilities and are very, very driven. Vitally important, you must have a good team of people around you to support you throughout.

Trust

In a freelancer's marketplace the employer must have trust in who it engages (you). A company is at the mercy of those it employs at all times! When teams of freelancers work together it can be competitive to say the least and sometimes their competitive natures can cause problems.

Freelance CP Specialists are an elite breed of their own and when working together as a group (especially for the first time) it can be very testing. Jealousy of position, who has a better relationship with the company or boss, who gets paid more and lack of respect for the Team Leader can be a breeding ground for problems and resentment, even more so if someone thinks they are more qualified than another.

If you work in a team like this it is a very difficult position and you will have to 'play it by ear'. Reporting it to your company is the wise thing to do. However when the company investigates it will probably come out (or team members will guess) that it was you that reported the problem. If the company doesn't make the necessary adjustments the problem will only become worse. A company has a duty to protect its Client; if the company does not solve any in-fighting it will certainly fail in this primary task.

How to Invoice

If you are freelance you must raise an invoice to get paid. Different companies will have different terms of payment for different assignments. It is quite normal that if you raise an invoice for work it can be up to 30 days before you get paid. This is an industry standard as the company will have to raise an invoice to their Client first before it can pay you.

It is vitally important that when you invoice you ensure the details are **absolutely** right. If you send an invoice to the company and you have made a mistake, it is your fault, not theirs. The company concerned may not review your invoice until it is time to be paid and notice this error - you may need to re-invoice, meaning it will take even longer before you see any money.

Expenses

Expenses will only be permissible if they have been agreed by the company in advance. I forget how many times freelance Operators have tried to charge us expenses without our agreeing to it. If we haven't agreed to it – it doesn't get paid and no assumption should be made by you that a company will pay expenses. If expenses are agreed, it will be to a certain level of expenditure. If you exceed this level you must get prior authority from the company or be prepared to pay for it yourself.

If you incur expenses while on a task, this needs to be notified to the company as soon as is practically possible; you must always provide receipts. The company will need to know this in order that they can charge their Client. If you forget to charge expenses when you invoice and try to claim at a later stage it will often be too late and it can look grossly unprofessional for a CP Company to charge an expense bill to their Client when some time has passed since the completion of task.

Presenting the Invoice

I have included a basic template that will assist you when you present an invoice. The most important points are covered but some companies may ask for more information.

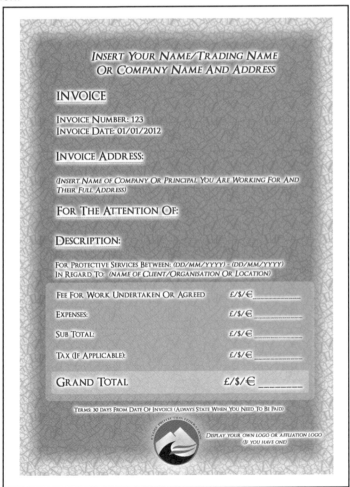

CHAPTER FIVE

THE PRINCIPAL

WITH ACTOR - MICHELLE RODRIGUEZ

IF WORKING WITH A CELEBRITY PRINCIPAL; THEIR
PRESENCE AND INTEREST WITHIN THE MEDIA IS
A SERIOUS CONSIDERATION

CHAPTER FIVE

THE PRINCIPAL

WHO EMPLOYS CLOSE PROTECTION?

The Rich

These are the primary clients of a Close Protection Operative.

Rich people come in different guises from *"old money"* to *"new money"*, aristocracy, the super rich, the desirable as well as the occasional undesirables.

An example of new money can be seen in the rise of 30 something's created from the information technology and computer games business over the last few years. The huge increase in popularity of television game shows offering huge cash prizes and national/international lotteries and their increased participation are creating new millionaires every day. Although lottery and TV game show winners may not be *'serious'* wealth, it is new to them and most find the adjustment of winning difficult to cope with. From the world wishing to be their friend to the novelty factor of employing a CPO, this is not the work of choice for a seasoned professional. Jealousy and envy of someone who has publicly won money, especially in deprived areas can make this difficult CP work.

Credible new money employment rests within the IT industry. The world is changing and it all comes with a press of a button. A few years ago the internet changed everything and the internet and IT business will continue to boom making those involved seriously wealthy. Close Protection does not just lie in protecting an individual or business it may also be a document or a programme or computer game. The release of top flight computer games now has the same release status as Hollywood films. Never close off any of your avenues or your thoughts to what can be protected and what needs to be protected.

Working with the rich is the most desirable end of the CP employment scale. Why? Because they can afford the service. I don't mean for that to sound as obvious as it may; but they can afford a professional service and operational procedures can be achieved properly rather than making mistakes on 'shoestring' budgets.

A really important factor if you are working with *'old money'* is that they are used to the lifestyle and the intrusions that inevitably come with professional Close Protection.

One of the defining factors for CP Operators and successful CP operations is how things are completely different between the two styles of money and how the intrusions are handled.

Firstly if you are working with new money and the Principal has never had Close Protection before you will be a certain inconvenience. For a Principal to have to tell a CPO where he is going and almost 'asking permission' will make him feel very uncomfortable and that they are being watched all of the time. The other scenario is that you will be a status symbol and will be introduced as the *'Bodyguard'* with a big grin, there to solve 'problems' rather than providing resolutions.

Old money may have used this service for a long time. They understand your role and what is required of you and would very rarely abuse that fact. Rich people have been the primary source of employment to the Close Protection industry for hundreds of years; this is unlikely to change and is the ideal environment for the specialist to work in.

"Passengers onboard a private tender prepare to join their ship in Monte Carlo"

The Celebrity

Overview

Working with celebrities and the entertainment industry generally can be a very interesting but pressured way of life; it is certainly an education on the ups and downs of a business that can change rapidly. It can have many perks and as long as you keep a level head and don't get personally involved in this type of lifestyle you may do very well.

However, like everything in life there are pitfalls and it can be a very large dark one if things go wrong when working with celebrities.

There is a distinct difference between the celebrity that needs Protection and those that think they do, (but don't). Celebrities have been employers of the Close Protection Industry for many years and CPO's are becoming more recognised as a necessary 'tool' or function of being a celebrity. To work with celebrities you must have an appreciation of status as there is a complete difference from the old status and graded celebrity to the new status that has just emerged on the block.

"Celebrity interest is still as big as it ever was. A whole street had to be closed in New York when this picture was taken of the actor Will Smith, on the set of I Am Legend"

Old Status

Old status may be someone who has either been successful as an actor and has made a lucrative living from it or someone in the music and entertainment industry who has stood the test of time.

If you were considering the status of a celebrity think how long they have been successful for or at the peak of their career, or have they reached that yet? Think of a celebrity that has been famous for over ten years and you may have a celebrity that could be defined as "old status".

Old status is the more preferential Client as they are so much easier to work with and although a generalisation they are not inclined to burn their money as much as new status. Old status have achieved where thousands of thousands have not. How they did it or if they are really that good to be there is irrelevant. Behind each successful celebrity is a very good agent.

A known celebrity does not just have a good personal agent but may pay thousands in fees to Public Relations (PR) specialists. Media PR agents are/can be separate from performing agents and representatives. Media PR agents can manage a story or manage someone who is in the press but will only be involved for a short duration. Celebrities can pay tens of thousands to the best PR agents each month and that agent's job will be to keep them in the press. Press exposure can be very lucrative for the celebrity, from being paid for media features or scoops (often called splashes) or for keeping their exposure high to gain more employment, sponsorships or endorsements.

Celebrity old status employment is by far the more preferred option and there can be many professional perks and long lasting contracts.

"Meeting a Principal for the first time, being introduced to the actor Hayden Panettiere"

New Status

For someone who has just hit international fame with their first block buster or landed a television presenting job, or their first top 30 hit, such new status often brings the desire (and sometimes the necessity) to employ a Close Protection service.

This new status can however be problematic and often requires considerable adjustment to this new way of life. It is an old cliché that you can be a victim of your own success. Nothing is truer than with a new status celebrity where pressures and lifestyle change overnight. If you consider what it may be like to suddenly come into money, (like winning the lottery) it may be an amazing but daunting experience. If you are 'new money' you may lose the value of money very quickly and problems associated with such new status can start. Every 'friend' they have ever met coming out of the walls, tabloid press digging out everyone that they have had a sexual relationship with, you can see the possible problems.

There is a potential that the new status celebrity, having found instant fame, may suddenly start to behave differently. Going out to clubs, being photographed everywhere, staying at the richest hotels, a new lover, divorcing your family and employing Bodyguards now become a lifestyle need.

One of the real problems with the new status celebrity is that they often do not employ well trained and disciplined Close Protection. Their friends and the local night club doorman who they met once stand a good chance of getting employed. This is rife particularly in the music industry.

You may think that I have painted a particularly bad picture of the new status celebrity. Not at all. Some are excellent Clients and have a level head and pursue their goals and succeeded where so many others have failed. Just be aware that if you work in this environment that many "new status" celebrities do not make it to "old status" and careers in the entertainment industry can be short lived and quickly forgotten about.

Pretending to be a Celebrity

Over the last few years the culture of celebrity has been pushed almost to the point of being forced upon us through frenzied interest in magazines and television. There are only so many genuine celebrities out there, so television has created its own through TV reality and game shows! These shows have a very short shelf life and those they feature......... even shorter.

For this short duration the media love them and everything about them and they will feature in the tabloid press with often low level sponsorship deals. The chances of these people who have found fame in this way really making a career out of their newfound fame is small indeed.

This brand of celebrity will usually have an agent within the first 48 hours of the programme finishing, but everything is as short lived as the 'fame'. Within 2-3 weeks the media that had loved them so much will turn on them and they will feature in the least desirable guest lists for parties and become a laughing stock, often referred to as the 'Z list'.

Why anyone should want their whole life probed in such a way is not easy to understand and they will never get any sympathy when it all goes wrong and ultimately disappear into oblivion.

Never forget this type of 'person' is seldom a celebrity in its truest sense. They have been on television and that is all. It is no more than an extended fifteen minutes of fame!

If you ever work with this type of *'Principal'* take all of the above into account and view the opportunity as experience only. A lasting contract is highly unlikely.

Agents and Public Relations People

There are many difficulties from a security perspective when working with celebrities and a primary reason is that you are <u>never</u> working with just one person.

Unfortunately PR people and agents often do not appreciate security risks. Why should they – it's not their job.

There are excellent agents especially at the upper tier of the entertainment industry. These agents are professionals in their own right who have had to work hard to get to where they are. If they have grade 'A' celebrities in their portfolio then they will definitely understand the role of CP.

An agent is an integral and necessary part of the celebrity's life and even at grade 'A' level you may be looked upon as a necessary evil. An agent or PR person may wish your Principal to attend a certain place and you know that this is a potential security risk. Never forget, unless you are greatly respected by your Principal or the agent (if you are employed directly to them), your opinion will come off second best. The difficulty here is that you cannot win. If you go to a certain place and nothing happens you have overreacted; if something does happen and your Principal is hurt, embarrassed or photographed in a way that they are not happy with, you may be blamed for this for not putting your foot down and being more assertive.

"With International Actor, Julian McMahon"

Celebrities are not always the decision makers. Although the most established will consider what particular roles they wish to work with, it may be the agent who is the mastermind in obtaining employment for them.

The professional agent can make an incredibly good living and may take 10-15% of the celebrity's fee. Multiply that by five top Clients and two films each a year and now you can see how much money is involved.

If you decide to pursue the entertainment industry for your CP work there must be an understanding on your part that if you work with celebrities you will be working with agents, as well as other professionals that are there to support the celebrity's career and profession.

Never forget that they have a living to make and that security may not be their top priority or primary concern.

Considerations

There are some celebrities that generally need Protection and there are some that don't.

A significant factor when working with celebrities is that the perceived threat can be constant and this can become very draining for them and you. You must also consider your own position and your former background. When you undertake celebrity work you need to consider that you may now become a figure of interest yourself. There are a high percentage of excellent CP Operatives that cannot risk this, especially those who have come from a Military or Special Forces background.

If there is no obvious threat then you may be working to elevate the status of a celebrity and as such this can be nice work if you can get it. The problem with 'status symbol' work is that you **may** tire of the work very quickly and the true professional will want challenges within his work, which this type of employment cannot provide.

If you are someone who has come from a specialist background before entering the Close Protection industry this type of work will probably not suit you as you may not wish to be photographed where ever you go. In some cases, if you are recognised you could be a liability to your Principal instead of protecting them. Always consider the paparazzi and the effect that will have on your Principal and you.

*"On the world famous Rodeo Drive in Beverley Hills, an area
used to the sight of Close Protection"*

Corporate & Business Executives

Corporate Business is the ambition of most involved in this industry. There are numerous perks and more reliability of full time employment. To work in the business sector is seen as very credible employment which can easily lead to full time and lasting contracts.

Such work is predominately the preserve of former Military personnel. The business executive will always be looking for someone who has been properly trained and there is no better training in the world than the Armed Forces.

It has already been explained why Military personnel make good Operators and are employable in this sector. However, the civilian Operative should consider that if you are to work in this sector, you will be working predominately with former Military people.

Working as part of a Close Protection team in the business community is not always a four/five person detail as many training companies would have you believe. You may be working by yourself and may have to undertake driving duties as well; your contract should explain all of this. This is far from ideal but nevertheless is a reality of this business. If you don't wish to undertake other duties such as driving – don't take the assignment. If you are by yourself or part of a smaller team there can be a lasting relationship with the Principal and this can lead to long term employment.

Working in the business environment can take you to many places and international travel may be commonplace. You will need to study the customs of a given country otherwise it reflects badly on you and your Principal. Regular travel abroad is not for everyone; you must be the right person for the job. Don't forget, travelling abroad brings with it new and additional risks!

A lot of corporate business is undertaken in 'difficult' climates where religious and political influences could be a very important factor. Working in your own country and protecting your business executive is one thing but working abroad may now be considered as 'High Risk'. Are you qualified to undertake this? It is for this reason that the Military specialist thrives and is so employable in this field. Weapons training, communication skills, working long hours on your feet and being vigilant is something that the average person just cannot do without training and practical experience.

You may find that if you are working for a CP company and you do an excellent job in your own country that they may replace you when travelling abroad. Don't take it personally. There will be a reason why they are doing this and you should consider what you can do to make yourself more employable in this field of work for the future.

You can pay a lot of money for specialist training because it is 'specialist' and the people training you are qualified in these unique skills. Only undertake the training if you really do need it. If not having these skills is costing you work then definitely invest in it. However, always check the credentials of the company that is delivering it and their reputation in the industry so that 'credence' of the training is valued in professional circles.

High-risk deployments (or being tested in some capacity) are the motivating factor for most; a professional wouldn't enter this field if he thought it would be all *'Driving Miss Daisy'*.

There is immense satisfaction from working in a high risk scenario and taking on the challenge. It's not just about protecting an individual (as you will see later in the book); it's much harder than that.

If you have never worked in a high-risk scenario, don't think you need to be an expert in jungle warfare or be a practitioner in close quarter battle *(most of the time, anyway)*. However, you will need mental agility and physical fitness and have the resources and ingenuity to take care of a variety of factors if things do go wrong.

Working in corporate business is the upper end of the VIP Protection market but it is not suited to all. If it is your goal to work in corporate business it may take some time and a lot of effort and dedication to acquire your goal; but if achieved it can have the biggest rewards.

Politicians & Heads of State

To work in this category of Protection is far removed from all the others. It is not normally open to the private sector and most falls under the auspices of Police Protection and Elite Units.

As with all categories of employment, things are changing as more work is outsourced to the public sector. It is a misconception that **all** members of Royalty and every Politician have Close Protection; this is not true at all.

I remember giving a lengthy radio interview for the BBC discussing protection of British Politicians and it comes down to simple mathematics. To protect each member of the British Parliament with just one CPO *(therefore not very efficient protection)* would cost the taxpayer over £1,000,000 British Pounds per week! The key word is "cost" – sometimes security just isn't affordable.

If every Politician at all levels was to be protected worldwide and this is to be paid for by the taxpayer there would be a public outcry. Other services such as teachers, fire-fighters and the medical professional *(which statistically have far more confrontation and history of being attacked)* are more at risk and they could call for their own Close Protection service – the list is endless.

The deciding factor is the budget and the appropriate use of public money. Priorities with public money often lay elsewhere and security in schools is one such example. Children being searched for weapons is not just reserved for inner cities but across a nation. The security industry and security 'acceptance' is more commonplace now and as such will continue to be a massive growth business for the foreseeable future.

"At Number 10 Downing Street, London"

"On the terrace at the Palace of Westminister, London"

However, in saying that, there continues to be an increase of attacks on Politicians around the world. When this happens it makes for massive media coverage with continual speculation and some accurate but also some inaccurate opinion from journalists. One may argue that by the very nature of politics and by being a Politician you cannot please everybody especially if they are in Government and therefore some risk 'comes with the territory'. They may disagree, but the financial facts are simple. Specialist Protection cannot be given to everyone.

Not many British Members of Parliament are protected and many do not receive even basic security training. It often surprises people that you can just ring up your MP for a chat or arrange a meeting. Members of Parliament are often grateful for any advice that you may be able to provide. However, do not go down this route unless you **really** know your job and can prove that you have the skills to offer professional advice.
Another consideration is that some Politicians are also becoming celebrities and continually court the media; they appear on chat shows that very rarely discuss political opinions or agendas, and some can be tabloid/celebrity based.

Be aware that if you work freelance and are ever involved with the protection of a Politician, you may become the subject of some focus as well. Always remember that if you are seen to be working with one political party, it is unlikely that you will work with another. We have Clients from varying backgrounds who have a broad spectrum of political interests. This is the reason why you should not get involved in politics directly. Imagine the damage you could do if you worked with two political parties at a crucial time such as an election!

Protecting the British Royal Family will always remain the preserve of the Police. I have heard people say to me in the past that they have looked after Royalty or the Prime Minister. What they mean is that they were on the security team at a venue which was being attended by them. This is not the same.

Business: Small & Medium Enterprises

For many years the Close Protection industry was the preserve of the rich and famous but changes in international business have made this a service that is now required by a much larger Client base.

Over the years I have given numerous speeches to the business community about the Close Protection and Specialist Security Industry and how security affects businesses in the modern era. I am there of course to promote our service and explain why the employment of specialists is necessary.

I have also spoken to smaller businesses that are shocked (to say the least) when I explain to them the dangers and pitfalls of modern business trading. From rogue traders and internal fraud to depreciation and industrial espionage. Despite these dangers many business people think:

1.   It will never happen to me
2.   We do not have a budget for this in our forecast figures, now or
       for next year
3.   We can't afford it

It's worth passing further commentary on all three points.

1.   It will never happen to me

Why? It happens to everyone else so what is different about you and your business?
This is what you should be thinking. You would of course present this far more diplomatically and choose your words carefully. Never scare businesses into employing your service. Bearing this in mind, you should make your point with tact and diplomacy.

Every business irrespective of what it actually does, will have a security related problem at some point. Admittedly many aspects fall more in to the investigation side of the business but do not close off your opportunities, as investigations and security protection are often linked together.

Sometimes in order to get an *'in'* with the company or business you are talking to you may have to promote the investigation route.

Footnote: never try to claim that you are something that you are not. Professional investigation is a career in its own right and if you do not have the experience to investigate, speak to another company that you know or the CP firm that trained you and seek their advice.

Be very careful when you promote yourself that you do not <u>scare the potential Client.</u> Horror stories of what has happened to other businesses can be used as examples but you must offer examples that are absolutely relevant and lessen the *'horror'* parts. Equally, stories of how you fought in combat, your martial arts skills and desert storm experiences may not impress the IT Company that think they have a rogue employee that needs investigating?

Never, never write to a company with your opening statement being *"did you realise that you could be a victim of terrorism'* or *'since 9/11…etc."* It amazes me how many companies really think this approach works. Bullying people into your service, scaring them or trading off events where people have been killed is completely unethical and grossly unprofessional.

Most people and businesses (unless they have had problems in the past or have personally received threats) think that it will never happen to them. This can make presenting yourself or your specialist services and skills difficult. When speaking to a business that may be considering employing a specialist for the first time, try to let them do as much of the talking as possible and look for a niche – there will usually be one.

2.   **We do not have a budget for this in our forecast figures now or for next year**

Quite right. No business will have an amount of money put aside with their accountants under the heading *"Resolving our Employee Problem'* or *'Hiring of Bodyguard to investigate our espionage issue."*
Most small and medium businesses will never plan for such an event; most trust their staff. Their goals are to expand their business. Unfortunately while pursuing this goal some things, especially the closer ones, are overlooked.

When meeting with a small to medium enterprise business it may be helpful to take a presentation with you on a laptop computer. If that presentation has 'bullet points' and photography it will help you to remember everything you need to say and the points to impress upon. This will help them to see your professionalism and give them ideas of how a specialist service may help them.

When you meet a potential business Client you must create an impression of absolute confidence (not arrogance) and show that they can trust you with business secrets and security related matters. If you can do this you may have sold yourself far better than you realise. I know many excellent Operators who cannot project themselves, train people or promote the service.

3. We can't afford it

What exactly can't you afford? The crash of your business because a rogue element stole your Client base behind your back? You can't afford for your competitors to know everything about you and your fees? You can't afford to investigate the thousands you have lost in stock that you think has gone missing but are not sure? You can't afford to employ us to send your vital document or programme that if lost could lose you a major contract and would rather use a standard delivery service? *And the list goes on.*

Never forget that *'Protection'* does not just mean the protection of an individual or a team of people. Effective protection requires the whole of an image, brand, business, products and secrecy to be maintained. As the majority of small & medium businesses would never consider engaging specialists *(particularly bodyguards)* to assist them, you must tread with caution, don't scare them or seek to over-impress them. Be honest, and advise – if the problem cannot be resolved, tell them honestly.

A true Close Protection specialist is one that can work in all environments and can adapt to all avenues of employment.

Victims Of Crime

This may sound like an area of employment to keep away from. Not necessarily so, but it is one to be cautious of. Some assignments, particularly anti-drug and child abuse cases can be immensely satisfying to work on. Out of all the assignments that you may undertake over the years these are the ones that you never forget or are the ones where you may think that you have made a difference.

A 'Protection organisation' can work in this field, usually in conjunction with official departments for the area in which the assignment is based. For these types of assignments you will often be working with the Police as well. A Close

Protection Company must have been trading for some years before being able to undertake this sort of work. Credibility and trading history must be proved due to the sensitivity of such assignments. For a company or an individual to work in this sector it requires skill and experience.

You will be required to know:

- The law and its implications
- Your rights, your Principal's rights and the rights of the Public (including the rights of defendant/s)
- Surveillance and evidence gathering skills
- Understanding and presenting physical and documentary evidence
- Excellent communication skills and understanding of the problems involved
- Basic knowledge of criminal and abnormal psychology (not essential but useful)

You will observe that protecting someone in this situation can be somewhat different from the 'norm'.

In most cases it will not be the victim that will call you for help; the majority of Principals in this sector cannot afford the service and require the government to pay. If the state is paying, you may well be expected to work in a variety of roles rather than just straightforward *'Close Protection Services'* and may have to try to obtain some evidence surrounding the Principal that you are protecting. This borders on a service which in the UK is called a *"Professional Witness"* – this is where you gather evidence. It is completely different from providing 'normal' Close Protection duties.

This type of work is incredibly challenging and a developing area of specialist security services. Some of the reasons include:

1. It is not the job of the Police to protect people. The generalisation of "Protect and Serve" is different from physical Close Protection services. This comes as a surprise to many but Police protection is not an every day service; this is also a considerable use of Police resources and is only used in rare circumstances.

2. The local authority does not have the ability to undertake this service themselves and certainly does not wish to use any extra Police or expend their Policing budget. For reasons of bureaucracy they often cannot act very quickly, unlike a commercial CP business.

3.   There are far better working relationships in the modern era between the Police, local authorities as well as outside agencies such as a CP company.

4.   Threats of attacks, intimidation and stalking (to name a few) are taken very seriously. Although there is legislation to assist those that are victims of these crimes, the lack of Police resources and overworked Police Officers swamped in paperwork does not necessarily mean that the legislation can be implemented or enforced. Therefore any outside assistance available is far more welcomed now. Private security is viewed far differently (and positively) by Policing and local authorities than it was several years ago.

Whilst this is not an exhaustive list it will give you some understanding of the positive views towards modern day specialist security services.

Point number 1 is of the most interest.

Despite public opinion, the Police are not there to protect people from a Close Protection point of view. This sounds like a contentious point, but it is not their main function and if it were so would be a complete waste of Police resources and core Policing would suffer.

Police Officers have a warrant of power to enforce the law and that is their duty and sworn oath. This is the fundamental difference between law enforcement and Close Protection/Private Security.

Working with a victim of crime is different from witness protection (in its truest sense) and often when a crime is investigated the level of 'Protection' is little as it is not the Police's job to do this.

You often hear of someone claiming to *"having Police Protection"*, usually because of some lowlife of an ex-boy/girlfriend or family member threatening someone. Usually what he or she means is that they have a phone line to the Police and may have a quicker response time than most.

For the Police to protect an individual as a victim of crime and not witness protection *(which is completely different)* would have to be an extreme case where there is already some substantial evidence and the expense would be justified. Budgets are always a consideration even with law enforcement.

There are a lot of negatives of working in this line of Close Protection.

- The risk level is usually high.
- You will very rarely have the resources of a team and will often be by yourself.
- You may be working with serious criminals or low life's who are the victims, you may have to protect someone like this.
- You may observe things and witness situations that are against your personal principles and you may find difficult to identify with, deal with and accept.
- You will definitely have *'difficult'* Principals from time to time as Principals in this sector do not understand your exact role and don't know what to do with you or what to say.
- Work will usually be of a short duration.
- Work will often not be very highly paid *(depends on the victim and their status)*.

And the most important – You cannot help but get involved

You can be the best of the best but if you are working alone and protecting a female who has to testify against her family for abusing her or protecting her from a rapist, pre-trial, you will always get involved in some capacity.

Never forget that a victim in this situation will see you as someone to talk to and to confide in. This is completely unavoidable and you will get dragged in and may be the *'new best friend'*. It is difficult because you must be professional but not rude. Nearly every time I have worked in this type of situation, the 'friendship' continues, fine in some cases but others can be a real problem and they may ring you every day and out of hours. Without sounding too materialistic – you are never paid for this!

My comments may sound very mercenary but you don't want to get involved. If you do, your professionalism will inevitably suffer and things may become personal. If things do become personal you will lose perspective and get angry with the case and what has happened to your Principal; it will lead to certain poor judgements. This is easier said than done and when I work on cases like this, I often take a little time off at the end to regain some clarity.

NEVER GET PERSONALLY INVOLVED

Nevertheless, this can be a very rewarding area of work. Whilst not perceived as *'top end'*, it will give you experience that hopefully you will learn from and it is a valuable insight into a different aspect of Close Protection duties.

"Evidence gathering as part of an anti-drugs assignment"

Crime & Drug Syndicates

It is a misconception that criminals and the "underworld" are not entitled to be protected. In the main this is not true, as everyone has the right to protection *(dependent on the country you are working in)*.

The public image of a *'Bodyguard'* can also be of someone that is on the edge and therefore associated with the criminal underworld; but it is a fact that underworld characters do use Close Protection, especially in the organised drug trade.

This type of lifestyle is fast and dangerous and appeals to some individuals, especially those who want to be a *'face'*. I have met quite a few over the years and with all *'faces'* they eventually make mistakes. The other fact is that it is easy to get into this line of business (at low end initially) and you will get work with no problem as long as you earn your reputation as someone who can be trusted.

It's the **type** of work that is the concern; firstly you will have to prove yourself to earn the trust and start to run small errands, which can only ever become bigger.

There are some genuinely naive CPO's out there who fall into the criminal trade by accident. Upon realising what you have gotten yourself into you may have already seen and done too much; the next thing you know, you are an enforcer. What started with the small debt collection may progress to you becoming the recognised muscle.

In this temporary world of *'glamour'* it is easy to forget who you are and where you initially came from, but it is always short lived.

In the real world the *'king pins'* of the drug syndicates and those that employ you often never get caught because they have people like you to do the dirty work for them. All work is usually cash paid, as crime is a cash rich industry with no records, therefore no comeback to them and the buck stops with you when eventually you get caught.

When it hits the fan you will be the first to know about it and your reputation will never be forgotten as someone who protects criminals.

If you ever work in the criminal trade and respected professionals in this industry find out about it, it's all you'll ever be good for; doing the jobs that no one else wants.

It may sound like a cliché but when you work with crime and organised gangs, once you're in your never out.

Never enter this line of trade under any circumstance - or on your head be it if you do.

CHAPTER SIX

CONSTRUCTING A RÉSUMÉ
AND
INTERVIEW TECHNIQUES

SIGNING CLEARWATER AS PRINCIPLE MEMBERS OF
THE BRITISH SECURITY INDUSTRY ASSOCIATION (BSIA)
CLOSE PROTECTION GROUP

STUDENTS COMPLETE THEIR TRAINING NOW AS
QUALIFIED CLOSE PROTECTION OPERATIVES

CHAPTER SIX

CONSTRUCTING A RÉSUMÉ AND INTERVIEW TIPS

After completion of your training, a well constructed résumé is the next essential point in obtaining employment.

It should be an outline of your professional education and personal history and offer a potential employer an understanding of your abilities and suitability for employment.

A résumé is your opportunity to present yourself in the best possible light where first impressions are all important. It is an introductory text that should be written specifically for the Close Protection field, indicating your strengths and why you should be selected for interview.

Irrespective of your background, a résumé should always be kept updated and should be circulated to the most prominent employers on the CP circuit. We have files of résumé's in our office and it is important for us to see how a potential candidate is developing in their career and what their range of skills and latest work experience is. If we are looking to recruit new Operators, reference to a résumé that is a couple of years old is no use at all. Résumé's need to be up to date, especially if the contact numbers and locations of Operators have changed.

What should the résumé include?

Many résumés don't make it past our filtering process. This is generally when there is not enough detail, irrelevant details, too much waffle, too much detail of work that should be confidential, name dropping and lack of presentation etiquette.

Golden Rule:

When you are applying for work you will be competing against other qualified people. Research the company you are applying to and identify with the employment you are seeking. Formally introduce your letter with *'Dear Sir'*. Find out who is the head of recruitment or Operations Manager and mark it for their attention. Always present a covering letter of introduction. A résumé that comes in the post (or worse by email) with no covering letter is lazy and un-professional. Frankly, this type of approach generally goes straight in the bin.

Emailing a Résumé

Documents/attachments that have to be opened by the viewer are the easiest way of virus transmission in computer systems.

As a rule we do not accept any résumé's that are submitted to us by email unless permission has been given by us in advance. The fact that we still get so many is an indication that applicants have not researched us enough or read our websites properly; therefore the approach is unprofessional and is often deleted at source.

If you wish to email a résumé, ring the company in advance and ask permission – this is basic etiquette. The recipient will then be expecting your email and this reduces the chance of it being deleted. The document can then be scanned to ensure it is safe from any potential virus. If permission has been granted, make sure you still have a note of introduction and in the first line a comment along the lines of *'following our conversation'* will be helpful as the potential employer should remember you.

Do not bulk email your résumé.

You may apply to many different employers but each application should be sent individually to each company. We receive many emails where our email address is one of 20 or more in a list. This allows us to see who else you are writing to.

Your contacts are yours and we do not need to know who else you are applying to. Sending a résumé by email to a list of companies is not a good way of introducing yourself to a potential new employer.

As a guide a résumé should contain the following points:

1. Full name and any other professional titles
2. Education and any qualifications
3. Work experience
4. Interests and Achievements
5. Skills
6. Referees

1. Full name and any other professional titles:

Your full name should be bolded and centralised at the top of the document. Abbreviations of your name are acceptable, such as Jonathan becoming John if you prefer. For formal identification reasons you should state if this is not your real name but an abbreviated one. If you have formal qualifications or professional memberships you can use your titles here, such as Dr or PhD. However do not exaggerate this. Having a string of the alphabet after your name will always raise questions. If they are professional qualifications – fine, if not, you will look very Walter Mitty. Some of our students who are members of the Close Protection Federation like to use CPF after their name. This is not a problem but if you list every CP affiliation you have an association with after your name, it will appear unnecessary and irrelevant.

2. Education and other qualifications:

Take this opportunity to inform the potential employer that you are qualified to work for them! If you reside in a country where licensing is mandatory include a photocopy of your licence, if not, always provide a copy of your training award with the application. A Close Protection employer is one of the rare trades that will base a decision of potential employment not on how well you did at school but how qualified you are now. Use this section to quote facts of how suitable you are and quote grades from schooling after you have got your main relevant qualification(s) clearly listed.

"Receiving the Approved Contractor Status from the (then) Heads of the Security Industry Authority. Clearwater were the first Close Protection Company to achieve this standard."

3. Work Experience:

Keep this accurate but brief. If you detail absolutely everything from a previous operation, the potential employer may view this with some concern. Work on the old basis of KISS *(keep it simple, stupid)*. State the employer and a rough description of the role you had. **Never divulge other employer's Clients on a résumé.**

4. Interests and achievements:

A potential employer is interested in you. Use this section to inform the employer about your interests. This gives an idea of what you do when not working and can be a talking point with an employer who has similar interests. Keep this section brief. For example: if you are a graded black belt this is a very notable achievement, however do not list every qualification that you went through to earn it. We have had many résumés like this; these details are irrelevant and distract from the main facts.

5. Skills:

You may have a particular aptitude for something associated with the industry – you can use this section to demonstrate what you will bring to a team or if you are capable of working by yourself. It will highlight your ability to work under pressure and what level of responsibility you can work to. Only quote skills that are relevant.

6. Referees:

Referees are very important. You should quote at least two and possibly more if available. Ideal referees are former employers and if possible the head of training of the company you gained your qualification with. Every student that passes through our training centre has an evidence verification file. This contains all of the student's course work and training comments and is a vital part of the qualification and evidence process. Although the information is confidential, if you give written consent for its release, the training manager can quote from it.

Other Important Information

At the start of the résumé you should also include your date of birth, your home address (and possible region) and contact details (including your home number). Always provide an address. We still get résumés that state *"address available on request"* – this is a considerable insult to a known Close Protection company. We get many résumés from people in a variety of specialist backgrounds that trust us with their contact details – so what makes you so different?

A personal statement of no more than a few lines is also useful at the start of the résumé.

Useful Information

- Height/Weight
- Your health condition
- Blood type
- Marital status
- Rank on leaving service *(if applicable)*
- Whether you are computer literate
- Foreign languages and competence
- Membership of professional bodies

Making an Impact

Generally speaking, a résumé should be no more than two or three sides long; if it is longer it should only contain accurate facts that are verifiable. Make the presentation clear; well spaced with a standard reading format and a standard font size. The resume should have relevant copies of certificates attached. A passport picture is also useful just in case the employer wishes to make an ID card for you.

Each page of the résumé should be on a separate piece of paper, do not use double sided sheets. You may wish to put your name and contact details on each sheet.

Be honest – a professional employer will check the validity of statements you make on a résumé.

Put your résumé in a hard back envelope. A résumé folded three times and crushed in a small envelope does not give a good impression.

The Job Interview

Always arrive early. Punctuality is immensely important in this line of business. Report in and sit patiently until you are called.

Always be dressed appropriately for the interview with a clean and plain coloured suit paying particular attention to clean and tidy shoes.

When called into the room, demonstrate an air of confidence not arrogance. Do not sit down until instructed to. Do not move your chair forward from where it is; it is placed there for a reason.

Interviews can be tough, as you would expect in this profession. A potential employer must be 100% certain that they can trust you with the safety of their Client and the rest of the team. If selected you are an ambassador for that company and the way you work is a reflection upon your employer.

There should be a set format for interview ensuring that each candidate is treated the same and with fairness. Answers should be brief and to the point, never waffle as this could be interpreted as indecision or that you are making it up.

Answer the questions by looking the questioner in the eye; this demonstrates confidence and that you have knowledge of the subject. Looking at the floor and constantly fidgeting is an example of bad interview conduct.

I have seen many professionals fall apart at interview. If you know your subject do not worry about it. Answer clearly and concisely but think about your answer before you give it.

Do not be nervous

It is natural to be nervous but it can sometimes be your downfall. When I see potential CPO's get nervous in interviews my initial thought is that they are taking the interview seriously and this is a sign of wanting to be successful. However, this thought process is short lived. If a candidate are still showing exceptional signs of nerves a few minutes into the interview I will start thinking about how they would react under pressure? Nerves are natural – but get rid of them quickly or you will not be employed.

Employment Etiquette

If you work as a freelance Operator you are dependent on good Close Protection companies to offer you constant work.

The CP industry is a freelancer's industry and all employers know this. Regardless, employers will still look for loyalty where possible. It may be that a company has a good seasonal contract every year and they may 'earmark' you for a position. It's good for you if you can work on this contract as the employer will constantly come back to you every year. Many Operators have been earmarked for contracts but turn it down at the last moment because they have been offered more money elsewhere.

This is a constant industry problem. If the original employer is let down by you because of money they may say that they understand but will probably never offer you work again.

Every time we are let down by a freelance Operator we never forget and they may be moved from the top of the employment list to the bottom. If you commit to a company in this business you should mean it. Your word is your bond and what you stand for.

At the completion of an assignment always thank the company that employed you. This may sound like commonsense but it does not always happen. A simple phone call of thanks is all it takes. If we are employing freelance Operators who have been working for us for a few months on a continuous contract, we would expect a thank you at the end of the task. If this is not forthcoming, it will be noted. It may sound a little petty but if we have had the courtesy to employ you and pay you well for a few months, the least you can do is say thanks. For those that don't the bottom of the pile awaits.

Conclusion

It cannot be emphasised enough how important the résumé is and yet the presentation is simple. If you do not have any previous experience you will have to state this. However this does not mean that you are not employable. Many résumé's end up in the bin because they have missed the basic principles of résumé construction. Remember the Keep It Simple Stupid rule, be confident in your interview and keep your nerves at bay.

CHAPTER SEVEN

TEAM OPTIONS

At Some Stage In Your Close Protection Career
Responsibility Will Fall Directly Upon You;
Working Solo Is Highly Likely

CHAPTER SEVEN

TEAM OPTIONS

Working Solo

If there is one statement that will be constantly repeated it is 'the budget determines your ability to perform successful Close Protection'. Most training organisations train people in 'box' *(five person)* formations. This is because it is the most efficient from a security perspective and reduces the risk of a threat approaching your Principal.

"An example of the 'Box' formation"

Despite this, the budget will make it unlikely that you will always be working in this type of formation with the luxury of such manpower. The reality of this business is that on many occasions you will be working alone. The majority of assignments range from 1 – 3 Operatives in a standard 'mid level' risk team.

As with everything in the Close Protection industry, there are pros and cons in whatever you do. This especially applies when working as a solo Operator.

Good Points

One of the main benefits of working as a solo Operator is that it is usually a low threat level assignment. Some Operators only like to work in high-risk environments although, if we are honest, a lot say this but many don't always mean it. Being tested from time to time, yes! Being tested every day – definitely not. Irrespective of an Operator's background or what their goals are, all enjoy working low risk from time to time.

Sometimes the Principal just cannot afford the cost of additional Operatives. You may advise him that you think more security should be employed but if the Principal cannot afford it or does not think it is necessary you are unlikely to get more. Always make sure that you understand why you are working by yourself. When you ask for more resources you are going to have to justify it; but remember, never scare your Principal. If a threat is elevated and the Principal does not know how significant this may be, you are probably going to have to make him aware of it. Be diplomatic but be firm if you must. If you are still unhappy and your Principal is the type of Client that does not like to be advised; speak to your employers and let them take some responsibility for arranging a more comprehensive service.

Footnote: Generally speaking, if you are working for a company, financial matters should be discussed between them and the Principal, as the Principal is their Client, not yours. If you are working directly for a Principal, this is different.

You may not be aware if there is a budgetary limit as this is confidential business between the Principal and your employer. Never ask a Principal directly about financial affairs when trying to justify extra security. However, there may be occasions when compiling a threat assessment, that the financial affairs of the Principal will be a <u>very</u> relevant factor.

One aspect that is very apparent when working alone is that you can become a close and trusted colleague of the Principal which can border on friendship. Although you will often find throughout CP texts and training courses that it is grossly unprofessional to become close or *'too close'* to the Principal, when working by yourself it is inevitable that this will happen.

Working solo and the inevitability of getting to know your Principal very well can also mean long term employment and occasionally some of the perks mentioned in chapter one.

A definite benefit is that the *'relationship'* can become more relaxed and this isn't always a bad thing as it creates an easy working environment.

Being relaxed and calm can create an excellent atmosphere for everyone involved. Just make sure you remain sharp at all times and never slack. If you relax once, you will do it again, as we are all creatures of habit.

If it is a low level threat you may be on first name terms with your Principal. If you are, don't ever abuse this or refer to it in public (where others can hear) unless permission has been given; your dress will be appropriate to the task and may be very informal.

If the threat can establish that you are a lazy CPO who has a lazy approach to your work, you can earn a year's money in one day and find out what it is like when things go really wrong.

Bad Points

For all of the good points of working solo there are just as many bad points.

If you are working by yourself you have to depend fully on your own judgement. This requires you to use all your skills, often improvising to cover every eventuality. This means that you will be on call 24hrs a day, seven days a week with very little time off for sleep or relaxation. Working by yourself means you will have to cover all of the facets of a Close Protection Operative, i.e. you will have to work as a:

P.E.S.   **Personal Escort Section –**
The term given to the team that protects the Principal

"Solo escort protection"

A.S.T.   Advanced Security Team – often called S.A.P. (Security Advance Party) –

The term given to the team that goes ahead of the Principal

R.S.T.   Residential Security Team –

The term given to the team that protects the residence or place that the Principal is staying in

Working in all of these roles for a couple of days or even a week and you will quickly tire. Even our students on training exercises tire very quickly after a couple of days when put under this amount of pressure. The fact is that you will have to get on with it. Imagine working on a contract like this for a couple of months! Always consider what you are taking on at the outset because you will burn out if you do not get some *'down time'*.

Although it is unprofessional to complain, a company will not object to hearing from you if your Principal is putting you under too much strain or if there are other factors that are hindering your work. By not saying anything you could be making the situation much worse and the longer it goes on the more tired you will become. It is when you're tired that you are likely to make mistakes.

An employer does not want to hear about every little problem. At the end of the day you are a professional Bodyguard so deal with it. However, there are limits and if you are being stretched too far every day you must report it to the company you are working for. This is for the benefit of your Principal's safety, your safety, and the reputation of your employer.

Another point that you should consider is how comfortable the Principal is in employing you? Strange but true. If this is the first time that he has employed Close Protection he may not be fully conversant with your role or responsibilities.

True Case

I have worked with Principals in the past who have never employed a CPO before. They continually asked me if I was OK and started to work their day around me. You don't really want this to happen as in no time you will become more of a hindrance and your presence will become very inconvenient. In this scenario some Principals often feel that they have to ask your permission to do everything. Try to make them as comfortable as you possibly can and give them assurance that:

a) You can look after yourself.
b) You are there to assist them, not the other way around.

Multiple Clients/Principals

One of the main difficulties of working alone, even with Principals who are used to the service, is that it is often not clear exactly who the Principal is, i.e. the person that you are protecting.

You may think that this is a strange thing to say, but when you are working solo you will sometimes be required to protect the whole family who now regard you as *"THEIR BODYGUARD".*

When you work by yourself, especially if you are freelance, and working directly for a Principal (not through a company) you may not have a contract document *(unless it is a full time position)*. The danger of not having such a document is

80

that if things go wrong it is your word against theirs and you will have few rights or 'comeback'.

In the event of not having a contract document that specifies exactly who you are protecting, you will be required to protect:

- The 'Principal'
- The 'Principal's' family
- The 'Principal's' property
- The 'Principal's' business interests and business secrets

This can create confusion for the lone CPO who may feel he is being pulled in different directions. Imagine if something happened to a family member while you were in the property or vicinity and you say to the 'Principal', *"it's nothing to do with me, I only protect you"*. Join the unemployment queue.

If you see this scenario arising, you must speak with the Principal and explain the situation. They need to make the decision who or what is your priority. Working solo has as many disadvantages, but it can be as good or bad as you make it. Don't ever let a Principal take advantage of you. Always ensure that you get proper rest breaks and some time for yourself. If you don't it will become a very unhealthy lifestyle and you will burn out very quickly, becoming a danger to yourself, let alone anyone else.

Working A Two-Person Team

There is an obvious benefit in working as a two-person team, by splitting the tasks in half.

When working in a two-person team you will still have to perform all of the three main functions of Close Protection. You will certainly work together in an escort section capacity but you may take it in turns to undertake advanced and residential work.

Two-person teams can work very well and some Operators may stay together for many years and will come to understand how each other operates and what are their strengths and weaknesses.

You will certainly earn the trust and respect of each other, enough to watch each other's backs.

"Working as a two person team eases some of the pressure"

Irrespective of how many are in a team, there must always be a Team Leader, as someone must take overall responsibility and be the decision-maker. That person will take the glory when all goes well but will also have to take the blame when things go wrong – the standard responsibility and definition of leadership.

Benefits

Apart from the obvious benefit of sharing the workload, you must also consider the skills of the person you are working with. The ideal combination is for each other to have different skills for the benefit of the Principal. It is not uncommon for a team to have different specialist skills such as advance driving for example. In order to cut costs, more Principals are now employing those who have driving skills to double up as CPO and chauffeur. This is not an ideal situation and where possible (if the budget permits) security drivers should be employed in their own right.

Although there will be a Team Leader who will make command decisions, most plans will be discussed when working in small teams. Threat analysis and countering will always be more successful having discussed it with your team partner and this is an obvious benefit compared to working solo.

Responsibilities and Considerations

Regardless of what size of team you are working in, the Team Leader will always take responsibility. This applies equally with two-person teams. If you make a mistake the Team Leader will have to take the blame for you but in smaller teams problems can be solved very quickly.

The difficulty when working in such a *'close proximity'* is that the Principal will always have a preference between one CPO and the other. It's human nature. Whilst some can work with this and accept it, some cannot. Imagine if you were the Team Leader and the Principle ignored you and always took advice from the other. Try to avoid these situations at all costs or work out your differences between the pair of you. In a competitive line of business this is a commonplace problem.

Benefits of a Full Team

Working in a full team is very satisfying when everything goes to plan with the added obvious work load relief. A full team should consist of Residential Operators, Advanced Specialists (who continually conduct reconnaissance) and the Escort Section. If a Principal is used to paying for a full team they will be used to this type of lifestyle and therefore you will not be an *'interference'*.

"A full escort section escorting their Principal to his vehicle"

Each section will have its own Team Leader or Shift Leader as well as an overall Team Leader who is responsible for everything. Each section will have Operators with different skills that should be utilised accordingly.

If you are working on a high-risk assignment the team should be used to working together and certainly be aware of the drill procedures. All teams should drill together when working for the first time and this should be undertaken prior to the commencement of the assignment. There should be Standard Operating Procedures (S.O.P.'s) and 'actions on' drills for every eventuality.

You should only be employed in one role and this may also be stated in your contract so there is no confusion. When working in one defined role there will often be a set working day or shift (usually of 12 hours duration) so you can have a period of down time to get some rest.

In large teams there is the chance of promotion *(as long as it is not a one-off assignment)* as there will certainly be a chain of command as well as the opportunity of long term/regular employment and benefits.

You would also expect that in a large team the operational planning is more precise and the Principal's itinerary has been better planned.

There are many advantages to working on a four/five person team but the reality of life is that in the main you will probably be working in one to three person teams, unless working with the exceptionally rich or where there is an elevated threat.

Team Options Scenarios
(Do's & Don'ts)

The Professional & The Errand Boy

It is often forgotten by Principals and *(sometimes)* by CPO's what it is that you are there to do. **You provide Close Protection and Close Protection only.**

Bodyguards have been occasionally referred to as *"glorified man servants"* this is not the case. Admittedly there will be times when you will be asked to undertake other menial tasks such as to assist in carrying the Principal's shopping. Always consider the risk before carrying out such tasks; in essence you shouldn't do any. Some Principals come to expect you to carry out tasks which fall outside of the general boundaries of *'Close Protection'*. Discuss this with the Principal or take some advice from the company you are working for because there is being professional and being servile. Try to treat a Principal how you would like to be treated. Also consider that if you are new you may be replacing a CPO who was a lap dog. Right from the outset there should be ground rules; this is to protect you and to ensure that you do your job properly.

Footnote:

Your training will have impressed upon you that you should never undertake any tasks that are not directly for the Principal's Protection. All well and good, but imagine if you are working with a Principal for the first time. You are working by yourself and he asks you something simple such as to carry a bag. If you refuse and say 'this is outside my job description' – you won't last a week. Always use your common sense. However never forget that if you agree to do a menial chore once, it will happen again. Helping with bags is one thing, washing the car is another.

We all have bad days from time to time and the Principal may yell at you just for being there - some CPO's can take this and some cannot. Irrespective of the rights and wrongs of this, most Principals will 'usually' apologise *(at some point)* if they take something out on you unnecessarily but you may have to bite your tongue, and wait a while, quite a while actually!

It is human nature that if you are working in a close proximity to someone for a long time that at some point tempers can flare. This also happens between CPO's working together more often than you think.

Be professional and never be rude, always treat your Principal with respect but try to make sure that you are treated with respect in return.

The Family

At the outset of a contract or even in an informal agreement make sure that you understand who the Principal is *(the one who you are most loyal to)* and whom exactly you are protecting. There is a distinct difference between the Client and the 'Principal', as the Client is the employer i.e. a music agent. You may be employed by the music agent but it is *their* Client who is your Principal.

If you are there to protect the children, make sure it stays that way unless indicated otherwise by the Client, Principal or a Team Leader. Never split your loyalties.

When working with a Principal it is inevitable that you may become close to some members of the family as you will become someone that can be trusted. Family members may ask you for your advice or opinion on a situation. If you have served in the Armed Forces or Special Forces or have worked on the circuit for many years they may try to press you for stories and find out about your past and what '*really goes on*'. This is where things become problematic and a little awkward.

Never get involved with family issues. Try to be neutral in all situations.

Use your commonsense and discretion. If you are ever pushed for answers be aware of your surroundings and who is listening. Be diplomatic at all times even if you are itching to say something to the contrary.

Never forget: **YOU ARE ONLY AS GOOD AS YOUR LAST JOB!**

The Friends & Agents

The old saying of *'friends is friends and business is business'* is certainly true until you come between all of them as a professional Bodyguard.

All celebrities have an agent who is responsible for representing him or her and obtaining work for them. The agent is also the bridge between the celebrity and the public.

If the celebrity is under threat the agent will understand your role and what you need to do. There are excellent agents (especially at the top end of the celebrity business) and although they will understand your position, they may not like you being there. You get in the way, impede their movements and perhaps do not present the right image for the celebrity in question.

Celebrities often live in an insecure world - a world equally insecure for their management. If the celebrity doesn't work, no-one gets paid.

You can develop good relationships with managers and agents and this is well worth holding on to. For those that you can't, just try to do the best you can.

If the celebrity has recently attained this status, their friends will find you of interest and may like you being there, although, this very rarely lasts.

You will inevitably be required to work closely with your Principal and you will *(most likely)* get to know each other. Friends do not like this and they certainly don't understand it and in an insecure world can become jealous of you being there. In extreme cases they may even try to sabotage you to get you out of the way. A discrete word in the ear can work with friends but not with agents *(Unless you are absolutely right in what you are saying)*. Remind them what you do and why you are there.

The golden rule with friends is never under **any** circumstance do what they say or take instructions from them. They do not pay you and therefore they do not employ you.

Hotel & The Cars

If a Principal can afford professional Close Protection they can usually afford to stay in a good hotel. Five star hotels (or above) open your eyes on the first couple of occasions that you stay in them, but after a period of time you will come to appreciate that they are just a place to work from.

The same applies to cars. The Principal's cars may be top of the range. However never 'take them out for a spin'. To take the car off task and have an accident is too painful to consider. Cars are a necessary tool of the operation to aid you in getting from A to B.

Consider

If you are the sort of person who enjoys the trappings of five star hotels and luxurious vehicles and enjoys being seen in them – you are not what this industry is looking for. People who are 'wannabes' are always found out. Be aware that you are now playing a dangerous game with the hotels you cannot afford and the cars you may never own. This can affect your thinking and professionalism and if you are this type of person it may lead to a deep resentment of your Principal.

"Discussing routing plans with a security driver"

Chapter Eight

Foot Formations For Close Protection

FOOT FORMATION DRILL TRAINING

CHAPTER EIGHT

FOOT FORMATIONS FOR CLOSE PROTECTION
(THE PERSONAL ESCORT SECTION – P.E.S.)

A Principal is most vulnerable when travelling. Therefore the use of formation cover is a requisite of Close Protection.

Personal Escort Section (PES) formations take different shapes but formation selection will always be relevant to the:

■   Threat level against the Principal and the location you are in
■   Public profile of the Principal and what public area you are travelling in
■   Media intrusion
■   The budgetary allowance for physical Close Protection

Observation

When working with a Principal either as a solo Operator or part of a team you will be responsible for that person and their body cover. Naturally, the more in the team the less responsibility of territory (arcs of vision) apply. In the event of a possible 'confrontation' or 'contact', it is the responsibility of the CPO to avoid, diffuse, escape from, or move the Principal away from danger, or, if there is no other choice, to engage with the threat.

Arcs of vision are a term given to the area of your direct responsibility. If you are working as a solo Operator then you are responsible for what is in front, behind or at your sides. A full 360 degree vision.

An arc of observation is the extremity of your peripheral vision – as much as you can see without having to turn your head.

As a lone Operator the difficulties concentrating on a full field of vision are obvious. If your attention is focused on moving forward with the Principal (a natural thing to do), this leaves the rear completely uncovered and is a serious gap in the Principal's security and overall body cover. When you turn your head around to inspect the rear this will leave you vulnerable at the front and your concentration will be continually distracted.

Most training courses concentrate on the classic 'box formation'. This is the use of 5 Operators giving cover with a team leader (TL) in the centre directly behind the Principal. The TL is sometimes still referred to as the BG (The Bodyguard), i.e. the one in charge and the decision maker. This is the most desirable of formations as it covers every position in the arc of vision. However, from a budgetary point of view this does not always happen due to the expense of employing such a large team as well as other practical considerations e.g. transport for such numbers.

Formation Structure

Formations may be taught slightly differently at every training school as the leading instructor and directing staff will have their own preferences.

This chapter offers you practical guidance on how to provide cover for your Principal. These techniques are tried and tested and **they work**. They are however for predominately low to medium risk assignments. For high risk assignments, these techniques will have to be adapted to suit that environment.

One Person Formation

The one person formation is usually the territory of those who are not at risk or require security at a very low level (not when but if). A Single CPO is responsible for complete all round protection of the Principal. The CPO in this formation assumes responsibility of being the team leader (TL). In all formations, irrespective of numbers, the TL should always be within arms reach of the Principal.

A simple rule: If you are right handed stand on the right hand side of the Principal, if you are left handed – stand on the left.

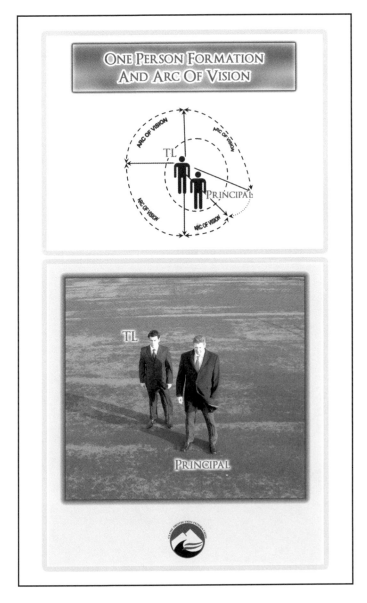

Footnote: I have seen many training videos where it is encouraged to touch the Principal gently on the back when escorting them through doors and in and out of vehicles; this is meant to guide them in the direction you are wishing to go and provide some reassurance. This is completely wrong and the Principal should not be touched at any time. In many circumstances it is considered very disrespectful and with some Principals may be considered a dismissible offence.

Responding to a threat:

In this formation removing the Principal to a safe area is practically impossible unless you recognise the threat very early on. The threat therefore has to be engaged and you will need to put yourself in front of the Principal.

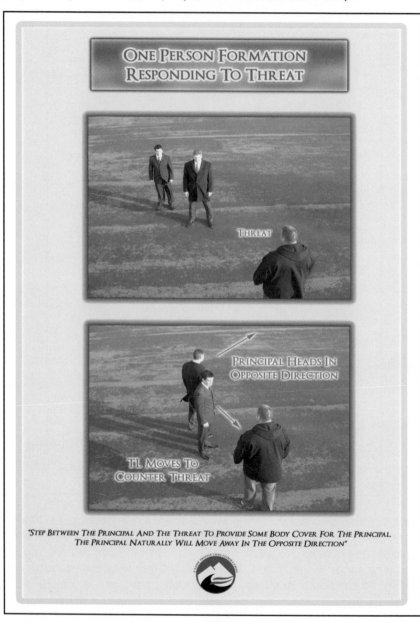

ONE PERSON FORMATION
RESPONDING TO THREAT

THREAT

PRINCIPAL HEADS IN
OPPOSITE DIRECTION

TL MOVES TO
COUNTER THREAT

"STEP BETWEEN THE PRINCIPAL AND THE THREAT TO PROVIDE SOME BODY COVER FOR THE PRINCIPAL.
THE PRINCIPAL NATURALLY WILL MOVE AWAY IN THE OPPOSITE DIRECTION"

Snatch Technique

Sometimes simply stepping around your Principal will not be enough and you may need to react quickly by 'snatching' the Principal out of the direct line of sight.
This can be done by putting your hand on the Principal's shoulder and holding their shoulder tightly and pulling quickly so the Principal is 'snatched' behind you.

Footnote: There is a time and place for employing such techniques. The snatch is exactly as it sounds, crude but effective. It will be very uncomfortable for a Principal and clothing and public status can be damaged, especially if they are in the media eye. You will have a split second to make a decision as to what technique you should use. Remember if you employ a technique like this and have cleared your Principal by force out of the way of someone who was completely harmless, this overreaction could cost you your employment.

Do not do:

I saw a programme some time ago that advocated the CPO stepping in front of the Principal and delivering an elbow strike to the Principal's solar plexus. The *'reasoning'* for this is so the Principal would 'bow down quickly' and therefore be out of the line of a possible strike. What the programme failed to say (as you have just assaulted your Principal) is that you now have a winded and weak Principal who will struggle to have the ability to stand, therefore clearance, let alone engaging a threat, is nearly impossible.

Proceeding through doors

On your approach to a door you will need to move slightly ahead of the Principal. You will have to do this as you are about to enter an area out of *'safe vision'*. It will be your responsibility to open the door for the Principal and in doing so take a look around the door, looking both left and right for assurance that you are happy to proceed inside. A common mistake in training is the holding up of a Principal at a door. This movement needs to flow and should be practised in training regularly. The Principal should not be detained at a door and wait for you to say "Ok, sir". Move ahead of the Principal allowing enough time to open the door and confirm clearance in your own mind. You do not need to tell your Principal that it is ok for them to walk through a door. This movement should take a couple of seconds to complete. If you are unhappy or not comfortable in any way a Principal will know that you will prevent him from proceeding through the door. Therefore words or instructions to a Principal such as "Ok Sir" are unnecessary.

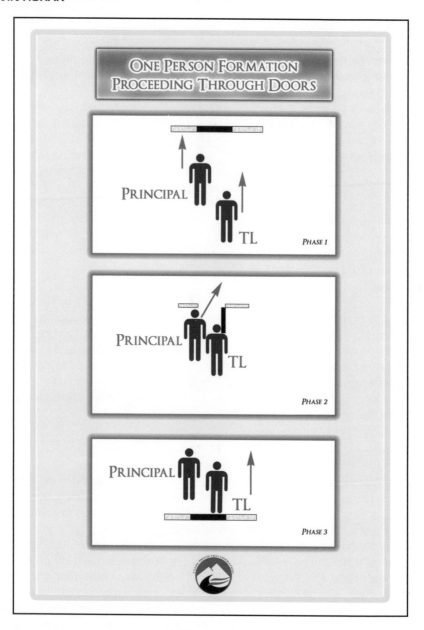

ONE PERSON FORMATION PROCEEDING THROUGH DOORS

PRINCIPAL

TL

PHASE 1

PRINCIPAL

TL

PHASE 2

PRINCIPAL

TL

PHASE 3

When the Principal proceeds through the door, you move back into your original position. Do not move ahead too early and check around you before you do so to ensure you are not leaving your Principal at risk. If you are entering a building with good vision and you can see no threat, move ahead just to open the door.

Two Person Formation

This is a more ideal formation and eases some of your arc of vision responsibility.

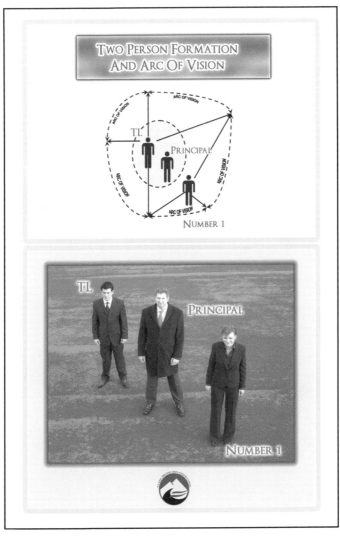

In all formations there must be a TL. The TL will always take the senior position within arm's reach of the Principal. The other is called number 1. Number 1 will take a frontal position and be at the opposite side to the TL. If the TL is right handed, the TL will be to the right hand side of the Principal and therefore number 1 will be on the left (or vice versa if left handed).

Responding to a threat

It is the responsibility of the TL to protect the Principal. It is therefore the responsibility of number 1 to engage with a potential threat if it cannot be avoided.

It is also the responsibility of number 1 to provide cover when the Principal wishes to move through people, e.g. if your Principal is walking down a street and is recognised by someone who you know that your Principal does not wish to meet, it is the responsibility of number 1 to shield the Principal to allow uninterrupted passage.

If the person approaching is a potential threat and is approaching from the front, number 1 needs to observe this first and inform the TL immediately. If time allows, this instruction should be given across a radio discreetly to the TL. If not then it has to be told openly to the TL to save time. The nature of a threat, who they are, and the manner of their approach will determine the reaction.

Number 1 will have to provide cover to stop the threat getting close to the Principal. The TL will need to either take the Principal forward and around number 1 and keep proceeding in the same direction (as 1 is giving cover) or more likely move the Principal away in another direction completely.

The TL will generally make the assumption that retreating in the direction he has come from is the safer option as this is ground that you have already walked through. The TL should be aware that if the threat is organised and motivated then an attack from multiple threats could be waiting and anticipate such action.

To clarify: If number 1 is countering with threat number 1 and the TL moves backwards away from number 1 they could run directly into a new threat. A TL must always be vigilant and be expectant of these situations as baited attacks do happen.

Proceeding through doors

As the formation approaches a door it may be difficult on occasion for number 1 to know whether the door opens automatically, outwards or inwards.

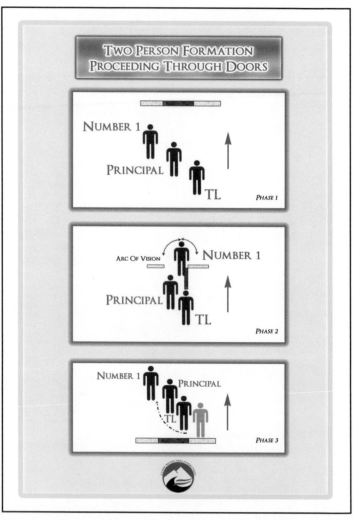

It is the responsibility of number 1 to open the door. If the door opens outwards he will need to proceed through and look left and right into the building and give a practised clearance signal to the TL. He can then either a) go forward but still hold the door open with his left arm (refer to picture) or b) hold the door open, remaining outside the building. (Some teams have preferences as to how they do it).

If the door opens inwards, number 1 can proceed through, give a clear sign when he is happy and remain with the door and re-close it once the TL and Principal have passed through. When the TL and Principal have passed through, number 1 will retake the forward position and resume the original formation.

Three Person Formation

Three person formations can take three different forms:

Formation 1

In this formation you will have a strong frontal position with number 1 and 2 being ahead of the TL and Principal. The reason for this formation is the assumption that you are walking into the unknown and the route that you have passed is 'clear', so rear cover is not so necessary.

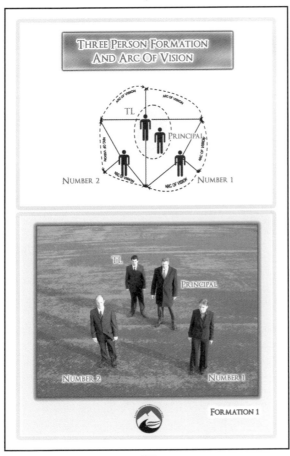

Formation 2

This is a staggered formation where number 1 has responsibility for the front and number 2 has responsibility for the rear. This formation does ease the burden of responsibility of the TL from watching the rear.

Both of these formations are effective and it should be the TL who makes judgment as to which formation to use.

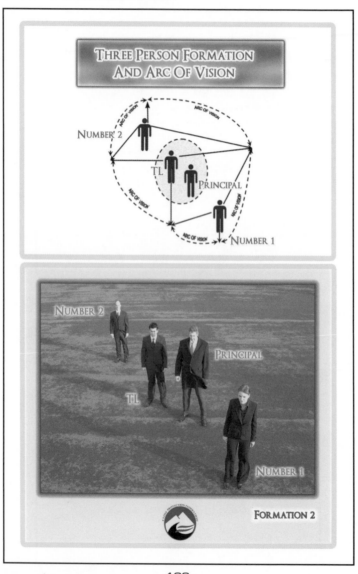

Formation 3

This is a reverse of formation 1 where we now have strong cover at the rear. This formation may be a necessity in some cultures where it is inappropriate to walk in front of the Principal.

Formations, irrespective of numbers, are not *'set in stone'* and must be flexible. Rigidity is not always necessary and a combination of formations could be used on the same assignment, the appropriate one must be selected to suit the scenario.

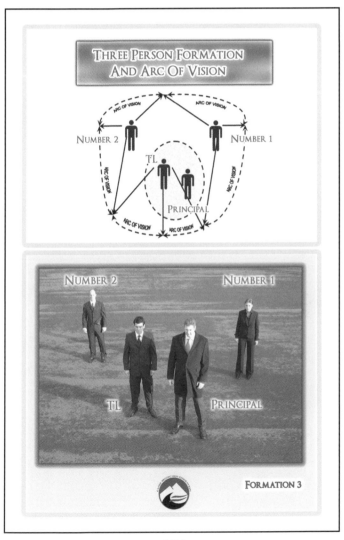

Responding to a threat using formation number 1

If the threat is approaching the formation from the front then number 1 will engage with the threat. Number 2 now has a decision, he either gives support to number 1 (as in the picture) or will assist the TL with the removal and clearance of the Principal away from possible danger. Although the TL is in charge overall and therefore makes decisions, situations have to be responded to on the spot and have to be judged as they happen. In the sequence above number 2 is supporting number 1; but on many occasions number 2 would retreat with the TL and Principal. Number 2 in this type of situation should use his own initiative as to how he should react. If there is more than one threat (approaching from the front), number 2 would definitely assist number 1.

If the threat assessment indicates that a possible attack could happen from multiple assailants (In different directions) then formation number 2 (staggered) is far more appropriate.

Footnote: If the threat assessment has reached this possible conclusion then a larger formation should be advised.

Proceeding through doors

Using formation number 2 (staggered).

When approaching a door, follow the same initial procedure. Number 1 will open the door and look inside giving the all clear to the TL. The Principal and TL will walk through the door and number 2 will follow to the rear. Upon moving through the door number 1 will close the door and rejoin in his original position.

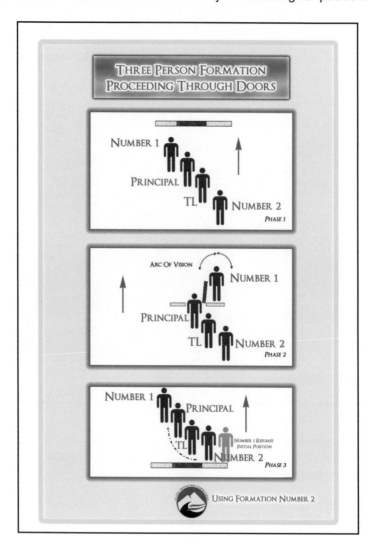

Four Person Formation

This formation takes a 'scattered' appearance. The formation is staggered with number 1 taking the front position, number 2 covering the rear and number 3 being offset to the left of the Principal and TL.

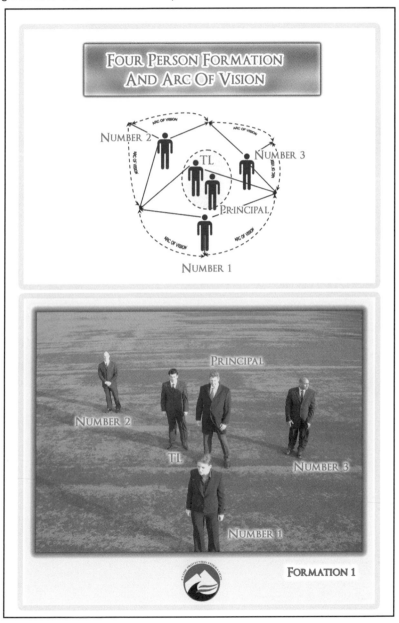

This is a very flexible formation and number 3 can move on the left hand side between the front and rear position as is necessary. He can also work on the opposite side if necessary. Generally number 3 will always be on the left hand side of the formation as there is already number 2 and the TL watching the right hand side.

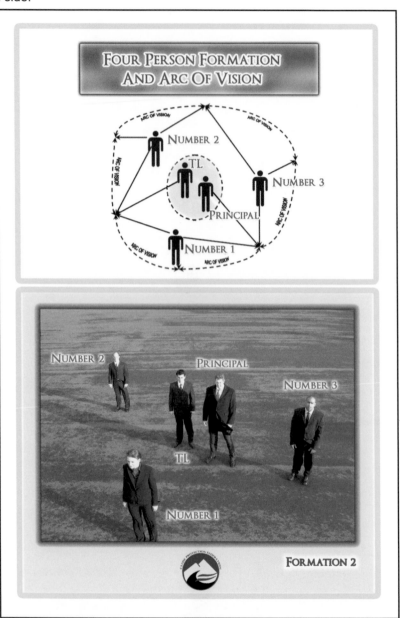

Proceeding through doors

In this formation number 1 is still responsible for the opening of the door. Number 3 will pass through and remain on the other side of the door. Number 2 remains at the rear and moves forward with the TL and Principal.

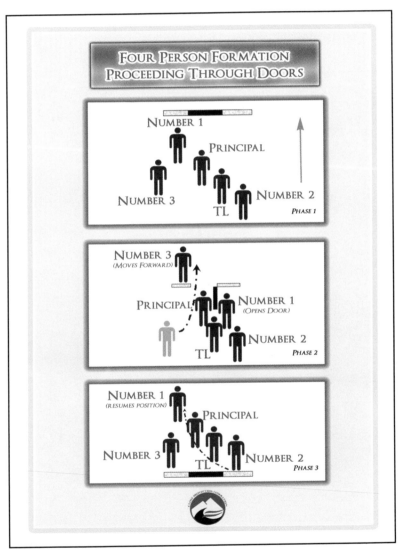

Once through the door number 1 will close the door and one of two things can then occur dependent on the preferences of the TL. Number 1 will resume his position or number 3 will now become number 1 and vice versa.

5 Person Box Formation

The 'box' is the classic training ground formation. Most training centres concentrate on this style of formation but as aforementioned in the real world this is a very expensive service indeed.

The box covers all of the arcs of vision and each team member has a clear responsibility of the area that they are responsible for.

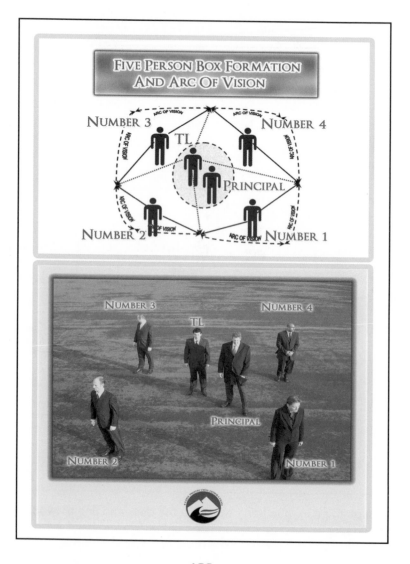

Responding to a threat

In this scenario two threats have come into sight of the box, 1 from the front and 1 from the rear.

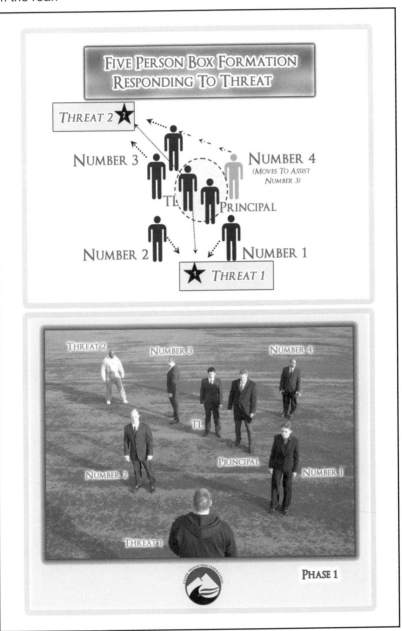

In this situation, the rear is vulnerable as well as it is being potentially targeted by the 2nd threat. Numbers 3 and 4 have to confront the 2nd threat, stopping him from getting close to the Principal. 1 and 2 will have to counter the frontal threat.

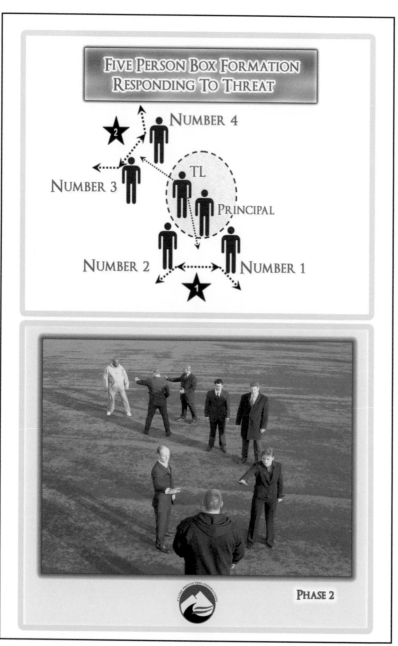

110

FOOT FORMATIONS FOR CLOSE PROTECTION

This leaves either the front as a direction for escape for the TL and Principal and they will pass by numbers 1 & 2 or they can retreat to the rear in the opposite direction (as in the photograph and diagram).

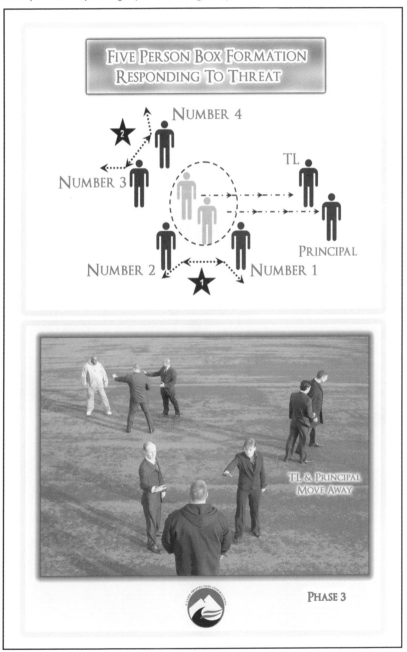

Proceeding through doors

There are two favoured methods for a box formation door entry.

Method 1

In this scenario 1 and 2 have approached the doors. They both turn around facing 3 and 4.

Number 3 moves up ahead and opens the door. Number 3 observes both left and right inside the building and gives indication for number 4 to proceed forward. Number 4 passes through the doorway taking a position on the left of number 3 and he waits for the TL and Principal to move forward.

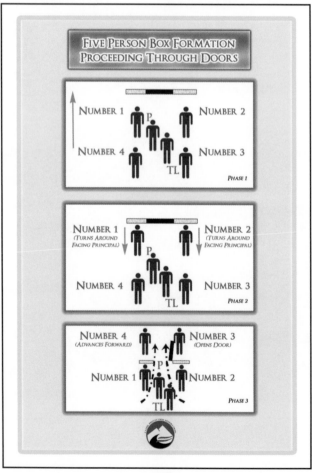

When the TL and Principal have moved forward and are level with 3 and 4. 1 and 2 come through the door and 3 and 4 move forward taking the original formation position of numbers 1 and 2.

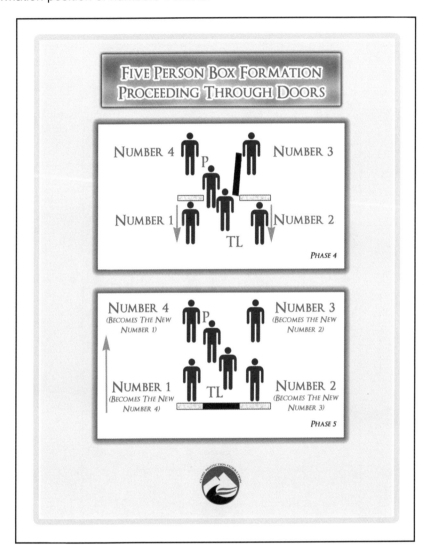

This particular formation takes a lot of practise for it to flow easily. Once you have practised and become used to it; it is second nature.

Method 2

In this scenario 1 and 2 approach the doors. Number 2 opens the door and, if it stays open by itself, he will move forward level with number 1.

Number 2 will still give a signal to the others to proceed and the remainder of the box will move forward together as one. Number 3 will close the door.

This is a far easier method of door entry.

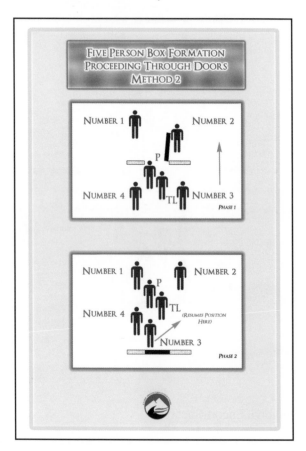

If the door does not stay open, number 2 will have to remain with it and number 3 will have to move forward slightly ahead of the rear of the pack. He will pass through and hold the door as the remainder of the team come through. Whilst this happens number 2 will move forward into his original position level with number 1.

Crowd Line Formation

This is the most commonly observed formation in Close Protection. This is used when protecting those in the public eye – from politicians to celebrities. This technique is used when there is (planned) public interaction. Your Principal may wish to 'meet the public' and this is where very close attention needs to be paid as the public will be within touching distance of your Principal.

This is a staggered formation that walks with the Principal, often at a very slow pace.(Refer to diagram on next page). The TL will still be within arms reach of the Principal with 2 and 3 keeping a very close vigil on what is being passed to the Principal. Documents have to be checked (so the Principal knows what he is signing) and the Principal should have one pen that is used for all signings. Do not take a pen from the crowd. This situation has a huge potential of going wrong as everything is in such a close proximity.

While the TL and 2 and 3 are concentrating on what and who is directly close to the Principal, 1 and 4 have to observe their arcs of vision as well as the deeper crowd. There is a genuine danger that too much concentration is given to those who are really close, but those who are a few feet behind the front line often go unobserved.

Responding to a threat

If a potential threat jumps over the crowd barrier you will need to look for instant cover. This could take the form of vehicles, premises or the direction you have come from. These situations happen in seconds and you must be really sure that the threat *is an actual threat.* Overreacting to a non hostile situation, especially in front of the media is a PR disaster, for the Principal, for you and the Close Protection industry.

Conclusion

Formation training cannot be underestimated; working in formations is a key function of the Personal Escort Section.

Concentration must focus on protecting the Principal in fluent patterns, not making mistakes because you were concentrating on getting the formation right. A book is a useful learning tool, but there is no substitute for training hard and practising diligently until it is absolutely right.

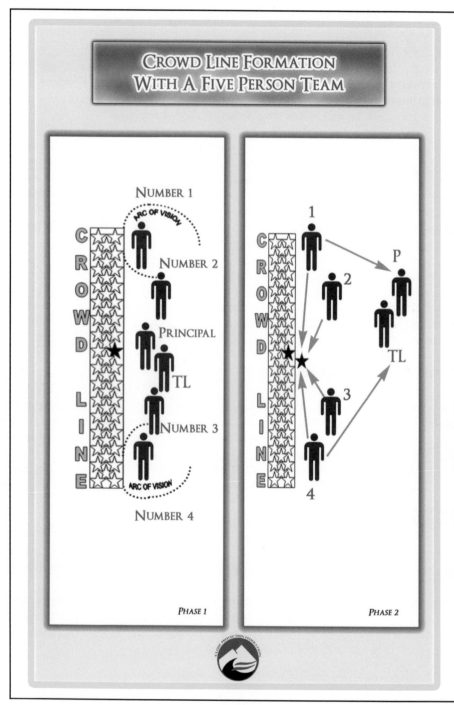

CROWD LINE FORMATION WITH A FIVE PERSON TEAM

PHASE 1

PHASE 2

CHAPTER NINE

RESIDENTIAL SECURITY TEAMS

RESIDENTIAL SECURITY IS A VITALLY IMPORTANT
FACET OF SUCCESSFUL CLOSE PROTECTION

ALLOW TIME AND ENSURE PRIVACY
WHEN SEARCHING VEHICLES

CHAPTER NINE

RESIDENTIAL SECURITY TEAMS

If you work on large or more organised assignments you may have up to three operating sections.

1. The Residential Security Team - (RST)
2. The Advanced Security Team – (AST) also called SAP's (Security Advance Party)
3. The Personal Escort Section – (PES)

The role of the Residential Operator

The residential team work in a fixed location only. Their duty is to protect that location and its contents. Dependant on the size of the team and the resources to hand they may also have to protect the Principal within that location as well.

Some duties may include:

- To detect a threat
- Monitor access
- Monitor postal deliveries and other items
- Maintain existing security systems
- CCTV surveillance
- Vehicle control measures
- Maintain perimeter security of the residence
- Provide a physical presence to deter unwanted visitors

"An example of a vehicle control measure"

Being an RST team member is often seen as the starting point of a CP career and it can be generalised by those in the field as an *"easier"* role. This is not always the case and RST work can be very demanding and the hours quite intensive. Most who work in this section are usually from the manned/static guarding sector or rookie CPOs.

Working residential detail is excellent experience but can be very tiring. Dependent on the size of your team and your role in it you may assume a lot of responsibility and this is also very good for your résumé. I have employed excellent RST that are highly experienced and enjoy working in RST. It is certainly a dedicated facet of the CP business that requires commitment and concentration.
In each of the three main operating sections of a large CP team there should be Standard Operating Procedures (SOPs).

The term "SOPs" is very well known to Military Operators and is used by all experienced CPOs.

Standard SOPs for Residential Security Teams

Each new team member must have a detailed knowledge of the main residential building, outhouses, garages, vehicles, entry and exit points and the inner and outer perimeters, especially any perimeter/cordon weaknesses.
This assessment is the <u>primary</u> point of any residential operation.

The following list is not exhaustive but if you are working in an existing team, there should be the following in place:

1. Details of team members and where they can be contacted at all times.
2. There must be an overall Team Leader and shift leader – someone must be able to take absolute responsibility. *(Most shifts are generally 12 hours and the overall Team Leader would usually be on the day shift).*
3. Details and contacts for other Team Leaders i.e. The PES Leader and AST Leader.
4. An organised shift rota with provision for emergency staff cover.
5. Understanding of existing security systems – a guide to understand existing measures and any countermeasures, to include essential security codes that you **need to know.**
6. Response procedures for intruders. There must be an overall response procedure in the event of an intruder as well as measures for an 'extraordinary' intruder that threatens serious harm – i.e. a stalker who has planned entry to the finest detail.
7. A log for the recording of visitors, including regular guests. Continually stopping regular visitors can antagonise not just the visitor but the Principal as well.
8. Essential communication systems between the team/s; Principal and family or senior guests.
9. A direct line of communication and details of all surrounding emergency services including the company responsible for fitting the existing security alarm and CCTV system as well as security measure auxiliaries.
10. Mail sorting room and a procedure for dealing with suspicious items *(refer to Chapter 21 for more information).*
11. A Secure/lockable key cupboard with a log for responsibility and record for signing in and out.
12. A security room and workstation (The OP's room).
13. On some assignments there may also be a room capable of withstanding forced entry (sometimes referred to as a panic room).
14. Gate/Access control room with a log for entry and exits.

Access Control

The majority of attacks against a Principal happen when they are mobile. This is when your Principal is more vulnerable and because residential security, when employed correctly, is very successful.

One of the key areas of the residential Operator's duty is access control. This is not just monitoring the existing security system but also the vetting of visitors.

"RST can be as covert or overt as a Principal requires"

"Clearwater team members providing access control to a large private estate"

Types of Visitors

If working a large residence there will be a continual flow of visitors and you must be decisive as to whom you will allow access.

You can classify visitors in five categories:

1. Friends, family and associates of the Principal
2. Associates of the residence staff
3. Maintenance people for house and vehicles
4. Deliveries
5. Unwanted visitors

121

"Knowledge of permitted visitors is essential"

Intruders

You must know what to do if somebody breaches the security perimeter, or worse, the residence itself.

If an intruder is detected on the premises and you are working alone you should consider the following:

1. Are you sure that you are dealing with an intruder? Should you wait to be sure? – Has an alarm tripped or do you think that you saw someone on CCTV?

2. When you are sure *(and only if you are sure)*, the Principal must be informed. There should be an SOP for this. You only inform the Principal directly if on a small team and there is no Escort Section Team Leader. If there is, tell the Team Leader who will notify the Principal and that Team Leader should become directly responsible for the Principal.

3. If you are alone and you inform the Principal you may (will) lose sight of the intruder, *(dependant on what resources and communications systems you have).*

4. Consider that; once you inform the Principal it is a human reaction for the Principal to go directly to the person or object he cherishes the most (wife, children, treasure). This can cause its own problems. This is a very important point and should be considered in detail beforehand. A Principal may not always listen to you and may panic and want to get to the children first. Make SOP arrangements for this eventuality.

5. If you are by yourself and assume responsibility, then you should accompany the Principal to a safe/panic room or the most secure part of the building.

6.   You should inform the emergency services (If your Principal is in the public eye this may leak out and lead to press coverage).
7.   You will then have to decide what to do about the intruder:

- Do you try to find the intruder?
- Do you confront?
- Do you remain with the Principal?

Finding The Intruder

You must always secure the Principal first before you even consider pursuit of an intruder. You should then return to the point where you first observed the intruder – this will probably be the operations room on CCTV screens or a central point where an alarm trip has registered.

If you go on to search you are not providing **any** direct protection to the Principal and you may be making them vulnerable. In a claims culture society, every move in this situation will be examined especially by:

1.   The Principal
2.   Your Employer
3.   The Media if it is a celebrity
4.   The Principal's lawyers

By leaving the Principal alone you may also be causing him stress as he would expect you to remain at his side. The eventuality of a whole variety of scenarios must be thought through and considered beforehand as part of your RST preplanning. Everyone will always have their opinion on what they think is right in a given scenario. Ultimately it is you that makes the decision and you have to do what you believed to be right at that time.

Do you Confront?

Before you make the decision to find the intruder, you need to consider and quickly evaluate what you are dealing with? Do you have sufficient abilities and resources to counter this threat and if so do you know what to do with the threat?

You must consider the following:

Is the Intruder Alone?

Can you be absolutely sure that what you have either seen or heard is just one person? In organised threat scenarios where gangs or multiples are involved, one person may go in to test the presence of the security first. Never assume

that what you have seen is the full and overall picture.
If you are dealing with multiple intruders and irrespective of how confident you are, you should not engage with multiple threats at any one time.

This statement is made with the assumption that you and the intruders are unarmed. There have been numerous cases when armed CPO's have engaged with multiple threats and the outcomes of those engagements are constantly debated.

To be an expert in the Close Protection Industry, before you can learn to protect anyone else you must also learn to protect yourself. Never, ever, rush into something until you are aware of the facts. Common sense is your best defence here.

What powers do you have?

CPOs are not Police officers. It is true that there are close links between the Protection community and law enforcement agencies, but in a legal sense it stops there. Having a good relationship with the Police is vital to allow them to be able to do their job, not for you to try to emulate them. Study the powers of arrest for the country or state you are working in and the consequences of exceeding what is *"reasonable force"*.

What will happen if there is a confrontation and you are hurt?

You are now effectively a useless Bodyguard.

Who is looking after the Principal?

If you made the decision to engage with the intruder you must be responsible for your actions. If you are working solo there will be no one looking after the Principal. If you get hurt or injured, the intruder may then have access to the Principal or try to force information from you to disclose where the Principal is.

If a Principal is hurt through your actions or negligence, or by you trying to be a hero, there will be certain reprisals. Not just from the Principal, where being sacked is a certainty *(the minimum you can hope for)*, but from the company you are working for. A CP company will always look to protect its reputation and if that means you are sacrificed for a bad decision in order to maintain a contract this will certainly happen. It's a harsh reality of business. You may also face a lawsuit for being negligent.

The CP industry can be a difficult industry to get into but is very easy to get out of. You will hear it many times – you are only as good as your last job. CP companies do talk to each other and news of a bad decision by an Operator will travel quickly through the industry. Bad decisions lead not just to a loss of work, but possibly a loss of career as well.

What will happen to you if you hurt the intruder?

It is not the most diplomatic way to answer a question but it will depend on the country you are working in. In the majority of 'Western' countries, if you hurt someone the Police will have to determine whether you acted lawfully. Legal processes can take not just months but years, with you, your Principal and the company's name being dragged not only through the Law Courts but also the mire of the media. Lawyers can make the vilest criminal seem angelic. Always look for reliable defence and corroboration *(witnesses)* before engaging with intruders.

Do you remain with the Principal?

If you are working alone the sensible (and safest) action is to remain with your Principal; you should secure the area and wait for emergency assistance. Be an effective CPO – be seen to be vigilant, show experience and be exceptionally calm *(even if your heart is racing inside)*. In these situations, by doing the right thing and being seen to be proactive can lead to a job for life. Your calmness in a stressful situation will always be remembered by your Principal especially when you have made positive and accurate decisions.

A Close Protection Operative is responsible for *'Protection'*. Try to protect by creating obstacles for the intruder and by making sure that security systems are in place. Successful protection means that there should be no contact between the Principal and the threat, especially in residential areas.

After the intruder or threat has been either apprehended or left/escaped, make sure that you prepare reports for use by the Police. The report must detail everything that has happened: times, events and witnesses are a few vital points. If you are ever in a situation where your Principal has been hurt or you have hurt or injured an intruder, there will be a whole different legal process to deal with.

Take advice from the company you are working for.

In the event of an intruder entering a 'secured' area, your Principal will certainly want your account of events. If a threat assessment has been undertaken and implemented but has not worked, the situation will have to be thought through again. Counter-measures will need to be undertaken to ensure that such a breach never occurs again.

Chapter Ten

Indiana Jones
and the
Kingdom of the Crystal Skull

The Advanced Security
Team

ADVANCE PLANNING FOR THE RED CARPET IS ONE THING,
ADVANCE PLANNING FOR HOSTILE ENVIRONMENTS
IS SOMETHING ELSE

CHAPTER TEN

THE ADVANCED SECURITY TEAM

Advanced Security Teams (AST's); often referred to as The Security Advance Party (SAP's), is the final piece of the three main sections of a full Close Protection team.

Advance work is an essential part of a well organised operation and from the Principal's viewpoint makes everything appear smooth and professional.

The costs that are incurred employing three sections of a full Close Protection team are enormous and are only implemented in larger operations to include VIPs, Royalty and very high profile celebrities. CEO's of global companies and the exceptionally wealthy may also require such a service.

"Advanced planning can be immensley time consuming where every situation must be considered. The Queen is giving a speech in the background of this picture; security arrangements have to consider every eventuality"

If you are working solo then you will not normally get the opportunity to perform any advance work to an efficient degree. The closest you may get is:

■   Checking hotel bookings.
■   Making sure that the vehicles that you will be using are arranged in the correct order.
■   Confirmation of Travel plans and itinerary (but no on the ground physical reconnaissance).
■   Rough overview of the venue layout and entry/exit points.

You will normally make or confirm these arrangements by phone

Considerations of booking and checking arrangements when using the phone

- Mistakes are inevitable when you have to rely on other people (no one will ever be as good as you).
- You will not have been able to vet the safety of a hotel, the hotel rooms, vehicles or travel routes.
- Gaining co-operation over the phone can be difficult and may not provide a trustworthy and professional relationship.
- You will not be able to observe threat areas and make counter-action plans.
- You will not be able to vet hotel staff or check public areas.

Footnote: It is practically impossible to vet all hotel staff or other members of the service sector. Be careful not to upset hotel management by questioning the integrity of their employees. Obtaining information on key personnel may be possible, but checking the background of others could prove to be a lot more difficult.

This is by no means an exhaustive list but will indicate some of the problems that may be encountered when there are no formal advanced preparations.

Remember if mistakes are made – you may take the blame!

Working The Advance Team

As an advance team member your job is to provide safety plans and routes, secure hotel and vehicle bookings and all auxiliary travel arrangements from a security point of view. A Principal's personal assistant or manager will take care of general day to day concerns. You will also need to check flight arrangements and the full travel itinerary. You may also have to sweep hotel rooms for listening devices – especially if you are working with the entertainment sector and CEO's of corporate concerns.

"Undertaking some advanced planning in Malibu, California with Clearwater employee Ian Dewsnip"

Your task and responsibility is to secure all preparations prior to a Principal arriving at a given destination.

Hotels

If a hotel has been booked that has not been used by the Principal before, make sure that it is suitable, in respect of status, facilities and location.

Selecting a Hotel

Principal's generally have their own favourite hotels. If however they are to attend a business engagement or travel or holiday in a generalised *'unknown'* area, you may be responsible for finding the right hotel.

When selecting a hotel for the first time, make the following checks:

- How did you hear of the hotel?
- What reputation does it have? – *(don't take a web site for granted).*
- Confirm with others (if you can) about the quality of service, food and rooms.
- Ask discrete questions about a hotel or area with colleagues of yours in CP (your personal loop of information).
- Ask for floor plans to be sent to you before your arrival

Footnote: In the current security climate with increased threat levels and presumed hostilities, you will have to put any requests for floor plans in writing. Any formal written request may have to be signed by your Principal or the company CEO or Operations Manager. Do not be surprised if a hotel is reluctant to provide plans to you.

- Arrange a line of communication between yourself and the Manager (or Assistant Manager) and the head of security if the hotel has one. Try to arrange to meet at least one of them upon your arrival.

- Upon arrival also meet the catering manager, (If you stay warrants it) as well as the concierge and the doorperson and tip them appropriately.

Always try to have a 'slush fund' for tips. Most VIPs will expect this and provisions are made. Never pay tips out of your own money and then try to claim them back, as by the very nature of tips there is no receipt and therefore no proof of expenditure.

- Make sure that when selecting rooms or a suite that they are of the standards that your Principal would expect.

- Ensure that surrounding rooms are available for the escort section (Dependent on an approved budget). Remember that as an AST you will probably not be staying in the hotel and you may have moved on to the next location by the time your Principal arrives.

- Make sure that any special requirements for the Principal i.e. dietary needs are taken care of and provisions made available.

True Case: I recall a couple of scenarios with Clients. One had a serious health condition if he ate cucumber; even the slightest amount would make him violently sick and would leave him ill for many hours. Another situation was in a very expensive hotel suite in London. The Principal about to arrive, was insistent on jelly beans being available in the room – no jelly beans, no stay at that hotel.

- Check the rooms for vulnerable areas i.e. balconies and their views

Do not get carried away and overreact. To not use a hotel suite because it has 'possible line of sight' is not acceptable in a low level situation. However, long lens photography from the paparazzi may be a consideration.

A good CPO will be able to make accurate judgements relative to the situation. A CPO who overreacts and makes a Principal's life difficult will soon find himself out of employment.

- If relevant, check the rooms for listening devices. This is very important for business executives and protecting company secrecy as well as celebrities especially at the tabloid/low level end) who are sought by the media.

- Arrange that the Principal's check-in is swift and that he is not subject to unwarranted attention.

Footnote: Many top end hotels have VIP/Executive services and if you request this you can prearrange check-in so that the Principal can proceed directly to the room.

Travelling and Airports

The most common role of advance work is the preparation of travel plans. To ensure a smooth operation consider the following:

- Have a copy of the Principal's full itinerary and travel plans.
- Have communication with the Escort Section Team Leader.
- Establish if there has been any threat towards the Principal and if he/she is vulnerable while travelling. Has the threat status been elevated?

- Establish who is in the Principal's party and their requirements? If you are working with celebrities, especially in the music industry, the amount of people in the party can increase and decrease rapidly. If your Principal has a fanatical fan base then fans will appear around every corner and if your Principal is so inclined they may join the party.
- Check flight times well in advance to include cancellations and diversions.
- Make sure that the vehicles are in the right place and correctly parked.
- Meet the Head of Security (if possible) at the airport and explain who you are and why you are there – do not loiter around airports without identifying yourself.
- Observe if there are any local customs that you should be aware of?
- Arrange that the Principal is not unnecessarily detained in baggage collection – arrange elevated VIP priority services with the airline.
- Establish whether the Principal is flying privately or commercially?
- Check the terminal that the plane is landing at. Private jets may land at

a different terminal. Introduce yourself beforehand and check what procedures are in place for meeting/escorting a Principal from a private terminal.

- Do you have to book the tickets?
- Make sure that the tickets are what the Principal wants i.e. class of ticket, window seat or aisle. Always ensure that the escort section is booked in the right place.

True Case: I heard of a team who made flight arrangements for their Principal and his family, but the Escort Section was booked not just at the other end of the plane, but on a different level!

Always double check tickets. Make sure that security vehicles and chase cars are ready well in advance of arrival.

"Henry undertakes some ariel advance work prior to a Principal arriving"

- Establish that the drivers are suitably qualified and know the area of travel and have driven the routes beforehand.
- Never, ever, photograph airports as part of your advanced work. Claiming that you are a CPO or even a *'plane spotter'*. Neither will help you in some countries and can be seen as a serious inprisonable offence.

"Conducting some resarch in Gothenburg Sweden"

Conclusion

These are the basic principles of working in the role of AST. As you can imagine there are many other considerations, which you will have to take into account in a variety of places that you will work in.

Being part of the Advance Team can have many benefits and unless working at very late notice is not nearly as stressful and pressured as working in the Escort Section.

I have only selected hotels and airports as examples. To be an expert at advance work you will need experience in the following locations: (As examples)

- Shopping Centres
- Restaurants
- Bars and nightclubs
- Theatres
- Cinemas
- Casinos
- Travelling to meetings
- Clients visiting the Principal – (arranging travel for them)
- How to plan and accommodate a full entourage

You will see from the above that there are implications for every route and venue relative to every possible type of Principal and every type of threat. An advanced specialist can be worth his weight in gold as he should have the ability to plan for each scenario. Use the basic principles as listed earlier and create your own system and standard operating procedures for what works best for you.

"Advanced planning is essential to ensure success at special events"

Chapter Eleven

Vehicle Drills

If You Are Arriving At This Hotel With Your Principal
Consideration Must Be Given To:

a) Vehicle Barrier - Where Does The Vehicle Go?
b) No Space To Debuss The Vehicle Safely
C) General Members Of The Public Can Walk Up To The Vehicle
D) In The Event Of An Incident - Is There Anywhere To
Retreat To?

CHAPTER ELEVEN

VEHICLE DRILLS

"A classic Executive car - the Maybach 63"

"Inside the Maybach 63, a very luxurious vehicle"

There are four main considerations when working with vehicles:

- What type of vehicle and why?
- Seating Positions
- Travelling Difficulties and Observations
- Search Procedures

"Often a choice of a business professional - A Bentley Arnage"

What type of vehicle and why?

Travelling in a vehicle is a time when the Principal is most vulnerable. This is the time you need to be the most vigilant. Statistically 95% of kidnappings happen between the home and the office.

Travelling creates exposure; this is inevitable and often unavoidable. Your risk/threat assessment should determine your reaction with a full coverage of Standard Operating Procedures (S.O.P.s) and actions on drills.

"On the left Henry with a BMW X5 and an Audi Q7 on the right"

It may surprise you that most VIP vehicles are not normally 'protected' and are often just expensive vehicles. Most chauffeur driven vehicles have very little built-in countermeasures. If a vehicle is armoured or protected it will require a specialist driver as the sheer weight of the vehicle is increased dramatically and will be more difficult to handle.

"An un-armoured executive vehicle"

"An armoured vehicle for hostile environments"

Unless you are working with a Principal who is at extreme high risk, *(especially in areas where kidnapping is a regular occurrence)* or a country of some instability, you will probably work in standard, non-secured vehicles. It would be unusual for you to select the type of vehicle that you are going to use as preferences are usually determined by the Principal but if you have the opportunity and security takes priority over preference; you should consider the following:

- A Powerful Engine
- High Performance Handling
- Power disc brakes or ABS braking
- Power steering
- Full air conditioning system to allow windows to be kept closed
- Locking petrol cap
- Locking bonnet and boot
- Alarm systems
- Electric windows and central locking
- Non accessible spare tyre
- Type of Glass

On larger assignments, especially where the Principal is travelling into a different country *(not of their origin)* it is usual to provide a vehicle and driver for their use.

Driving as a Close Protection Operative

As a lone CPO you may be asked to undertake some driving duties where there is no chauffeur or nominated security driver. You should also consider that there are some Principals who like to drive themselves. Not many, but some.

"One of Clearwater's professional CPO team undertaking driving duties"

Points to Consider

If you are driving you will never be able to work properly (for what you are contracted for) and you will certainly be distracted from your primary objective of providing 'security'. You should also bear in mind that in the event of kidnap it is often the <u>driver</u> that is targeted first.

Where budget allows it is always preferable to have a security driver with his duties being solely for driving.

Note: Some drivers occasionally 'stand in' and become temporary CPO's as well, often without formal training and just 'assume' this role. Always be on the lookout for those drivers who want to turn their hand to something they are not trained or employed to do and what is their motivation for doing this anyway? On many occasions they can be more of a hindrance than help.

<u>Seating Positions</u>

If you are working solo (*and there is a security driver*) you would usually sit in the front passenger seat. The Principal will be directly behind you as you are providing some body cover and you are in the frontal line of sight in the event of an attack.

If there are two Operatives then one would sit in the front passenger seat with you *(as the Team Leader)* sitting next to the Principal in the rear. This, of course does not always apply to limousines and larger vehicles where the internal layout can be considerably different. Use basic principles and common sense when selecting seating positions.

Travelling

Always brief the driver where you are going

To sit in the car with the driver unsure of where he is going is very embarrassing and very irritating to the Principal. The driver should always know in advance and should be conversant with the area you are working in, as well as back up routes. Global Positioning Systems (GPS) are **no** substitute for localised knowledge.

Avoid the same routes

In the event of a higher risk scenario use different routes when travelling to the home and workplace even if it takes you out of the way and makes the journey that little bit longer.

We are all creatures of habit and get set into routines too easily. Vary the way you carry out the most basic of procedures and remain sharp and focused. This point is easier said than done. Your planning will always be with the best of intentions but a Principal may not see it that way. To explain to the Principal that you are taking a different route and that it will take an extra half an hour to get to work will be frustrating for him and he may not accept it or allow it. In this situation, your tact and diplomacy will be called upon.

You are a professional CPO and your view must be respected; never lose sight of what the threat actually is and, if actioned, what could happen. If you start to try to change routine and the 'threat' does not warrant it, you will end up antagonising a Principal. This sounds like common sense but there are individuals out there who do exactly this to try to justify their income and position.

Avoid Publicity

Some celebrities (often at a lower grade) will often court the media but this certainly does not apply to the business executive. Avoid the media at all times when working with corporate executives and celebrity Clients if they do not wish it.

Try to keep the vehicle moving as much as possible

When we deliver personal and professional safety lectures, this statement usually raises a smile or a raised eyebrow.

When moving through city centres where there is a constant build up or slowing of traffic it is far more sensible to move at a slower rate than the speed limit to keep the vehicle moving. As soon as a vehicle becomes stationary you become a more vulnerable target. The type of person that hits the accelerator very quickly to move a short space is only burning tyre rubber. On approach to roundabouts and traffic lights if you can see the traffic lights ahead are red, slow the vehicle to keep moving and very importantly do not go too tight to the rear of the vehicle in front. Always leave enough space to move around it quickly if you have to. An experienced security driver will be an expert in keeping a vehicle moving and quick to recognise obstructions that will slow the vehicle down.

Make sure the advance team plans a map and travel plans for you

If you have an advance team they should plan a suitable route for you to travel.

The route plan should show the direct planned route of entry as well as back up plans to include escape route/s. It should also include building entry and exit points. The route plan should also display travelling observations such as one way streets and choke points. Aerial photography is also very helpful and free from the internet and this will offer some further guidance.

Make sure that the driver remains with the vehicle at all times

If drivers (especially non security drivers) know they are going to get some down time, they often park up the vehicle and go elsewhere, such as take a lunch break. This is fine until they are working in a high risk scenario where the vehicle could be under surveillance for exactly this reason. If residential security and your escort work are very good then this may be the opportunity the threat is looking for. You cannot watch your drivers all of the time and most who have been on the circuit know that in many situations you don't leave the vehicle unattended. If they do they will at least make sure that they search it on their return. However, there are some drivers out there who are set in their ways and they must be reminded appropriately.

Time must be made available if the vehicle has to be searched regularly throughout the day. Always make provision for this and ensure that your driver does as well. A standard vehicle will take you a **minimum** of 20 minutes to search thoroughly. The last thing you want is for your Principal to remain by the car while you search it. He won't stand for this and you will be getting into an unchecked and non-sterile vehicle.

Travelling Observations

Road appreciation and critical observation of road surroundings is very important when travelling with vehicles. Travelling through cities to the open and exposed diversity of the countryside all pose their own problems.

Take your own car out and practice how many times you have to stop in a journey and observe where you became vulnerable. Pay attention to 'choke points' where you have nowhere else to go and have to proceed in one direction, visualise and plan escape routes just in case you need them.

Heavy Traffic

This will delay your journey and if your Principal is time critical this could become a problem. You will also have to continually stop, and it is when you are stationary that you are most vulnerable.

Be conscious of traffic behind you and of becoming 'boxed in' (from the front and rear) and therefore unable to move away in the event of an incident. When in a stationary position in traffic always leave enough space in front of the car to allow you to escape if necessary.

Roundabouts and Junctions

Roundabouts and junctions pose natural barriers and at these obstructions you will need to be prepared to stop.

Consider your position in traffic lanes at larger roundabouts where there are traffic lights as you can become trapped in the middle of multiple sets of lights. Positioning yourself in the middle lane could result in you becoming boxed in.

If in a vehicle procession extra care needs to be taken where there are obstructions so that you don't lose your lead or chase vehicles as well.

One way streets

Some maps do not identify one way streets and you can become lost or stuck quite easily. This is where local drivers are worth their weight in gold. Never forget that once you are on a one way street you have to proceed in that direction. If possible it is best to avoid such routes in the first place.

Bridges and tunnels

Tunnels are reasonably obvious as to why they should be avoided, however this is **only** if the threat determines it. Such an overreaction can distress a Principal if you have to explain why you are not using tunnels in a low threat assignment.

Your threat analysis should determine is the threat *seriously* going to attack you when you are in a tunnel potentially full of other people? Not just from the crudely termed *"collateral damage"* point of view but all of the witnesses that would see such an event? Is the threat really that determined, motivated and resourced enough? If so how are they going to do it and how are they going to escape and not get caught? – Or *is that not their intention, which is a whole different rationale.*

When driving under bridges you should be conscious of the roof as this is one of the most vulnerable points of the vehicle. You should pay attention to what is overhead and what can fall or be pushed upon you. It is not unusual for youngsters to throw things from bridges, especially on motorways. Your brand new executive vehicle makes for a nice target!

High structures & Observation points

In high-risk assignments you will need to pay attention to surrounding structures when entering and exiting the vehicle. Your threat analysis should determine what level of reconnaissance is needed and 'actions on' counter measures in the event of a contact.

Traffic lights

Try to get to know the area you are travelling or working in and where traffic lights are located along your route as well as on back up routes. Traffic lights in city centres are difficult to avoid. Keep moving as best as you can, keeping enough distance between you and the other vehicle in front. Be conscious of traffic lanes and your position in them if delayed at lights.

Unlit Roads

The countryside is very rarely lit and there are many potential dangers. Country lanes can be easily cut off and are perfect ambush points.

Level/Train Crossings

If possible try to avoid level crossings. It is *'almost inevitable'* that the lights will change as you approach. If you do get caught at a crossing don't go fully up to the barrier as often the barriers are not particularly strong and you could be rammed by another car from behind and your vehicle pushed onto the track.

Sharp bends & gradients

Fairly self-explanatory. Drive carefully and safely. Keep to the side of the road that gives you maximum visibility around the bend.

Areas with large buildings either side

In some areas you may lose radio communications when surrounded by high rise buildings.

Search Procedures & Avoiding Sabotage

Vehicles should be searched frequently as a matter of routine but in the event of travel and unsecured parking you will have to make extra provision for this.

Never overreact if the threat does not warrant this. Searching a vehicle for an hour at a time will take an incredible amount out of your working day and will become an irritant to your Principal.

"A search mirror is an extremely useful tool"

Stripping the car down when working on a low level threat assignment can completely unnerve the Principal and can do more harm than good. When you take something apart make sure you know how to put it back together again.

Vehicle Safety

Keep the vehicle locked at all times including when travelling. Do not leave equipment on view, especially when approaching traffic lights and roundabouts.

Wherever possible try to garage the vehicle when it is unattended and ensure its safety even at respected hotels.

Never take 'secure' car parks for granted and always check your vehicle when it is brought up to the front for you – especially if it is brought up by someone other than the security driver.

Footnote: Generally speaking it should always be the security driver who brings the car up. However, in some hotels no-one outside of hotel staff or their in-house security are allowed in secure areas, irrespective of your position or the status of the Principal.

Consideration must also be given if the car is being brought up to you at the front of the hotel. It would be highly irregular to start doing vehicle search procedures in view of everyone and the hotel guests. For the respect of your Principal and the hotel's professional reputation this should <u>never</u> happen.

Have the car moved to a more private area to conduct your search and ensure that it is brought up to you in good time.

Car Jacking

Car jacking is not a new phenomenon; in some countries it has been taking place for many years. In some European countries it is still rare *(statistically)* but it is on the increase nevertheless.

Car jacking requires some consideration. When you are working it is a probability that you will be travelling in executive vehicles. It is these types of vehicles that are often targeted by thieves.

*Footnote: In a car jack it is often the vehicle that is wanted and **NOT** your Principal. In these circumstances your Principal would have been the victim of crime and nothing more than. However, your threat assessment may have concluded that an area of travel is prone to car jacking but with the best will in the world, circumstance cannot always be planned for.*

The car jack is often an opportunist crime generally carried out by organised criminals. Their most common method is driving another car into the back of yours in an attempt to get you or the driver to get out. Admittedly, a potential car jacker being confronted by a team of CPO's will probably think twice. However, you must be aware of this tactic. In many places in the world, whether working solo or in a team, getting out of the vehicle will not deter an organised car jacking team. You will simply be just another obstacle that needs to be removed.

The car that the jacker will use to drive into the back of yours will almost certainly be stolen and reporting the vehicle registration to the Police does not guarantee any apprehension of the culprit/s.

Do not approach traffic lights with visible unlocked doors, which will allow an attempt to be made to open the doors and drag persons or property out.

Another tactic used by thieves is to leave a piece of paper on the rear windshield. If there has been no vehicle searching prior to entry, the driver gets into the car, starts the car and then looks into the rear view mirror. In doing so he sees the piece of paper and gets out to investigate. While he does this he will often leave the engine running and he and the car are rushed as soon as he gets out.

What to do in the event of a genuine accident?

What happens if someone drives into the back of you, whether you have the Principal in the car or not? You have a duty to investigate and if necessary report the accident.

This is a very difficult situation.

If the Principal is with you and you are working alone you will have to think carefully but quickly. Use your common sense; if you look in the rear view mirrors and five big men are getting out, the chances are you have a problem. If it is one sole person and you are sure that this is not a diversionary tactic to get you out, then proceed to deal with the situation as you would in your own car, exercising due care and attention. If you are in a team of 2, only 1 should get out and the doors should be locked behind him. There should always be contact between the CPO and the driver. If necessary the CPO may have to give an instruction to the driver to move off without him.

A Principal will always look for decisive decisions with their Close Protection but this is one instance when, if the Principal is present, you may even suggest to him 'do you want me to get out'. If you are working on a serious risk in a volatile and high crime area you certainly would not do this, but by asking, at least you are putting the ball in the Principal's court.

Observe the body language of the person who has hit the back of you. If it is a lady in her seventies – chances are she's not going to jack you! If someone looks shocked or has their head in their hands it could well be genuine. It is a human reaction for the person who crashed into you to get out of the car – to check that you are ok and there is no damage to your car as well as theirs. If someone just sits there with no expression on their face, you should regard this as suspicious.

The Principal may tell you to get out and find out what has happened? You will have to make a judgement. If you think the situation is dangerous you will have to tell him (politely) of your concerns and suspicions.

Chauffeurs and Using Their Own Car

This is a problem when in a possible car jack situation. If you are the CPO with or without a Principal, and you are using a private driver and it is his car that is hit, he may get out without thinking. The car, after all, is his livelihood.

Some chauffeurs undertake CP training. This is a bonus but far from ideal. Having separate Close Protection is preferable as the two functions should be kept separate. A 'trained' driver however, should have awareness skills for situations such as this.
If you are in an area where car jacking is known to take place, discuss this with the driver first – trained drivers should always know better and read a situation before getting out and acting on impulse.

Car Jacking Conclusion

You should never get out of a car unless you are absolutely sure there is no danger to you or your Principal. The fact of the matter is that genuine accidents do happen and there will be an insurance procedure. To simply put your foot down and drive off will not help your insurance claim when asked what happened – your judgement will be questioned and you could be seen as someone who overreacts.

The fact that your Principal is a millionaire does not always mean that they will accept your decision to just drive off on the basis of safety. They may actually encourage you to find out what has happened and more importantly who is responsible for the damage to their car.

Principals in countries where car jacking is more commonplace should have a better understanding of these matters and should accept your professional judgements far easier.

VEHICLE SEARCHING

SOME POINTS TO LOOK FOR:

- CUT BRAKE CABLES
- OBJECTS THAT YOU DO NOT RECOGNISE
- OBJECTS THAT MAY BE AN I.E.D. *(IMPROVISED EXPLOSIVE DEVICE)*
- LOOSE WHEEL NUTS
- MAGNETIC DEVICES - OFTEN ATTACHED TO FUEL TANK
- LOOSE PLUGS
- CHECK BRAKE AND CLUTCH FLUIDS ARE NOT DRAINED
- CHECK PETROL OR OTHER FLUIDS HAVE NOT BEEN PUT IN THE WINDSCREEN WASHER BOTTLE
- CHECK FOR SIGNS OF TAMPERING OF THE BRAKE-LIGHTS AND HEADLIGHTS
- PHOTOGRAPH THE ENGINE AND STRUCTURE FOR FUTURE COMPARISONS

Vehicle Searching - Detailed

If a threat level is minimal, basic searching will take place usually once a day in a workable area such as the Principal's garage or estate. On a basic search you are looking for vehicle disturbance and smears and fingerprints that were not there the day before.

The vehicle should be kept in a 'secured' and protected/alarmed area. It should also be lit to assist you in searching, as well as to ensure better quality CCTV images.

Try to utilise the driver for vehicle searching, as he will always know the vehicle better than anyone else. Try to have two people searching the vehicle so they can check over each other's work. The ideal number is three with the third person being a Team Leader or someone working in an advisory role to make sure that nothing is missed.

Search the vehicle in a clockwise direction with both Operatives at opposite ends to each other. They should keep moving around until the whole vehicle has been covered and both Operatives work has been checked by each other.

Order of Search

- Have knowledge of the surrounding area (dependant on being garaged or not) i.e. car parks, garden areas, dustbins, hedgerows etc.
- When satisfied that the surrounding area is contained – move to the vehicle.
- Observe the bodywork of the car.
- Look on the paintwork and chrome for fingerprints and oil/grease smears – VIP cars should always be clean!
- Check mirrors and windows for the same.
- Search the wheel arches and wheels.
- Look for sharp objects at the rear of the wheels; check spare wheel if located outside of the car. Check wheel nuts.
- Search underneath the vehicle and look for oil and fluid leaks, loose wires, cut cables and foreign objects.
- Examine the engine from underneath with particular attention to the radiator and front of the vehicle as well as the underside where the Principal would usually sit.
- When satisfied, proceed to open doors, the bonnet and the boot. (As part of your initial research you should know where the release catches are).
- When working as a two-person team use the assistance of the other member to open doors and the bonnet. When opening the doors

148

make sure the other member is observing in a different position from you. When opening the bonnet and the boot, one can hold down on the hood while the other pulls the lever. Check around the edge of the bonnet and the doors before fully opening.

- Search the interior with particular attention to where the Principal will sit. Try to keep 'loose' items in the boot to a minimum.
- When happy that the vehicle is safe – you can start the engine.

"A vehicle offers a great hiding place for an I.E.D."

"Demonstrating hiding places inside a vehicle to students"

"Checking students progress on a search exercise"

"The looks on the students faces say it all - an I.E.D. missed underneath the car"

CHAPTER TWELVE

EMBUSS AND DEBUSS

CHAPTER TWELVE

EMBUSS AND DEBUSS

Embuss and Debuss is the term given to getting into and out of a vehicle(s).

The way that a team gets into (and out) of vehicles is a coordinated movement that takes a lot of practise to perfect.

Footnote: The photographs in this chapter were taken in the UK. The principles of formation positions however remain the same. These tactics apply irrespective of which side of the road you are driving on.

Working Solo

Solo embuss procedure - and where you and your Principal should sit in a vehicle.

KEVIN HORAK

Entering the vehicle

The CPO will walk in a standard one person formation where he is behind the Principal. Upon approach to the vehicle he will take a forward position and open the door for the Principal.

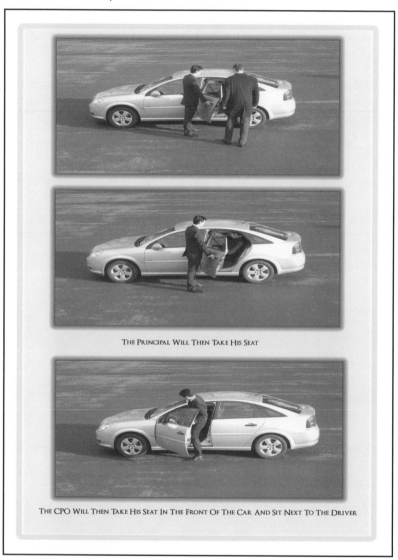

THE PRINCIPAL WILL THEN TAKE HIS SEAT

THE CPO WILL THEN TAKE HIS SEAT IN THE FRONT OF THE CAR AND SIT NEXT TO THE DRIVER

Exiting the vehicle

With all vehicle formations you do the reverse of the formation getting out as you did getting in.

153

Two person formation

There are two different ways of entering the vehicle.

Formation 1 (working with one vehicle)

Number 1 moves out and walks to the vehicle and opens the rear door. He gives a premeditated all clear signal to the TL, this would generally be a radio instruction or discrete gesture. He remains holding the door as the Principal and TL approach the vehicle.

The Principal will take his place in the vehicle; when he is sat the TL will walk around the rear of the vehicle and take his place next to the Principal.

THE PRINCIPAL WILL TAKE HIS PLACE IN THE VEHICLE; WHEN HE IS SAT THE TL WILL WALK AROUND THE REAR OF THE VEHICLE AND TAKE HIS PLACE NEXT TO THE PRINCIPAL

NUMBER 1 WILL CLOSE THE DOOR AND TAKE HIS PLACE IN THE FRONT PASSENGER SEAT

Formation 2

Number 1 moves out first and walks around to the other side of the vehicle. When he is happy he turns around and gives a pre-arranged signal or radio instruction to the TL to proceed forward with the Principal. The TL then opens the door for the Principal and closes it when the Principal has sat down. The TL will then walk around the rear of the vehicle and takes his place sitting next to the Principal. Number 1 will sit in the front passenger seat. When the TL has sat down in the vehicle and number 1 hears the door close, this is his cue for him to take his place in the vehicle.

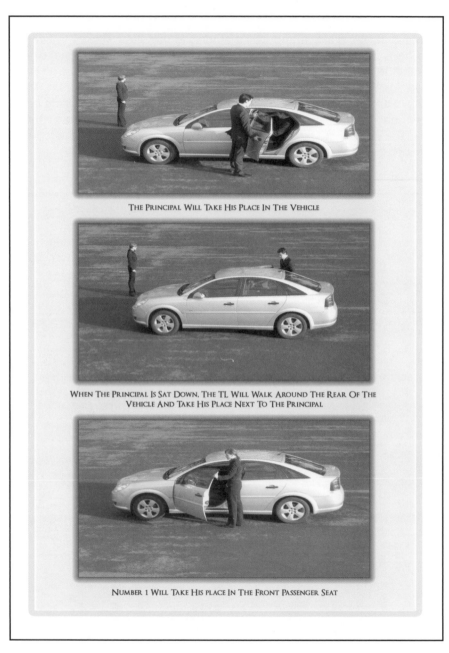

THE PRINCIPAL WILL TAKE HIS PLACE IN THE VEHICLE

WHEN THE PRINCIPAL IS SAT DOWN, THE TL WILL WALK AROUND THE REAR OF THE VEHICLE AND TAKE HIS PLACE NEXT TO THE PRINCIPAL

NUMBER 1 WILL TAKE HIS PLACE IN THE FRONT PASSENGER SEAT

When you have a two person formation with only one vehicle available the TL will always sit next to the Principal.

Two person formation (using 2 vehicles)

If you have two vehicles the formation will change significantly.

Number 1 takes the position at the front thereby providing cover to the Principal's car. Number 1 will give a premeditated signal to the TL to proceed forward. The TL then opens the door for the Principal.

THE TL WILL THEN TAKE HIS POSITION IN THE VEHICLE IN THE FRONT
PASSENGER SEAT

WHEN THE TL HAS TAKEN HIS PLACE, NUMBER 1 WILL TAKE HIS PLACE IN THE
CHASE CAR, THIS WILL ALWAYS BE IN THE FRONT PASSENGER SEAT

Three person formation

In all formations there are always other variations of vehicle entry and exit. But generally either the TL opens the door for the Principal or a team member does. The TL who gives the briefing prior to assignment should inform the team how he wants the formations to work.

For the duration of this chapter we will concentrate on the TL opening the door.

In a three person formation there is not enough comfortable space to use 1 standard size vehicle.

In this formation the front car is the Principal's car. The Principal, TL and number 1 will sit in this car, number 2 will sit in the chase car.

Number 1 and 2 will walk out of the building together and take positions at either end of each vehicle. Number 1 will give a confirmation signal visually or through his radio to the TL to proceed.

THE TL WILL WALK TO THE FRONT CAR AND OPEN THE DOOR FOR THE PRINCIPAL

WHEN THE PRINCIPAL IS SAT DOWN, THE TL WILL WALK AROUND THE REAR OF THE VEHICLE AND TAKE HIS PLACE NEXT TO THE PRINCIPAL. NUMBER 1 WILL TAKE HIS PLACE IN THE FRONT PASSENGER SEAT SECURING THE PRINCIPAL'S VEHICLE

NUMBER 2 WILL TAKE HIS PLACE IN THE CHASE CAR IN THE FRONT PASSENGER SEAT

Footnote: This formation can change easily and this will be dependent on your Principal and the threat. For instance you could have numbers 1 and 2 sitting in the chase car and the TL could sit in the passenger front seat.

When debussing, this formation is still the same in reverse. Number 2 will get out of the chase car first quickly followed by number 1 and they will resume their positions at either end of the cars. 1 will still give the signal to proceed to the TL. When the TL and Principal have left the vehicle, 1 and 2 fall back into the standard foot formation.

Important Fact

The Principal can be at their most vulnerable when entering and exiting a vehicle.

The vehicle formations demonstrated here show the Principal's vehicle at the front. However, when the driver of the Principal's car is moving and cannot see in front of him, *(such as a blind bend in the road as an example)*, it is common practise for the chase car to overtake and take the forward position. It will then retreat to the rear when necessary and safe.

The Principal's car cannot wait for the chase car to Debuss.

Upon approaching your destination, the chase car should overtake the Principal's car so the Debuss procedure is quicker and safer. If you are using a formation that numbers 1 and 2 are in the chase car, 1 and 2 will get seconds worth of valuable insight by being on the ground and getting out of their vehicle first. They will do this just before the TL and Principal get out of theirs. If 1 and 2 are unhappy they have these valuable seconds to radio a signal to the Principal's vehicle telling them not to Debuss and to keep heading straight or turn around and meet at an emergency rendezvous.

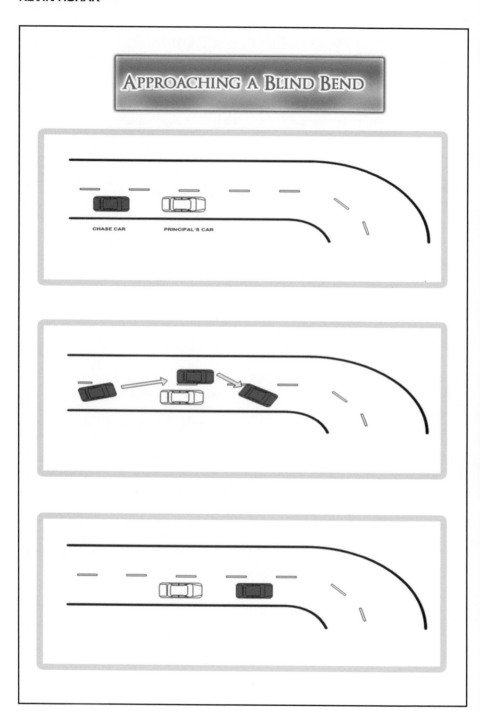

APPROACHING A BLIND BEND

CHASE CAR   PRINCIPAL'S CAR

Four person formation (using 2 vehicles)

NUMBERS 1, 2 AND 3 WILL LEAVE AND TAKE POSITION TOGETHER.
1 AND 2 WILL TAKE POSITION AT THE OPPOSITE ENDS OF BOTH VEHICLES.
NUMBER 3 WILL GO BETWEEN THE VEHICLES OR SLIGHTLY IN FRONT OF THEM

THE TL ESCORTS THE PRINCIPAL TO THE FRONT VEHICLE

THE TL THEN TAKES HIS PLACE NEXT TO THE PRINCIPAL.
NUMBER 1 TAKES THE FRONT PASSENGER SEAT

NUMBERS 2 AND 3 WILL TAKE THEIR PLACES IN THE CHASE CAR.
NUMBER 2 WILL SIT IN THE REAR OF THE VEHICLE.
NUMBER 3 WILL TAKE HIS PLACE IN THE FRONT PASSENGER SEAT

Five person formation (using 2 vehicles)

We now have the luxury of a full box cover for the two vehicles.

1, 2, 3 and 4 will leave the building together. Number 1 and 2 will go to the far side of each car. They are in line with each other covering a full field of frontal vision. Number 3 and 4 do so the same but they are on the near side of the vehicles and thereby both sides of the vehicles have cover.

In this formation all team members will indicate that they are happy with their arc of responsibility by using their radio and clearly stating "1 ok", followed by "2 ok" until all 4 have reported in. The TL on the same radio net will now leave the building with the Principal and escort the Principal to his seat.

Always remember: When securing a vehicle, all team members must take the nearest seat that they can; this saves an unnecessary waste of time. The Principal's vehicle must and without exception always be the first vehicle to be secured.

AFTER THE TL HAS TAKEN HIS SEATING POSITION NEXT TO THE PRINCIPAL. NUMBER 1 WILL THEN TAKE HIS PLACE IN THE FRONT PASSENGER SEAT OF THE PRINCIPAL'S VEHICLE.

THE REMAINING TEAM MEMBERS WILL TAKE THEIR SEATS IN THE CHASE VEHICLE. NUMBER 2 WILL SIT IN THE REAR PASSENGER SEAT. NUMBER 3 WILL SIT NEXT TO HIM. NUMBER 4 WILL SIT IN THE FRONT PASSENGER SEAT

LINE FORMATIONS

IN THIS FORMATION, THE CLOSE PROTECTION TEAM ARE MORE STAGGERED WHICH ALLOWS A PRINCIPAL TO WALK OR BE ESCORTED TO THE VEHICLE WITH COVER ON BOTH SIDES

IN THIS FORMATION, THE LINE IS CLOSED. ALL ARCS OF VISION ARE COVERED AND THE PRINCIPAL AND TL WALK ALONGSIDE THE LINE DIRECTLY TO THE VEHICLE

THE REVERSE OF THE PREVIOUS PICTURE, THE PRINCIPAL EXITS THE VEHICLE

Conclusion:

These are the basics of vehicle embuss and debuss. Dependant on the Principal, risk and budget they will alter to suit.

Part of the advance planning should tell you what side of the road you will be debussing on and this will have an effect on the overall formation and how it flows. Also dependent on what country you are working in, seating positions will change. A Professional CP Team must practise formation drilling diligently prior to working in a different country where seating positions and driving on the different side of the road is a working reality.

If performing an unorthodox embuss/debuss always remember to position your team where they have the best visibility that is possible.

The principles of all formations appear to be straight forward but to perform them correctly on the ground is not. They need to be practiced as a team prior to assignment. Good drill work that is slick will look professional and will flow smoothly; done badly it reflects on you and your Principal.

"With embuss and debuss training, you will be expected to move very quickly."

CHAPTER THIRTEEN

BUILDINGS & STRUCTURES

ALL BUILDINGS HAVE THEIR OWN COMPLICATIONS

THEATRE SEATING & ENTRY AND EXIT POINTS

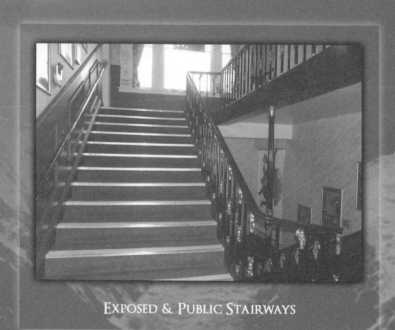

EXPOSED & PUBLIC STAIRWAYS

CHAPTER THIRTEEN
BUILDINGS AND STRUCTURES

To plan a successful operation and provide the best possible all round protection you must understand and appreciate the construction of buildings.

With every building you need to consider:

Outer Walls – Thickness, construction, penetrable.
Roof – Roof space or attics, material, construction, dormers.
Rooms – Number and location.
Inner Walls – Partition, load bearing.
Floors – Type of material.
Ceilings – False, lighting (carry electrical cabling) – often voids above.
Doors – Internal (often flimsy), hinges, locks, panelling, handles, alarmed.
Windows – Breakable, can be opened, (security), double-glazed, gap sizes, laminated (non breakable), viewable, curtains or blinds, window as an exit.
Entrances & Exits – Door type, strength, (thickness), glass, on what level, locks, does the door open inwards or outwards.
Staircases – Width, length, accessible, private VIP staircases.
Utilities – Gas, electricity, water, sewage, power points, trip switches and fuse boxes.
Number of Storeys? How many and who has access.
Lifts – How many, lockable (private lifts), passkeys required, service lifts.

Types Of Buildings

To numerous to detail but include:

Restaurants – Kitchens, rear entrances, car parks, easily accessible, capacity, large windows, Principal visibility, fire exits, separate VIP exits.

Theatres & Cinemas – Large foyers, large stairwells, fire exits, capacity, staffing, stage doors, regular seating, private areas, dressing rooms and facilities.

Shops – Entrance doors, fixture density, alternative exits, staff, visibility, changing rooms, facilities.

Private Houses – Non-secured, grounds, perimeter.

Nightclubs & Public Houses – House Limit, communal facilities, cellars, rear exits, loading hatches, in house security and VIP areas.

For every building there need to be different considerations. In order to prepare effective safety/security plans you will need to study and examine the layout of such premises.

Every building has its own complications for the professional Operator.

Using hotels as an example

There are many elements to consider in your planning:-

Garages – Where are they? Inside the building or at a remote site? Who is responsible for the parking? Who has access to the parked area and is there private security watching it? What is the size of the garaged area? What are its height limits? What is the lighting like? Is there space for vehicle searching and if so, who can watch?

What assurances do you have that the vehicles are secure? Does the hotel take any responsibility?

The garaged area of a hotel can be one of the most vulnerable parts of the premises and unless your Principal or Team Leader appoints a team member to watch the vehicles, you are absolutely dependent on in-house security.

Over the years I have seen some appalling security at hotels. Before you return to the vehicles with your Principal it is wise to check the car first. This checking procedure will draw attention to you and the vehicles as most garaged areas in hotels are under CCTV. If the garaged area is under the watch of in-house security, be courteous and try to be tactful as you are searching the vehicles that they have been watching. This may be seen as insulting and demonstrate a visual lack of trust. Diplomacy in these situations goes a long way for future co-operation with outside security teams.

CCTV coverage & other security control centres or central stations, alarms, (Security & fire) – some teams also carry a portable CCTV system; these can be set up easily outside a hotel door and are very cheap to buy. You can buy a useable system from most electrical or DIY stores.

Footnote: Be careful that if you 'install' a CCTV system that it doesn't damage the hotel doors or walls or this could lead to a compensation claim from the hotel. It will also have a certain affect of the reputation of your Principal.

Corridors and passageways – Where do they lead? Who has access? Where does each door take you?

Foyers & Receptions – Doorways, toilets, shops, lifts, stairways, private access areas which avoid the public.

Kitchens – Fire escapes, delivery entrances, hatches, store rooms, freezers.

Bathrooms – Source of water supply, one way in/out, extractors.

Fire escapes & back passages – Clearly marked, positioning, lead out to where?

Lifts – Access, weight limit, number of, private lifts and separate pass keys or key codes, alarm systems, manned? – Never use in an emergency such as a power cut – what is the back up plan?

Outbuildings – e.g. Stables, barns, leisure facilities.

Escalators – Every floor, slow, moving? (Not to use in an emergency).

Basement or cellar – Escape route, rear passageways, car parks, storage.

Others considerations - using hotels as an example

Major city hotels are used to working with high profile guests using Close Protection and this usually makes movement and assistance far easier. However, in smaller country hotels they may not be familiar with the concept of CP and you may become the gossip of the hotel. Do not ever let this interest affect your focus. If you are ever working with celebrities and you visit a small town or village, even if you arrive unannounced, the local media interest can be intense and at times can be difficult to work with. It is not uncommon for small towns to promote themselves off the back of a celebrity visit; in fact they will use this to the maximum limit to promote an area.

Other guests – Unless your Principal is of considerable wealth and books a whole hotel, there will be other guests. Some celebrities and the very rich who wish privacy book whole hotel floors for themselves and their entourage.

Guests are entitled to be there and their privacy has to be respected. Do not make a habit of removing guests out of lifts and bars and restaurant areas. If your Principal wishes this you have to make an acceptable judgement. Guests cannot be vetted. Approaching guests of a hotel and asking them probing questions is equally un-acceptable and will cause certain bad feeling. Guests however are to be watched when on high risk assignments, particularly if your Principal is of a religious or political background.

You must keep vigilant by watching other guests (without obviously staring and making them uncomfortable). Look at body language and if they *'fit'* the hotel – are they dressed appropriately? What baggage do they have and where are they carrying it to etc.? Maintain vigilance without being aggressive or adopt a stance that makes guests and hotel staff uncomfortable; if you need to speak to guests for whatever reason be polite and courteous.

Footnote: Some celebrities are not welcome and are 'banned' from some major hotels as their presence and the media interest is not always good for business. All press being "good press" does not apply to the running of an executive hotel. In major city hotels there may be a hundred other guests to consider and their business overall is of far more 'worth' to the hotel than that of a celebrity Principal staying.

Doorperson – The doorperson sees everyone who comes in and out of the hotel. They are to be respected and *"tipped"* when appropriate. During breaks it is good practice to speak to the doorperson who is often worth befriending. Do not get too personal with the doorperson as you are there in a professional capacity. However, if your Principal is under a substantial threat some non-confidential information may be worth mentioning and they can keep you informed of any suspicions they may have.

"A doorperson at a London hotel"

174

Manager – The manager of a major city hotel will be used to the sight of CP Operators and advanced team members. This doesn't mean that he will have the time to help you. If you want to meet directly with the main manger of a hotel make sure you use the time to its best advantage. Find out everything you need to know to include his personal assistant and assistant managers as they will always have more time to help you. Do not make a habit of ringing a senior manager for the slightest thing when an assistant will suffice.

Security Manager – Many large hotels employ security managers. Check if the hotel has any resident security and whether any of them could be at your disposal. The security manager will know all the pitfalls of the hotel and can be of considerable benefit to you both in planning as well as during your stay.

Footnote: We were recently hired to protect a very high profile celebrity Principal and the general manager and security manager put all his staff at our disposal and actually brought in more. This boosted our team considerably and ensured that the media and crowds were controlled as well as performing a valuable RST role. This allowed our team to concentrate on their jobs and was extremely helpful and ensured professionalism.

Concierge – The concierge is also worth speaking with as he will see too many of the personal needs of your Principal; from bringing cars around to the front, handling baggage as well as using his local knowledge if your Principal is looking for something in particular. If you need to arrange extra cars or rooms he will know appropriate companies and other good hotels. The concierge is also one to tip to ensure good service.

Porters – There is sometimes natural suspicion of some porters. They can see who goes into each room and their appearance on any level of a hotel is often not questioned. If tabloid journalists want to know what is going on in a hotel, the porter is the one to ask. As a rule of thumb, tip porters well and hopefully they will keep a lookout for <u>you</u>.

Footnote: In some places porters are used as spotters for who is staying in which room and whether there are items of value in them which could lead to a possible theft.

Other Staff – In large hotels there will always be many other staff in various support roles. Large hotels often have a high turnover of staff. In a recent marketing exercise, my Senior Operations Manager contacted most of the 4 and 5 star hotels in London to discuss security. It was a considerable surprise to us that many who answered the phone did not speak good English at all. Many did not know who the hotel manager was and next to no one knew who the security manager was.

Imagine now asking for a hotel risk assessment and floor plans and what type of people has been staying there recently.

Restaurant Managers – Obtain the name of the manager and visit him before dining. Discuss the menu and ensure it caters for your Principal's dietary needs. The restaurant manager can be of great assistance for a smooth operation and your Principal will notice the extra efforts you make. You may wish to ask for tables around your Principal to be reserved for your team if they are likely to be joining the Principal in the restaurant. If not, a discrete table maybe reserved.

Restaurant Managers can also be of help when it comes to getting meals and refreshments to your team and it is always best to keep them on your side.

Surrounding area to your hotel – Be aware of the surrounding environment and consider this to what threat your Principal is under. Do not overreact and advise the Principal against staying at a hotel, especially if the hotel is his choice. Consider routes in and if there is any vehicle choke points. Can others observe you entering and especially leaving a hotel to waiting vehicles? Your actions are always dependent on threat but do not overreact.

Revolving Doors – Revolving Doors are a real problem for effective and flowing CP formations. They are difficult to walk through in any formation and to move a full escort team through can take a minute or two especially if other people are trying to come through. Revolving doors are very dangerous and it is easy for the team to become separated for a brief period. A lot of hotels will have a side door next to the revolving door. Try to take advantage of this where possible.

Checking the room(s) that will be used – If you are carrying out a full search of any hotel room or suite you will have to declare them safe or sterile when completed. An advanced team may be responsible for this, but if anyone enters this area, albeit it very briefly to deliver or clean something, this is now a contaminated area and the full search will have to be done again. This is immensely time consuming.

Vetting of visitors at entrance – To vet people at the entrance to the suite or floor (if your Principal has booked them) is perfectly acceptable. However, it is not acceptable to stand at the front of the hotel and question everyone who comes in. You must appreciate the need of both the hotel and its other guests.

Communications – Have a line of communications with your control room – you may use a hotel room as a temporary security station, this is a good idea when working with a large team.

You should always have communications with this room and team from either your mobile phone or a radio. In built up city areas with high rise buildings and with very thick steel walls or floors, radio signals can be impaired. When using communications in these areas make sure you call in for a radio check on a regular basis.

Vetting of Staff – You have no rights to do this. Speaking to staff and asking them personal questions or enquiring about them to the management can cause considerable resentment. Any enquiries about staff will have to be handled very tactfully. Suspicious behaviour of staff is one thing and this should be brought to management attention but anything else may cause considerable friction. As a rule do not do this.

Surrounding rooms – It is always best to have a team together and surrounding rooms should be taken by the team. This sounds ideal but in a 5 star executive hotel this will not always happen as budget can take precedent over safety. You can observe who enters surrounding rooms and if you have any uncertainties then post a member of the team on corridor watch. There is nothing wrong with creating a presence in these circumstances.

"Surrounding rooms may be as luxurious as these. The budget may not allow for this"

Select rooms above the 2nd Floor. For safety from entry and media intrusion, always stay above the first floor, this also prevents too much noise from the lobby area. There will always be a fine line between safety and the Principal's needs. If the opportunity arises, generally select a room on the 2nd floor as you have to consider fire hazards in a hotel as well. However, the 2nd floor may not offer the Principal what he wants in terms of the quality of the room as historically the best hotel suites are on the top floor.

End of Corridor – For similar reasons try to have rooms at the end of a corridor.

This is not a definitive list but it will give you some idea of the necessity to understand buildings and how they affect Close Protection. If you have any uncertainties when working in new buildings, create a check list to make sure everything is in order. If, *(as an example),* you move to different hotels on a regular basis it is easy to become complacent. Try to be vigilant at every venue. Each building will always have its own complications.

"Clearwater employee Ian Trevor about to enter a London hotel with the actress Lindsey Lohan"

CHAPTER FOURTEEN

PERSONAL SEARCH TECHNIQUES

Search Techniques in Close Protection Must Be Thorough.
However, An Individual's Private Space and Belongings
Must Be Respected At All Times

CHAPTER FOURTEEN
PERSONAL SEARCH TECHNIQUES

With the exception of travel, searching is one of the most time consuming phases for the Professional CPO.

Searching is vitally important and is dependant upon disciplined routine. There is a sequence that must be followed to search vehicles, buildings, inner and outer cordons, as well as people.

Searching can be very tedious, thankless and monotonous and it can certainly be dirty – *never search under a car in your best suit!*

Searching is about detail and professionalism. If you become complacent in the way you search this will eventually be noticed by the people around you, and more importantly, your threat may suspect as much.

Searching should be handled by professionals who have been properly trained and know exactly what to look for. They require knowledge of device concealment and an understanding of the vulnerable parts or places of a building or vehicle.

Searching is a considerable responsibility. The Principal trusts the word of a professional who assures him that the building, vehicle or people around him are safe.

"A professional Military dog handler, an excellent resource if the budget allows for it"

"However, some do not react well to strangers"

Search Routine

External Search

- The Garden – and garden objects/ornaments.
- Outhouses – and who has access? (Use RST knowledge).
- Garages – how many garages and what vehicles use them? (To include other vehicles such as sit-on lawnmowers, buggies, children's vehicles etc).
- Outer Perimeter – the workable perimeter and physical boundaries i.e. fencing and security systems.
- Outer Cordon (Visual only), non-physical boundaries and public rights of way.
- Entrance/Exit, emergency routes, accessibility to you as well as others including potential threats.
- Search for signs of tampering. This applies throughout the external area and includes each building or object within that area.

Internal Search

- Entrance/Exits (all doorways) – underground passageways.
- Hallways – and objects inside hallways.
- Basements – to include those that are not used.
- Items that have been moved or disturbed – you cannot know this until you have worked in a residence or hotel area for some time and such disturbance will have instant recognition. Time spent in situ will develop your natural instincts and you will become accustomed to the décor, facilities and objects.
- Windows – open/tampered with, marked with finger prints or grease etc.
- Side rooms – who has access and how are these monitored?
- Main rooms – the main areas that your Principal uses to include areas of relaxation.
- Stairways? – how many and who uses them? Are there private stairways that the Principal uses that others do not or should not use?
- Below Stairways – some stairways have cupboards or small rooms beneath them.
- Loft/Attics – confirm that this is absolutely necessary to search here and bear in mind that you will get filthy dirty if you do so. It is good to be seen to be thorough but not to go to unnecessary lengths that will cause worry. Do not unnerve a Principal by carrying out actions that are not needed. If you determine that these actions are necessary, try

to do them discreetly. Clambering about in a loft can also be dangerous particularly if you are doing this in an old property. A false step and you can go through the floor and you can bet your life it will be right above where your Principal is sitting! Searching such areas and going to such extremes can raise serious questions of security *'professionalism'*. If a threat can get into the attic – you have many other serious matters to contend with.

■   Landings – and objects on it.

■   Bathrooms – how many are there and who has access? Some Principals will not want you to look in bathroom areas especially if they are en-suite to the main bedrooms. Bathrooms can be particularly dangerous territory for the CP specialist as they are very personal places, from objects inside them to walking in at the wrong moment. Ask yourself the same question as with lofts/attics *"can people really enter these areas anyway"*? If a threat has been able to get as far as the 'en-suite', serious mistakes have already been made.

■   Locks and Locked Doors – who is the overall keyholder? Bear in mind that your Principal may not carry the keys to a property or vehicles and this responsibility may fall to the team. Common sense should prevail if you find doors unlocked. It is good procedure to have a signing sheet detailing who has responsibility for keys and when the most important doors were last locked and by whom? By having standard operational procedures, any disturbance can be far easier to manage, as well as being able to point an accurate finger at the team member who may be responsible for leaving locked doors open.

Time Management

The biggest factor in searching is the time involved and the practicability of the time invested against the perceived threat. Generally the bigger the team the ease of searching. Responsibility must be taken by those who search. I.e. if a Principal is to arrive at a hotel – the AST team should have taken care of the detailed search. However, if the team needs to move on how can you be sure that the area is sterile?

Some AST work days or weeks ahead and therefore escort section members may have to be used for the search. If any room needs searching within the general residence then the team leader of the RST team must take responsibility while watching team members carry out the search.

For a successful assignment with little interference to the Principal, time management of the search is a crucial factor and you must consider the following:

Risk Areas:

- Consider how many are in the team and how much time you have to search? If you are on an assignment of considerable threat and you feel uncomfortable that searching is not being carried out effectively enough (maybe due to a lack of resources?), you must raise it with the Team Leader. If you are the Team Leader then you must raise it with the PES Team Leader. If you are in overall charge then it must be raised with the employer – that is the company you are working for - **Not the Principal**. Let the company handle the negotiation with the Principal if more team members are needed. Never go straight to the Principal to ask for more resources. This is not your decision to make and will antagonise the Principal and definitely your employer.
- Ideal numbers – the ideal number in a search team (for rooms and vehicles) is three. If in a room the Team Leader should stand in the middle directing and observing. The two team members will work at opposite corners of the room to each other and work in a clockwise direction.
- If the whole team is searching who is planning? – This is a very important question. If for example the whole of the RST team are involved in searching who is taking care of the rest of the whole protected area? Although assignment and threat related, professional searching is important, however it can dictate how much time you have left to spend on other phases of the operation.
- Save time by telling team members what they need to know – do not bother team members with tittle-tattle and make them search for something that is not going to be there. If you are the Team Leader only tell team members what you know to be fact based upon evidence and most importantly tell them only what they **need** to know.

Intensive Search Areas

- Is intensive search necessary? – do not waste time or overreact.
- What is the nature of the threat to determine the reaction? You cannot search for something that you do not know about or understand. If you are working with a business executive who is involved in, or maybe the victim of, a hostile takeover, you will need to give consideration to listening devices and what they look like and most importantly how they work.

- Never work in scenarios that you do not understand. If a threat is elevated consider taking advice if you are unsure. The company who trained you may be able to help here.
- What are you looking for? Know your enemy's tactics. Threat determination and knowledge of an enemy's capabilities and resources are paramount in answering this question.
- What needs intensive searching? i.e. one room or a whole floor with numerous rooms. Consider the necessity of this and the time involved.
- If you have to search a whole floor, this may take you <u>all day</u>.
- Which personnel are allowed to enter the secured area? An area is only secured when trusted members of the team have completed the search. In order for a team or team members to be trusted they will have to earn trust and respect from the employer, the team and the Principal. If you are working at a hotel and room service enters, observe them at all times. If cleaners need to enter the room then you may only wish to admit one at a time so you can watch them throughout the time they are present. Room service is generally only one person but cleaners can be in multiple numbers. A room is not sterile when someone unknown enters the secured area. If this happens you must start the search again. Look for hiding places, people and devices. Follow your routine and stick to it unless there has been a change of threat or an acceleration of motive.

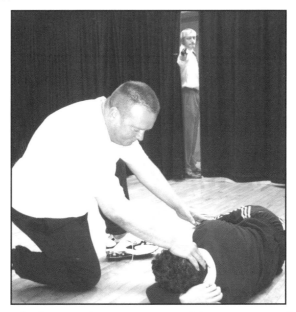

"Even if a Principal is down, never rush into a room until you know it is completely safe"

184

Routine

Construct your own personal routine
(The following tried and tested principles may help):

- Start with the doorway.
- Work in a clockwise direction (*always undertake all searching in a clockwise direction).*
- Check panels, seats, phone lines and everything moveable/liftable.
- If you have a full team, utilise the Team Leader by having him take the central position in the room. He must make sure that everything is covered in a painstaking manner.
- Switch on lights and electrical appliances.
- Check for new electrical appliances that have appeared – this definitely includes plug points and extensions (such as a three way plug block). Listening and film devices can be hidden in plug blocks and points and they will start transmitting as soon as they acquire a power source. have full permission for this *(especially in bedroom and bathroom areas).*
- Check windows and curtains for devices, tampering, the smearing of fingerprints and general untidiness.

Order of Search

1. Start with the ceiling
2. Search the floor
3. Work your way up from around the floor

Searching People

When can you search a person?

This will depend on the country you are working in but as a general rule you have no lawful authority which entitles you to search any person without their permission.

Searching people is a repetitive process and it can be very difficult as you may have to search awkward and sometimes offensive and rude people.

For a CPO who has spent his former years working in a Military environment or in civilian life as a door supervisor, he may think that he has left the searching of people behind – not necessarily so.

If you are working in the corporate sector you may have to carry out a search prior to an event or specific meeting. Searching is generally very poor business etiquette as it can demonstrate a lack of trust in the corporate community, but it does happen.

Searching a journalist who is to interview a celebrity or someone who is in the public eye is very tricky as the most non threatening objects can have transmitters and recording devices within them and *'conveniently'* get left behind. Never take an object for granted and if you have any uncertainties do not permit them into the room.

"When asking permission to search someone, never encroach upon their personal space"

Seeking Permission

If you touch someone without asking their permission you may have assaulted them. If you touch someone of the opposite sex you may be accused of sexual assault. Be exceptional careful:

Footnote: As a rule: Never search anyone without permission. Where possible try to have an observer and never search anyone of the opposite sex no matter what is said. If you are working on a long detail do not get sloppy. You must take action to protect yourself by advising your Principal that you cannot search anyone of the opposite sex. If your Principal then proceeds to allow this person to enter the room or area (after you have warned them of this) and they do something or leave a recording device (as an example), you can plead your case that you advised them not to. This may not be well received by the Principal but at least it is the truth and hopefully your employer or other team members (if you have them) will defend your actions.

Unlike the static guarding sector, provision is rarely made for searching.

This is true when travelling but there should be provision and SOPs when working on residential detail. If you are working at an Embassy (as an example) there should be search procedures in place although procedures will vary dependent on what the business of the day is.

Searching policies in the corporate community are not a good example of business trust.

This has already been referred to but it is very true. Be on your guard, if you ever have to search corporate Executives this will create a bad atmosphere before any meeting or event is to take place. You may be the victim of some abuse here despite saying that *'it is your job'* or *'Mr. so and so has requested it'*. Do not ever retaliate or speak back at a guest – just be professional and accept that sometimes in this career you have to swallow your pride a little.

Be vigilant of the threat and understand your role. You may have to make the decision to search or ask to search a person.

"A security detector is one way of minimising stress when searching people"

Searching At Events

For special events, a search policy can be requested, but usually it will fall to the discretion of the individual Operative. To avoid confusion put up a sign which can be clearly seen by all guests. – By doing this you can avoid the *"why are you picking on me"* type of question.

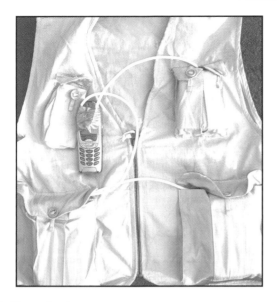

"An example of a body worn I.E.D. rig"

Ask Permission

If there is no search policy you must decide what to do.

First you must ask permission.

If consent is given make sure the Operative who searches is of the same sex. When *"padding"* someone *(In reality don't pad, squeeze gently)*, make sure that no personal areas of the body are touched – even if same sex. Professionally, the term *"padding"* remains in door supervision and nightclub security. In Close Protection it is called squeezing.

If you feel an object that you are not sure of:

1.   Ask to see it.
2.   Do not remove it yourself.
3.   Ask the subject to remove it and guide their hand (without touching) away from your body. Expert door supervisors and nightclub security are excellent at this. It is a natural reaction when someone takes something from their pocket that you naturally deflect it away from you. This can be done very gently and non-aggressively.
4.   Always examine objects. e.g. a pack of cigarettes. Look inside to confirm the contents.
5.   Always be on your guard for a *"double blag"*. A double blag happens when you search someone and find an obvious object, you then ask them to remove it but you do not recheck the area you have removed the object from. For example, you have removed a wallet and sitting behind it is a recording device that you may have missed.

ALWAYS CHECK OVER AREAS THAT YOU HAVE REMOVED OBJECTS FROM

"Searching should always be undertaken by someone of the same sex"

Bag Search

You do not have the power to look inside anyone's possessions unless permission has been granted.

Never remove a bag out of sight of the owner – **ever**.
Use your discretion with what you remove from the bag and be vigilant and courteous when people are around you.
Do not remove personal items from a bag if it can be avoided.
If hygiene products are in a bag use your discretion. You may ask the person you are searching if you can spray a deodorant or an aftershave and watch their reaction? If female hygiene products are found make sure that a female undertakes the search.
Use your skills of observation and see if the bag suits the person who is carrying it and does it fit their attire?

Be observant after entry. Make sure that the bag remains with them.

MAKE SURE THAT YOU ALWAYS THANK SOMEONE AFTER A SEARCH

HIDING PLACES ON A PERSON

1. HAIR, HAT OR TURBAN
2. SHOULDER PADS & LAPELS
3. IN THE MOUTH
4. LAPELS
5. COLLAR
6. TORSO
7. IN OR BEHIND THE TIE
8. ARMS
9. COAT
10. ARMPITS
11. WATCH
12. IN OR BEHIND THE BELT
13. HANDS
14. LEGS
15. ANKLES
16. FOOTWARE

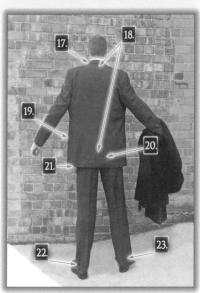

17. JACKET COLLAR
18. SPINE (FROM NECK TO BASE OF BACK)
19. POCKETS, LINING & PADS
20. BUTTOCKS (UNDER JACKET)
21. HEM OF JACKET
22. TURNUPS
23. SOCKS

* OTHER CONSIDERATIONS:
FACIAL HAIR - BEARDS
AUXILIARY ITEMS SUCH AS
GLASSES & HEARING AIDS

*"A receiver is found in a jacket
pocket"*

*"A transmitter is found hiding
inside a tie"*

"With the late Michael Jackson"

"Arriving At The Red Carpet, H.S.H. Prince Albert II,
the Sovereign Prince Of Monaco"

"Receiving Official Thanks from his Royal Highness The Prince Of Wales for Clearwater's Support of the Armed and Reserve Forces"

"At Buckingham Palace with Major Johnny Longbottom MBE HAC - Celebrating 100 years of The British Territorial Army"

"Paris Hilton in 2010, working with long term friend Ian Trevor"

"Working as a team can lead to long term friendships"

"At the Clearwater Head Offices with Lt. Gen Sir John Foley KCB OBE MC DL "

"Alicia Keys poses in front of a bank of the Paparazzi"

"With Formula 1's David Coulthard and Formula 1
World Champion Jenson Button"

"Working with Ian at the Cannes Film Festival"

"Mariah Carey in 2008"

"Jennifer Lopez in Monaco"

"With Ian and a selection of VIP Escort Vehicles"

"In Basra, Iraq, with Major General John Cooper DSO MBE and
Clearwater Reservist C/pl Lee Wickson"

"Clearwater Red Carpet Team 2007"

"Clearwater Red Carpet Team 2008"

"Clearwater Red Carpet Team 2010"

CHAPTER FIFTEEN

DRESS & BEHAVIOUR

AN EXAMPLE OF A VIP BANQUET

ETIQUETTE, EFFECTIVENESS AND PROFESSIONALISM
WILL BE QUESTIONED IF YOU EVER HAVE TO
PHYSICALLY RESTRAIN SOMEONE

CHAPTER FIFTEEN

DRESS AND BEHAVIOUR

Basic Principles of Conduct

Regardless of all the training you undertake, the achievement of specialist skills, and whatever experience and background you may have, if you cannot communicate properly you will not get employment in this business, or remain in it for very long.

The most common flaw in the Close Protection Operative is a lack of social etiquette. I have been embarrassed on many occasions with the way someone has spoken to a Principal, from either being too informal, too personal or commenting on matters not of their concern. From a smile that reveals a pierced tongue to bad breath and overpowering cheap aftershave, if you are unlucky enough you will get to see it all!

A Team Leader may not be the one who selects the team but he will be the one who is responsible for it as well as having the control of it.

A Team Leader must be respected and recognised as the decision maker and the figure of authority to get the best out of the team. A Team Leader who tries to 'befriend' the team or mix with the team while off duty does not bring out the best in his team. This can also damage the respect for the chain of command. For a team to do things together or socialise when on down time is one thing but as soon as the Team Leader gets personally involved with the team, respect can be lost and advantage can be taken.

That is not to say that the Team Leader cannot ever 'socialise' with the team, but he must not put himself in a position where he loses the credibility of the team or the respect for his position.

The company you are working for should guide you exactly on what is expected of you, this would usually be in the form of a working brief or assignment instruction. That brief should include your exact job description and detail what your overall presentation should be. This should include overall lines of communication and who you are directly answerable to.

When working in large teams, for example with a Principal and his extended family, there may be multiple Principals, from the main subject himself to the remainder of the family. In this scenario every family member is a Principal in their own right.

It is not unusual to have as many as 30 CPOs in a team for this type of contract. If you ever work on this type of detail it is the absolute responsibility of your Team Leader and the company you are working for to inform you of your <u>exact</u> duties and who is your immediate supervisor.

Behaviour

One of the most important attributes of a good CPO is his professional conduct and how he deports himself; this **will** have considerable bearing on what the Principal thinks of him and may ensure re-employment. It may have nothing to do with how well you *'performed'* as a good CPO but how you presented yourself, how you communicated and how you followed instructions.

This may come as a surprise to some, but sometimes judgements can be made on your etiquette and not necessarily your skills in threat analysis and other vital protective functions. There are many schools of thought that suggest you should not communicate with the Principal at all as this is unprofessional. This may be true, but you should always talk to a Principal if they are making conversation with you. By not communicating you will appear to be rude and possibly arrogant. Various Principals have commented in the past that he is *"miserable"* or conversely *"too talkative"*. If you are working full time with a Principal on a two month assignment it is inevitable that at some point you will end up in conversation with him. When this happens be courteous but not servile. Bad manners and a lack of etiquette will affect your reemployment.

A good CP Operative is not a servant but will always have to use his common sense when on an assignment. This will include the carrying of bags and other such tasks. As mentioned in Team Options; you should not involve yourself in domestic tasks but you will have to be flexible. Some will say that you should never carry bags (as an example) as your hands will not be free and therefore you are not providing cover – this is true. But refusing on those grounds will not be accepted by most Principals. If you have to accompany a Principal to a store and are asked to carry some of the shopping to a car, you will probably have to do it. By refusing you will be seen as unapproachable and possibly unemployable. However, try to find another way and try to arrange someone else to carry baggage if you can. The big department stores will usually have someone to do this and you should deflect this request their way.

When you are in this situation do not be over familiar or 'relax' too much. Always use the appropriate form of address.

If protecting a Principal of the opposite sex – for example, you are a male and assigned to protect the wife of a male Principal, make sure the rules of etiquette remain.

Be very careful if the *'relationship'* becomes too relaxed. If in a store she offers to buy a gift for you – refusal can offend, but accepting a gift can also place you in a difficult situation. Depending on what the gift is and if it is of 'small' monitory value it is usually best to accept *(after politely declining first)* – but be aware of what the main Principal will think of this when he finds out *(especially if his credit card has been used)*. To cover yourself you **should** mention this to your employer and disclose what was bought for you and when. Having gifts bought for you in some sectors of Close Protection can be quite common.

Job parameters – beware of taking on additional responsibilities or carrying out tasks not covered in your contract or working brief. If unsure, ask for advice from your immediate Team Leader or the Company you are working for. Items of value (such as assets) can be included here; for example - a Principal may ask you to transport an expensive piece of artwork. Are you covered in your contract to undertake this? A number of Close Protection Operatives would not think twice about carrying out this service, but if the artwork is extremely valuable are you insured for this? In most cases probably not. This is a difficult call as you do not want to appear to be awkward with the Principal. If you get into this situation you may wish to enquire of the Principal whether you are insured through their insurance?

Never transport packages that you are unsure of, or start collecting wrapped packages on a regular basis. Do not become an international courier service for your Principal. Where etiquette allows and there is no breach of confidentiality; always try to find out what you are transporting, this is for your own self preservation in Law.

Basic Principals of Conduct

Drink and Drugs – this should be obvious. If you are working for a company you would normally have to sign a code of conduct. The taking of drink and drugs whilst employed will probably be right at the top of the list of the things that will lead to instant dismissal.

This is not the same as having to take prescribed medication. You must inform the company immediately of any medication that you have to take. Consider that if you socialise the night before work and drink some alcohol it may not just be the smell of alcohol on your breath the next day that is the problem, you may also be over the limit not just to work but to drive as well.

<u>Important Fact</u>: My Company - "Clearwater", carries out random drugs tests on some assignments. We take this issue very seriously and all Operatives will have to sign a code of conduct where there is a clause stating that we have the right to do so. Failure to provide a drugs test when requested is instant dismissal.

Footnote: Some drugs are legal in one country but not necessarily in another. If you have to take medicine and are unsure of their legal standpoint, check this before travel.

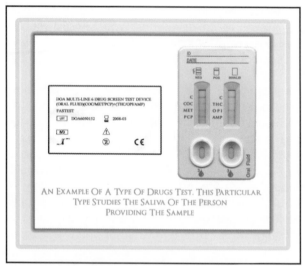

AN EXAMPLE OF A TYPE OF DRUGS TEST. THIS PARTICULAR TYPE STUDIES THE SALIVA OF THE PERSON PROVIDING THE SAMPLE

Swearing and coarse language – Swearing should never happen in front of a Principal or any of their associates. If you feel or are confident that you can have a conversation with a Principal and use bad language then clearly the *'relationship'* has become too close, too relaxed and unprofessional.

If relevant, try to gain knowledge of the Principal's religion and customs. If your Principal has religious beliefs they must be observed and respected. Every culture has different customs and you must have a good understanding of exactly what they are before you enter a different country or protect someone of a different Nationality. Always take advice on this through your network or carry out some research through a library or the internet.

Punctuality – This is of prime importance.
It can be very frustrating if a Principal is late but it is not acceptable for Close Protection Operatives to be late at all. Punctuality is always on my mind when employing CPOs and they usually have to report in to our Operations Manager when they arrive on assignments, especially for the first time or on the first day.

There are plenty of people who are good on the ground as CPOs but I do not employ them if I cannot trust their punctuality. In this business if you say you are going to do something or be somewhere at a certain time you must mean it.

Your Word Is What You Stand For.

Demeanour – It is important that you are presented correctly for each assignment and you must dress accordingly. Your demeanour says a lot about you; from the way you dress, your body language and how you conduct yourself as well as how you generally communicate with people. Aggressiveness and heavy handed approaches will not work in the Corporate sector and rarely works anywhere else. Your demeanour will also be reflected in how you 'display' your confidence. It is vitally important to be confident in this line of business but over confidence can lead to 'cockiness' and arrogance. Those who say that they do not fear anything generally do, or are simply dangerous people to work with. Having presence should be natural and not forced.

Appearance & Image – Surprisingly many CPOs wear earrings *(especially those working in the entertainment sector)* or other piercings that can be seen. They need to be removed or covered up.

Your hair also reflects your image and the type of person you are. Unkempt hair will reflect a scruffy personality and a completely shaven head can (at times) look aggressive. Principals will look for you to portray a professional image. First impressions count.

"Appearance and professionalism work hand in hand. Here Clearwater team members are dressed to suit the occasion"

197

After Work Hours – If on assignment and staying in a hotel, when you are stood down, you do not want to remain in the hotel for the whole of the time. This is not healthy as the hotel is 'a place of work'. Try to remove yourself from the place of work or where the Principal is staying. Wherever you go or whatever you do when working as a CPO, events can change at any moment and you may be recalled at any time. You should always be contactable and never travel too far that you cannot commute back very quickly.

Some team members out of hours may go for a drink. If you are under the influence of alcohol tempers can change suddenly as well as having obvious *'recollective problems'*.

Your movements will be slow as well as your reactions.
If you are part of a team that is known to drink socially together, this is a prime time for members of the public or journalists to get snippets of information regarding your Principal, as well as a potential threat by identifying your weaknesses.

In today's society, if you are unfit for the purpose and something goes wrong this potentially could come back against you, from criminal charges to a very damaging legal case and your career will come to an abrupt halt.

Corrupt practices – never accept a bribe for information. If you do this once you now have a price and have been 'bought', therefore you can be bought again. Bribes can come from the media for celebrity information but also from protected family members. i.e. if a son or daughter comes in late at night and offers you something of value in return for keeping quiet about it. Once you have been corrupted you will always be corruptible. Do not get carried away by being surrounded by wealth – it is not yours and it never will be. Once you have been bought, you will be bought again, and often for a cheaper price. The person who has 'bought' you will always have leverage over you.

Receiving objects as a gift or gratuity is not the same as taking something as a bribe. However be clear of the circumstances in which it was presented and who was present and can they witness or corroborate such actions?

Etiquette

Social inadequacy is not a myth and it can be very uncomfortable if you are caught up in something or somewhere that you do not understand, especially if you do not know how to conduct yourself in formal circumstances. The fact is that in all societies there is a class structure.

Integrating with different classes, especially the upper classes, can be very difficult, especially if you are someone who is more at home in informal surroundings. By nature, wealthy people will attend events and places where you are surrounded by their peers who will also probably be wealthy. It is on these occasions that etiquette flaws will show, especially when it comes to dining out.

"Working at a formal dinner"

Formal dinners and banquets

All events have practically the same service procedures where there is food or a formal meal involved.

After arrival at the event there will usually be drinks on reception such as champagne, Pimms, red or white wine and a variety of non-alcohol drinks. Pre- dinner drinks will be served from the time that is stated on the invite and will usually last for ½ - 1 hour. This time is used for socialising and general integration of guests. Unless you are your Principal's guest (very rare) it would not be usual for you to be involved at this point. You may be at the other side of the room or even at the front reception or outside with the cars. In the rarity that you are a guest of the Principal you will be expected to integrate with other people.

If you are ever in this position it is vital that you conduct yourself appropriately. Never try to 'overdo it' too much or pretend to be something that you are not. Someone who pretends to be rich, influential and travelled will often be caught out and *'old money'* will always be able to detect an impostor. However it is vitally important that you discuss this with your Principal before the event as dependent on the assignment and your role within it, it may not be in the interest to answer *'I am Mr. so and so's Bodyguard'.* Your Principal may not and probably will not wish for you to disclose who you are.

After pre-dinner drinks there will be the meal itself, often followed by speeches, presentations or words of thanks. There may be further drinks before departing.

At a formal dinner where an arrival time is stated it **must** be adhered to. For example the invite says 7.30 – 8.00 then 8.00 will be the sit down time and it will be very poor *'form'* to walk into a room after this time where everyone will notice you. It is possible at some formal dinner/engagements that you may also be refused entry – imagine your Principal is running very late, you are not ready with the car and your Principal is refused entry – you will certainly be blamed!

At this type of formal occasion you will probably not be next to the Principal or even in the room at all.

There will be a seating plan available and hopefully, if you have AST they will have helped make the seating arrangements, or liaised with those who do *(This will depend on the status of your Principal)*. The seating plan will be available for all to see and this will be outside the main function room or in the reception lounge. You should study this on arrival to note where the Principal will be in the room – *if you did not already know this?* You will of course be able to see on the seating plan who else is attending the function and if there is any known threat or other potential 'problems' in the room. If you are going to be present, each table will usually have a table number or object for you to look for, and your name will be on a name card at the table. It is customary to greet other people at the table. If you are going to be meeting people you will need to clear it with your Principal as to what you say as to your reason for being there. You may be on a security table with other CPOs in which case the evening will be full of interesting conversation (or not!).

The guest(s) of honour will sit at a top table and will probably be the last to enter the room. On very formal occasions with dignitaries in attendance other guests will remain standing until those on the top table have sat down.

The cutlery on the table will reflect the amount of courses there will be and this can be daunting for the rookie CPO who sits at a table like this for the first time.

Courses that may follow:

- Hors d'oeuvres
- Soup
- Fish
- Ice – to clear the palate
- Entrée (main course)
- Dessert
- Port & Cheese
- Coffee

Points To Be Considered With Eating Courses:

As a general rule start with using the cutlery from the outside and work your way in.

Eating can show the highest points of etiquette but will also show those who have none at all!

If there is a set menu you have no choice but if there is not, do not order the most expensive item on the menu, or what is the most difficult to eat, such as lobster or unshelled prawns.

Eating with hands will draw you a lot of unwanted attention *(such as de-shelling prawns and leaving lots of prawn heads on your plate).*

Do not make the mistake, as someone did, by taking a bowl of water from the waiter and saying thanks and then drinking it, when its purpose was for rinsing fingers. This was of considerable interest to the others on the table!

Drinking soup can be difficult, particularly if you are wearing a formal white shirt with bow tie and spill it down your top. If you spill food on yourself it can be highly embarrassing and it is a good idea to have a spare shirt or suit in the car outside.

Never complain about the food with comments like *"I've had better elsewhere etc"*, remember you will not be paying for this meal and as such is not your place to comment.

There will be different glasses on the table such as a water glass and a wine glass. Disregard the alcohol if you are working, but be careful with the amount of water you drink with the meal. Don't forget, especially if you have a long drive afterwards, that you may be desperate for the toilet on the way back and have to ask for the car to be pulled over. This can be embarrassing for you and annoying for your Principal.

If there are speeches at the dinner these will usually take place after port and cheese is served.

After port and cheese will be coffee. Dependent on the country you are working in, this may be the only time when smoking may be permitted in the room; although in an ever changing society this is becoming a thing of the past. If you are a smoker you should seek permission. As a general rule you should not smoke at all when working. The smell of smoke on your clothing and breath is not pleasant. If your Principal smokes he may not notice it, but if he doesn't he will certainly smell it on you. Some Principals stipulate that their CPOs do not smoke. This is why so many Résumé's from those looking for work make a point of mentioning that they do not smoke.

Dress

Always ensure that you are dressed appropriately for the occasion. In the event of a formal dinner this will usually be planned weeks or months in advance. You should therefore have plenty of notice.

Do not attend formal dinners wearing sunglasses. Some do this and irrespective of the reason, it looks aggressive and attracts far too much attention. Even worse is the *'poser'* type of Bodyguard (often with a 'Z' list celebrity in tow) who wears sunglasses in a darkened room, thus enabling him to see as far as 3 feet in front of his face!

Always wear a bow tie at a formal dinner; invitations will be clear about this. To attend a formal dinner in a straight tie or not wear one at all could get you ejected from some places and will certainly attract unnecessary and unwanted attention.

If wearing a radio rig, try to keep it discreet. Ask yourself if you really need to wear one at all? Is there an alternative method of communication that you can use?

The final consideration of dress code is your footwear. Make sure that shoes are always clean. They should also be comfortable as you could be on your feet for many hours. Always 'break' shoes in. Never buy a new pair and wear them for the first time to work as you could get blisters which will be very uncomfortable. Always pack spare socks to keep your feet fresh.

Mobile/Cell Phones

Always keep your mobile phone on silent vibrate or have the volume turned right down.

Mobiles are an essential form of communication. They can be discrete and a back-up communication source. However in these days of novelty ringtones, it is best to keep the phone quiet at all times. If you have to receive calls when you are working it is polite to ask the Principal or Team Leader first if you can take the call.

Appearance

Jewellery – Do not wear too much jewellery. Chains around the neck should not show. It is not a problem to wear a wedding ring but try to limit other jewellery.

Hair – Keep you hair neat and well groomed. Time permitting, try to wash you hair in the mornings to avoid greasy or dandruff hair. Dandruff on the shoulders never looks good.

Beards – Beards generally can look scruffy, although a well trimmed 'goatee' is ok.

Bad breath – You may not even know if you have this problem as most people are too polite and do not tell you. If I smell bad breath on a team member I will definitely tell him – get it sorted out.

Strong aftershave and perfumes – Do not use cheap products. If you wear aftershave at all make sure that it's a good one. In any event do not use too much so it overpowers people around you.

Body odour – The absolute worst. Keep some odourless deodorant in the car and your baggage.

General Cleanliness – You are there to protect the Principal, but your image will also reflect his standards so an overall 'clean' appearance will be required.

Overweight – An unsightly waistline, especially at the dinner table looks very bad and consequently makes you look unfit. Threats against the Principal from an organised and determined source may look for weaknesses like this. I can think of a few very famous celebrities who employ massive men to protect themselves from the paparazzi but who in reality would not be able to carry them a few yards, let alone escape on foot with them!

Sweating – Sweating looks bad no matter what, especially at the dinner table. If you have a condition where you overheat and perspire go and see your doctor and see if it can be treated.

Body piercing – Remove any piercing that will show.

Dirty hands and nails – Don't search underneath the vehicle pre-dinner as your nails will get filthy, Principal's and their Clients/guests do notice these things. Make sure your hands are clean at all times at a dinner table. If you ever have to undertake personal body searches ensure that your hands are clean for this. Keep your nails trimmed and clean. For females wearing nail varnish, use a low key colour, but chipped or half painted nails look unsightly.

"Glasses don't suit everyone!"

Conclusion:

You do not have to be an expert in etiquette to work as a CPO. However you will be working in places where your hygiene, appearance and communication skills will be on show. Good communication is one of the most underrated skills and a good CPO who excels in this will be respected by the Principal.

"A professional team should look like a professional team"

CHAPTER SIXTEEN

CLOSE PROTECTION AND THE MEDIA

Paparazzi Photographs

Ringo Starr

Curtis '50 Cent' Jackson

CHAPTER SIXTEEN

CLOSE PROTECTION AND THE MEDIA

"In this picture, the Queen is surrounded by as many cameras as she is security"

WHAT IS THE MEDIA?

The media take many forms but in relation to the Close Protection industry it can be categorised into four main areas:

Television
Newspapers (broadsheets)
Newspapers (tabloids)
Magazines

Television – The most powerful medium on the planet that has the ability to keep us informed of World events. It is also the singular and most influential tool for politics and news as well as a massive marketing tool for celebrities and the entertainment industry generally.

Newspapers (broadsheets) – Newspapers are printed in a variance of styles and cater for a variety of readers. Most broadsheet newspapers have some form of political belief and favour a political party. The main focus of broadsheets is serious news stories, business and financial markets.

Newspapers (tabloids) – Tabloid is the more generalised term for newspapers that concentrate more on celebrities and gossip rather than powerful news stories or events. Tabloids however can be the most influential of them all as they have the biggest readership, largest distribution and highest profits. A tabloid has the ability to promote a celebrity and just as quickly bring them down. Tabloids offer the most money for stories and because of their financial resources they have the ability to obtain information or gossip where others will fail.

Magazines – Celebrity magazines are massive business. They often compete with each other for stories, particularly photo stories and exclusives. Celebrity based magazines often have good personal relations with either the celebrity directly or their management.

Who works for the media?

- **Journalists**
- **Television producers and production crews**
- **Researchers and freelance agents**
- **Photographers**

Journalists

Journalists are immensely dedicated to their work and they often work under extreme time constraints. Their business is highly competitive and only those who get exclusives and the stories that people want to read are successful. In a higher turnover business than celebrities in the spotlight, their tricks, tactics and drive make them worthy adversaries. Some celebrities and their agents will only work with specific journalists from each magazine or newspaper. For those journalists who are successful they will have had to prove themselves at some point as being able to get and do whatever is necessary to succeed. For those who do they may often be labelled as being able to *'sell their own mother'* in order to get a story. In any event, once a journalist – always a journalist. Be careful what you say and to whom, and be mindful of the 'ears' that are listening around you at all times.

Television producers and production crews

People whose career is in television and film would not usually choose any other life. Many times I have heard comments to the effect that anyone who works outside of this sphere of work and lifestyle can be seen as *'lesser or ordinary'* as they are not in the *'business'*. The way they communicate and act is completely different from anyone else whom I have ever worked with. A considerable number of television producers, especially those who work in *'factual'* type of programmes (such as hard hitting, undercover documentaries) are former journalists. It is usually regarded as a career progression for many journalists to transcend into television and film.

Researchers and Freelance Agents

Those who wish to make a career in the media, (especially television); will usually have to start on the lowest rung of the ladder, often starting in a research related role. Television programmes rely on their researchers to obtain the information that is needed, especially those that are dependent on facts *(news based programmes as an example)*. Good researchers are worth their weight in gold. As with freelance journalists, they develop, over a long period of time, a pool of information and contacts from whom they can find out almost anything. From a CP perspective freelancers can be dangerous people, especially if they are only motivated by money. If they develop a big story, they will try to sell it to the highest bidder. A freelancer who has a distinguished contact list will be wise enough to syndicate stories and do so in various territories around the World.

A freelance journalist will often list the different newspapers that they provide stories for on their business card and it will give you an idea of where they sit in the media chain; this will also tell you the type of news story that motivates them.

Photographers

The paparazzi. - The highly visual and sometimes intrusive media pack.

The professional photographer is a highly skilled individual who can sell his pictures for incredible financial sums, especially in the celebrity based industry. Some work freelance or for photographic/media agencies or may work directly for a newspaper or magazine.

He/she will be immensely dedicated and have exceptional surveillance and some counter surveillance skills. Like skilled journalists, they have the ability of talking people into saying or doing almost anything. The photographer who takes photographs of your Principal when they are not looking their best will indeed get good money for the photos; however in this type of situation you may unfairly get the blame. This of course is unjust, but if the celebrity looks bad they will look for someone to blame and you are the "Security".

However, in saying all of this, celebrities and especially their agents often have *'relationships'* with some selected photographers. These 'relationships' will be of mutual benefit as the photographer may often be tipped off to where the celebrity will be. Let's not forget, without the media and successful promotion, the celebrity's career, may not flourish. This is why some celebrities pay thousands each month to specialist media agents to ensure their presence in the media.

Next time you look in a celebrity magazine you will see many grade 'C' celebrities who seem to make a career from being a celebrity but without much proven talent behind them. For every celebrity who gets continual exposure without being on the television or in recent films there will be a very good agent somewhere in the background. Photographers are an essential part of such celebrity success.

"When working with celebrities on the red carpet you have to be mindful of autograph collectors and the paparazzi. You will need to be close while the celebrity is signing, but the celebrity and the paparazzi will expect you to back away when the celebrity poses for pictures; this will usually be in a separate section out of the reach of autograph collectors and fans."

What do the Media do and who do they inform?

Public interest – The media in all of its forms (including radio and especially the internet) has the ability to inform us as well as misinform us. It makes us aware of situations but of course also has the ability to make us overreact. The media is an essential tool in political awareness and politicians court the media on a daily basis.

Wealth and influence – Media organisations are immensely rich and with this wealth comes power. The power to print, the power to inform and the power to influence, careers are made and broken in one news story.

By having such money it makes it very difficult for an individual to complain or successfully sue a wealthy and established media company. If something is printed or said that is disagreed with, the chance of it being brought to court by the complainant because he is unhappy is very unlikely.

The exception to this is the very rich and celebrities who can afford to make the complaint *(as some high profile cases have shown)* as they do not fear the publicity that may result.

To keep us informed (World Events) – Everything that we are influenced by comes from some form of media. News distribution through television, newspapers and the internet keeps us informed of everything we want to know, as well as much that we don't need to know. Security is the primary focus of current world news, with most leading news stories having some security slant or connotation.

Politics – With news events come political points of view and the occasional spin. The powerful medium of television allows us to witness events and for us to form our own views on them. This also allows politicians to give their views and use the media to sway our opinions. It is a priority of any political party to have media coverage and ensure they remain in the public eye.

With every general election we see increased media presence and campaigning. Now with live televisual political debates, the media is the way forward for modern politics.

"A British Politician often in the news. At the Palace of Westminster with Boris Johnson"

211

Where are the Media? – The media is everywhere and everybody. Everyone around us has the potential to be in the media *(their fifteen minutes of fame)* as well as being able to inform the media of potential news stories. The very famous British newspaper 'The News Of The World' has a common statement with its journalists stating that *'in every two streets there is a story for The News Of The World'*, if you think about it – they are right.

Selling Out

The media, especially tabloid newspapers, often offer huge sums of money for information. The sad fact is that some *'Bodyguards'* have sold information to the press or gone even further and written a book on their Principal. These individuals, (the same as former Special Forces people who make television programmes, giving away vital and confidential Military information and tactics) are selling out the industry, selling out their Principal/Regiment and of course are selling out themselves. They are not to be trusted. The consequence of these individuals selling out is that it affects us all in the industry. I have heard of grade 'A' celebrities moving away not just from Close Protection but nearly all security, including scaling down their residential security as they are worried about anyone getting 'too close to them' as they fear the media and leaks. This is becoming a serious problem, thanks to those who sell out. Any company can say that it is professional, but it takes a long time in this industry to develop a reputation of trust and integrity. Providing Principals or their agents with confidentiality agreements is a step in the right direction but you must make sure that it is enforced.

Can the Media help you?

Very Rarely

As part of your *"role"* in celebrity protection you may be asked or instructed by your Principal, to release details of your Principal's itinerary to a media source. This in truth would be a rare situation and is usually in the realms of working with grade "C" or lower *"celebrities"*, however it is worthy of some consideration. All celebrities have agents and celebrity agents work with the media. Arranging any publicity is outside your job description and should be tactfully declined. A Principal that asks you to do this is generally someone who has found fame from nowhere and is not used to having Close Protection. It could also be that something has just happened and your Principal is reacting to it on the spot. The Principal may want to be photographed with someone or be photographed in a certain place or wearing clothes or jewellery that they are being paid to promote. By the time the media show up your Principal may have changed his mind – too late!

Even consulting with journalists about possible stories either present or future *(if your Principal is asking you to do this)* is an appalling position for a CPO to be in. Once communication has started with a journalist/s they will always want something. For you to change your mind or for your Principal to come to you and say *"cancel that"*, will not go down well with members of the press, especially the tabloid press. They may still run a story anyway, now without your Principal's cooperation.

If you want to work with celebrities you must have some understanding of how things work from a media point of view. There is a fine line here. If your CV shows media experience that is fine, however if it is full of tabloid associations it can have the opposite effect and you could find yourself unemployable as you may not be trusted!

At the outset as part of your threat assessment, you should have gained some understanding of exactly why you are being employed. At low level, low grade celebrity protection it could be that you are being employed as a status symbol and you are there to attract attention to your Principal. Always consider the consequences of this as many CPOs that I have worked with and employed over the years would be horrified to find their photograph being in a tabloid paper – especially if they are of a former Armed Forces/Special Forces background. Conversely I have met many 'wanabees' that revel in this experience and regard it as something to boast about.

If you wish to work in the entertainment side of the Close Protection business it is clear that by having some understanding of the media you will be a better and more effective Operative. Some who work on the entertainment circuit know several journalists on first name terms as they will see them on a regular basis. There can be some benefit in this but you will always have to be careful what you say. Journalists can be a great source of information to you and can let you know what is going on, who is working where and what your competitors are up to.

"In the Viper Room in Hollywood California with respected entertainment lawyer Gill Baxter"

213

Difficulties With The Media

NEVER BREACH CONFIDENTIAL INFORMATION

At the outset, the rookie CPO will be a little naive. As aforementioned it would be a rare situation for you to be asked to communicate with the media. Don't ever take an instruction like this from an associate of the Principal, no matter how persuasive they may be.

We have all been in the position at some time when someone claiming the Principal has given them the authority to give you an instruction or that the instruction they are claiming (from the Principal) is entirely false.

Where the media are concerned, a wrong decision could be the end of your job and possibly your professional reputation.

In the current climate, security specialists and especially those with expertise in terrorism/counter terrorism are often asked for opinions in the media. As long as you know the field that you are talking about there is no problem with this, provided you really do. Even so, misquotes still happen and that's why live interviews are preferable so at least there is control of what is being said. I have heard of too many stories where a recorded interview took place and the interviewee is 'caught out'. The interview may take a couple of hours but only 20 seconds is used. This 20 seconds could be taken completely out of context and lead to a misquote. The true masters of interview techniques are politicians where they can talk for a long time and not answer a single question!

Contrary to what television may show, most senior journalists do not use dictaphones but rely on making notes. This can often lead to a misquote as many will write in shorthand and make notes on what they have interpreted you have said, not what they directly heard.

All filming is a form of documentary evidence. Once you have said or done something, it cannot be reversed. The media, *(as much now to protect themselves)* make people sign release forms which gives your permission for the Television Company or newspaper to use what you say. Once you have signed one of these there is absolutely no going back as well as no comeback whatsoever if you wish to complain about something you said or change your mind.

When an interview takes place and is recorded, unless it is a live broadcast, you will have no control of the final edit. If you are giving an interview for whatever reason you must be fully aware and be knowledgeable of the subject you are discussing.

"Two views of a hotel surrounded by paparazzi and autograph hunters"

Photographers

Years ago it was commonplace amongst the *'Bodyguarding'* community that if a photographer 'got in the way' and took unwelcome pictures then it was acceptable to snatch the camera off him, smash it or pull the roll of film out – times have changed. These days you could face an assault, as well as a criminal damage charge.

215

Cameras and their ability to take pictures have changed significantly as well.

The skill that was needed to be a photographer years ago was an art and a talent within itself. Where the brain was needed to control the camera, digital photography has improved so much over the last few years that now the camera does a lot of the thinking. Mobile telephones now being able to take media quality pictures or film, means almost anyone can now make images and this spreads the net of potential coverage and problems.

Never try to delete images from a photographer's camera. This is his property. It may be that he is breaking the law by trying to obtain the pictures; this is a different problem altogether. It will be dependent on the laws of the country you are working in and it maybe a civil offence, not criminal. If in any doubt always call the Police.

At celebrity functions there is a very good chance that you may get caught between the journalists and the photographers. Never lay you hands on either unless in an extreme situation when you have to escort your Principal very quickly through the media scrum. I have watched many CPOs throwing the media about, often unnecessarily. If you assault a photographer he will probably take a picture of you for evidence and pursue you. Don't ever give the photographer an inch by overreacting. He could always claim that you assaulted him and try to use this against you in order to get information from you about your Principal or getting that 'dream' shot. It is possible you may lose your career over an assault charge and you will find that this is considerable leverage. If you are ever in this situation you must inform the company you are working for immediately and move to a different assignment. You must protect your Principal and the interests of the company you are working for first.

Celebrity journalists and photographers are used to the sight of Close Protection Operatives but always remember that you are the line of defence between them and the celebrity as well as the line of defence between the story and the photograph. At a celebrity function such as a film premiere where you arrive before events start, photographers (if they recognise you or guess who you are) may try talking to you beforehand. The conversation may be pleasant but it is easy to drop your defences and as soon as the celebrity arrives they will try to dive in front on you. If you have been having a pleasant conversation with someone, to then try to force them back is very difficult and you will be more inclined to apologise. When at functions it is best to be pleasant and helpful but no more. Always maintain a professional distance.

Never forget that the media and journalists have a job to do and if the money is right the relationship that they may have had with you can be lost in order to get a front page.

"In discussion with respected photographer Frank Micelotta"

"Working in front of a bank of the paparazzi is not for the faint hearted"

CHAPTER SEVENTEEN

THREAT ASSESSMENTS

DELIVERING A SPEECH ON THREAT ANALYSIS FOR
THE SCOTTISH PARLIAMENT

DISCUSSING THREAT LEVELS IN BASRA, IRAQ

CHAPTER SEVENTEEN

THREAT ASSESSMENTS

If you are to succeed in an operational assignment you must have a clear understanding of the threat. A threat assessment should be the initial and primary focus of a Close Protection operation; however, in reality it does not always happen this way.

Many of the phone calls we receive are in respect of a problem that has already happened.

Too late then for a pre-emptative threat assessment.

Footnote: I recall speaking to a very influential and famous person in the television industry to whom we had been recommended. His quote was "when we have a problem we know who to call". A classic example of 'security psychology' – too late! Pre-emptive security is often overlooked in financial budgets and therefore reactionary security is needed when it all goes wrong. – Often at a higher price.

Financial constraints are a huge element in protecting someone properly.

A full team comprising of PES, AST & RST will cost a lot of money to support each day. To then explain to the Principal that you need pre-planning time or to employ a specialist to establish the nature of a threat is, in the eyes of some, just another expense. Nothing could be further from the truth.

Working in the entertainment industry where you are just there for status with no perceived or identified threat, is one thing. Working on a high risk assignment or in an environment where you and your Principal's lives are in constant danger is something completely different. To walk into a situation, (it is amazing how many people in this industry still do this), completely unprepared or unaware of what the threat may be is just about the most stupid decision that you could ever make. I have met many good Operatives who will take someone on face value just because he served with a Regiment, has a good car or appears to be financially sound or seems like a "good bloke", therefore surely he can be trusted. When he calls offering you an assignment you think "ok, no problem".

I cannot stress enough how important it is to have an awareness of the situation that you are walking into or working in. Failure to protect yourself will mean complete failure in protecting your Principal and your team.

If you are working on an operation that has been planned in advance you would normally have the opportunity to compile a threat assessment; in order to do so you must be fully aware of the facts.

The assessment will provide you with the basis for planning an operation. In other lines of business the term risk assessment is used on a daily basis. Health and safety requirements of running a business mean it is the law to have risk assessments in place. A threat assessment is where life is threatened or threats have already been made. This is completely different from a risk assessment where guess work is made about something that may happen. The threat assessment already has a presumption that a problem exists.

A threat assessment can be categorised and if you are assigned to an operation it may be for the following reasons (as some examples):

- A Potentially high-risk assignment, where the Principal or his family or business interests are facing threat or sabotage.
- A Principal is travelling to a dangerous region of political/religious instability or an area of high poverty.
- A Principal who is being employed in a high risk theatre because he has a specialist skill or qualification.
- Medium risk where threats have been made and have to be considered.
- The Principal is very wealthy and there is a risk of kidnap towards him or his family.
- Within the area being visited by a Principal or where the Principal lives there has been a significant rise in crime and disorder.
- A Principal is in the public limelight.
- No threat and you are being employed as a status symbol.
- Paranoia with no threat.

COMPILING THE THREAT ASSESSMENT

Primary Assessment

This section has been laid out in question format and will help cover the facts when compiling a professional assessment.

Q: Have threats been made?

On some assignments this can actually be difficult to determine.

It is human nature to keep things to yourself and Principal's can be no exception to this. If a Principal has not used CP before it can be very difficult for them to open up and admit that there is a problem. For them to discuss this with a complete stranger can be exceptionally difficult and sometimes you may only get a half truth. However, the fact is if you are to protect them **you need to know**. A lack of accurate threat information being passed to you is potentially negligent.

By a Principal not informing you and concealing a threat or an escalation of a threat they are not only putting themselves in danger but endangering you and others around them.

If significant threats have been made or life is threatened you will also need to consider with absolute honesty whether you are capable of handling this threat?

The threat assessment will give you an understanding of the threat and how to counter it. It will also, and very importantly, determine whether the budget for the assignment is what you need and if your team is capable for this operation.

If, in your research and detailed assessment you establish that team members are not capable for this task, or that you need a bigger team or need to replace those that are not suitable, you must inform the company you are working for. It is negligence on your part if you do not. What was the point in undertaking the assessment in the first place if it is not going to be acted upon?

Q: What would happen if these threats were successful?

This is the first and most important question in order to determine the reaction and it should tell you how you are going to address security. Is the threat centred on one person? Is it your Principal or his family or is it targeted against a building, asset or other valuable item? The threat may be to disrupt an event or the running of a business or a genuine threat to a life or lives.

Your assessment will consider and evaluate the worst case scenarios. When you have some understanding of them and what the counter reaction may be you will need to discuss it with those **who need to know** (i.e. Team Leaders). On many occasions this will not include the Principal. To inform a Principal of each worst case scenario of their possible demise is not good business practice and will make your task far harder. If your assessment concludes that you need to increase the team then you, or as a rule your company, will have to discuss this with the Principal.

If you are working for a company then an increase in the team means an increase in the budget. All financial matters should be discussed between the company and the Principal.

"How do you know that something is a threat? Do not overreact and always gather your facts first"

If you are ever in this position that you **need** to discuss threat related matters directly with a Principal you should still be diplomatic in expressing your concern for their safety. I have seen some CPOs discuss in length with a Principal what may possibly happen to them if the threat is realised. The horror on the Principal's face has just made the assignment 10 times more difficult and instead of protecting him, he has now become a nervous wreck.

A threat assessor is a skilled individual with experience in both planning as well as carrying out the execution of such plans. He will understand the threat and will also have the ability to inform a Principal of his concerns in a responsible, diplomatic and professional manner.

Footnote: There is a fundamental difference in protecting a Principal who maybe at risk, and working in a hostile environment when you are at certain risk. Principals, who work, live or travel in hostile environments will require some training of their own and they should know how to react in threat situations. They will require knowledge of what may happen to them in the event of a threat being realised or if there is a security failure. On low to medium risk assignments in generally safe countries you may require some tact and diplomacy. On High risk assignments you will need a much more positive approach.

Q: Can the threat change?

A threat level can change on a regular basis dependent on the Principal's line of business and their profile in the public eye. A celebrity who makes a personal statement on politics or religion can inflame the public immensely in the same way as a scientist who speaks out in favour of animal testing. When you have an understanding of your Principal and their needs for your service you will also have an understanding of how the threat can change or multiply.

Q: How many threats are there?

Can you be sure that you are aware of them all? A trusted relationship with the Principal can take a long time to develop before he will inform you of all that you **need to know**. If a Principal has regularly employed CP they should be aware of the need to inform you of an elevated threat or if they are about to engage in something that could change the number of threats or commitment of that threat. An example could be that of a CEO of a major corporation which is about to take over a competitor in a very hostile manner resulting in the loss of dozens or even hundreds of jobs.

Q: How do these threats affect the Principal's daily life?

Is the threat that significant that you have to work the whole of the Principal's diary (such as travel arrangements) around the threat?

We are all creatures of habit and some careful studies and practical experience of counter-surveillance is helpful when trying to outwit a significant threat. Our general habits make us take the easiest routes in all that we do. If the threat is significant you may have to start varying the routes to and from the Principal's work. If the threat has an impact on the Principal's daily life you will have to implement other changes. With all forms of security, change is not always appreciated or enjoyed. The 10 minute drive to work may now take 20 in order to disrupt the Principals pattern and habits, thereby lessoning the opportunity for attack.

Q: What is the Principal's line of work and professional life?

Your Principal's profession (unless they are "old money") will be a significant factor as to why you are employed in the first place. If you are gathering intelligence relating to a threat or trying to establish if there is a potential for an escalation of threat, you will need to assess and understand the Principal's line of business.

If you are employed in the corporate sector you may have to review your Principal's competitors, particularly if he is in a fiercely competitive line of business. Does the professional life cross over into the private life and therefore does the threat continually go with him wherever he goes?

It is not uncommon for the CPO to end up in a compromising position at some point in their Close Protection career. This is especially prevalent when outside factors have an influence upon the way you have to work. At the outset of an assignment there is no way of knowing what the Principal's personal life is. Such information is seldom volunteered. This makes the overall security a lot harder especially if the Principal conceals things from you until you are trusted. Earned trust may take some time.

Consider the difficulties if the Principal is having an extra marital affair and you may have to 'cover up' for the Principal as to where he has been. This is made even harder if you have a good working relationship with his wife and have to lie to her face.

Q: What are the Principal's assets? i.e. residence/s, vehicles and offices?

Asset determination is important, as an understanding of the Principal's wealth will give you a better appreciation of the threat, especially if the threat is financially motivated. This will also assist you (or your company) in terms of possible budget and what some of the constraints may be, not just financially but also from an operational perspective. If the threat against the Principal is financially motivated, such as extortion or a ransom demand, it is important to have an understanding of how much wealth is involved and asset values and where they are located.

If your assessment will be reviewing the Principal's assets you must handle this with great discretion, especially when determining personal as opposed to professional assets. Asking very personal financial questions regarding the Principal's wealth can be easily misinterpreted and may raise questions of mistrust by the Principal. If you are to protect the Principal effectively then you may need to review the security at all residences and work offices. Asking the Principal about assets in this way is the professional approach rather than asking questions about particular wealth. Overall protection may mean having to implement security at all of the Principal's residences (if he can afford it). Any property abroad that is currently empty may need a presence if the Principal is to use it in the near future.

Q: Review the Principal's existing security

Sometimes it is necessary to completely overhaul existing arrangements and security procedures. Pulling apart the existing security and telling a long standing team that they are doing it wrong requires a great deal of tact. In these circumstances the views of a specialist threat assessor employed for this purpose are invaluable and the team should recognise this fact. If you are part of the escort or residential team and attempt to change everything it will make you very unpopular and you will lose the respect or loyalty (or both) of the team.

If a new threat is apparent or an existing threat is elevated then a security review should take place in <u>any</u> event. This can sometimes antagonise a team as it will find certain faults, but it is in the interests of everyone's safety to get it right. If you have concerns then discuss them with the Team Leader and make him aware of why you think a review is necessary.

Secondary Assessment

After your primary assessment of the actual threat you then need to gather more intelligence about the Principal.

Q: Who is your Principal?

This may initially sound like an obvious question, but of course it is incredibly important. Who are they in relation to the threat and are they of old or new status, i.e. a consistent and established threat (such as Royalty, politicians and corporate executives) or new status and a new threat altogether?

Q: Why would he be facing threat?

Wealth, power, influence, fame, insecurity, paranoia or status? The assessment must determine which category best applies to your Principal. Has something happened that has just brought your Principal into the public eye? If so the threat may be from the media and you may have to protect the Principal from any further exposure?

Q: What is the Principal's line of business?

Does the Principal have multiple lines of business? If your Principal is from the corporate community it is not uncommon for them to have investments in a variety of different types of business.

In the UK some basic research tools are available and it is easy to find out who the Principal is in the business world. By accessing the Companies House website information is available on all company directors and you can find what other directorships they hold. This is a service that you have to pay for but is not very expensive.
Specialist researchers are available such as private investigators who have access to various research tools and databases.

Once you have an understanding of the Principal's business interests you need to establish how competitive their line of business is. If there is an elevated threat it could be from a competitor who is trying to ruin the good name of your Principal or his business (sometimes referred to as a corporate assassination - by trying to blacken the name of the Principal or his business). You will need to establish exactly who your Principal is? Are they a figurehead for their type/line of business and therefore known to the business world? If this is the case it will inevitably expose them as someone of success and wealth?

"Security planning ahead of a Royal visit needs to be extensive. In the picture Clearwater Senior Operations Manager Henry Pattison keeps an eye over HRH The Prince of Wales"

Q: What is the Principal's status in the Public Eye?

Public celebrity status will always attract possible threats and this comes with the territory. It is strange that some members of the public cannot distinguish between an actor playing a role and who they are in real life. Even with grade 'C' soap opera stars they have had to face volumes of public abuse if their character has done something 'nasty'. Their public status will increase with good story lines but it also has a knock-on effect in that the fantasists will come out of the walls.

Q: Does the Principal have religious/political beliefs?

The Principal's beliefs are their beliefs and they may voice these publicly and this may have some relevance to the threat. In any event you should not pass comment about their religious or political beliefs at any time. With some religious beliefs there will be customs of which you should be aware and research should be conducted by you prior to undertaking the assignment.

It is generally in politics that a new threat can develop when a Principal passes an opinion that may upset people. They may vote or legislate on laws that are unpopular or may cause debt or unemployment that affect masses of people. This may also be relevant if travelling to sensitive areas where your Principal has political/religious beliefs and is well known for expressing them.

Q: How many people are affected by the threat?

As part of your assignment you may be contracted to more than one Principal. You may, for example, be responsible for the whole family. Threat determination is very important at the outset so you or the company can select the right team members and make sure that you have enough on the team to counter/divert from the threat at large. If working solo and the threat increases from one to multiples, you cannot be expected to handle everything. As with all functions of Close Protection, if you become overstretched your quality of performance will decline and at such times the threat is most likely to be realised.

Q: Are you or your team competent to handle the threat?

Successful Close Protection requires absolute honesty. If you're not up to it you should admit this from the outset. Trying to 'wing' something and hope you do not become exposed spells disaster. It amazes me, even now, the number of people I meet in the industry who do not have either the skills or experience to handle difficult threat situations and as a consequence will place themselves, and their Principal, at risk. It is often only during training that many will comment, "I didn't realise that" or "I never thought of that" or even worse "I've been doing that wrong for years".

For those who have worked in the industry for many years they will know that, it is through training that mistakes can be identified. A considerable amount of people still work in this industry that has never been trained properly by an approved CP company. Training will bring out the mistakes, but the real learning can only come through experience. The more work you do, gaining experience in different scenarios with different Principals, the better all round CP Operator you will be.

A complimentary team should always be sought. This may not be up to you as ultimately it is the responsibility of the company you are working for. If you are a Team Leader you may get some say in who you would rather work with. Some teams work together because they know each other and trust each other, in fact this happens regularly. A good company should look at the team and ask if they are really the best to handle the assignment? They may trust each other, but will the Principal ultimately be able to be protected proactively by them?

Q: Have there been threats in the past?

Have any threats ever been attempted or successful before? Threats generally can take similar forms when working with the same Principal for a period of time.

If threats have been made before you must establish what they were, what they hoped to achieve and very importantly how they were dealt with on a previous occasion? Also what was successful from a security point of view in the previous threat situation and what was not preventative at all? This may not be as easy as it sounds. If you are replacing a Close Protection team that was sacked for poor performance you will get passing comments from the Principal or agent but not necessarily any more than that. A Principal may not object to a well mannered and experienced specialist sitting down with them in this situation and saying "we need to know what happened to ensure that it does not happen again".

If a team has been sacked there is a good chance that you will not be getting a full picture but an exaggerated or inaccurate report of why they were dismissed.

Q: How do you know there is a threat?

This can be immensely difficult to establish.

I know from past experience of a case where we were protecting someone, who, unknown to us (at the outset), was a diagnosed paranoid schizophrenic. It only became apparent after some time that there was no threat whatsoever.

Threats can take a great variety of forms and what is significant to one individual is of no consequence to another. You have to treat each assignment accordingly.

As part of your research in establishing what the threat is and where it is coming from, (e.g. a corporate competitor), you need to establish whether it is possible that such a competitor has the **actual** capability to carry it out.

Q: Has anything been received in relation to the threat, i.e. mail or phone calls?

There should always be SOPs in place to assist residential security in handling threatening phone calls and suspicious packages. Do not under any circumstance overreact to mail and packages. Even if a threat level has been increased and a package arrives in the mail room, it is not to say that it is a threat. Calling out a specialist bomb/IED team and fully evacuating the residence, the Principal and his family because of an unidentified object is totally unnecessary and if found to be harmless and a genuine delivery may well get you fired.

If you are protecting a celebrity they will get gifts from fans on a regular basis. Most of these will be thrown away. With other packages (upon observation) that contain a threatening remark or object, you must be very cautious in your initial evaluation and remarks as you are not a forensic expert. Generally the Police need to be informed but first ensure that this is what the Principal really wants. If the threat is sexually graphic and your Principal is a female celebrity this will need to be handled with an extreme amount of tact. Informing others could put this in the media domain – this may be exactly what the obsessive fan wants and instead of solving the problem, may escalate it.

In this situation it is not your job to discuss the nature of the threat with the Principal or pass expert opinion unless you are absolutely confident of your experience and that you are qualified to do this.

To walk straight to your Principal and say "I'm really concerned" will give your Principal nothing but sleepless nights and headaches. This is completely unprofessional behaviour and fails to provide a resolution. If in doubt always discuss this with your employer for some accurate guidance. In situations like this, the Company would now probably get involved in some capacity.

Footnote:

Never forget, we are professional CPOs and experts in security. We are not councillors, psychologists or criminal profilers. Excellent reading is available on these subjects and it is good practice to study a respected academic book on abnormal psychology. However, this is no substitute for a true professional in criminal psychology who will have a better insight of the criminal mind than us. Expert help is out there so use your network of confidants to find a trusted source that may be able to help. To provide a security review, counter or avoid a threat is our field of expertise, but to give first hand advice on the mental state of someone's mind is something else. If in doubt always seek guidance.

Q: Who profits from the threat?

This is an important question. People are not threatened just for the sake of it. There must always be a reason and an objective. Hopefully your primary assessment will give you some understanding of where the threat is coming from and how you can counter it.

E.g. if you are looking after a male bank manager who has access to a bank vault, he or his family may be targeted for a possible ransom (Tiger Kidnap). You are now in a position of almost having to split your loyalty between the family and the one who pays you, (the Principal). If it falls to you to provide safety guidance you will need to study how the wife moves around, what her itinerary is and most importantly what are the activities of the children. Children are sometimes the target in this type of threat situation and a threat to kidnap them could lead to the bank manager robbing the vault for the kidnappers.

Q: What is the medical history of the Principal?

This is vitally important. The health condition of the Principal may dictate the way that you work and the way you plan the itinerary. Unless you carry a medical qualification then you must be very careful in the way you provide medical assistance (especially in this claims culture society) including the carrying and administration of drugs and treatments. Some CPOs have paramedic qualifications and quite a lot of former Military personal have advanced medical training and field skills. Having these qualifications can make you more employable.

You need to be aware of the Principal's medical history so you can perform your task of keeping him safe. His fitness could be a major factor. Some medical problems will be strictly confidential to the Principal and at the outset of the assessment you need to be very careful in how you word your questions. You may also find that you are not being told a full and accurate picture. Use your gut feelings as to when you are being told what you **need to know**.

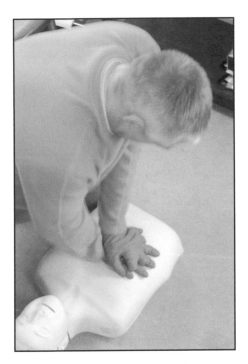

"First Aid and basic medical skills are an essential part of a CPO's training"

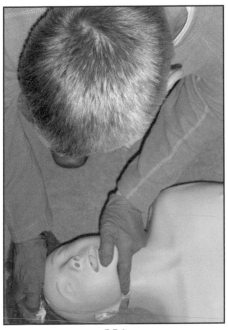

CHAPTER EIGHTEEN

THREAT ASSESSMENTS - ASSESSING THE BUSINESS & TRAVEL CONSIDERATIONS

DETAILED THREAT ANALYSIS MUST CONSIDER
EVERY EVENTUALITY

INTELLIGENCE GATHERING IN AZERBAIJAN

CHAPTER EIGHTEEN

THREAT ASSESSMENTS
ASSESSING THE BUSINESS
& TRAVEL CONSIDERATIONS

Assessing the Business

A common area of the CPOs detail will be in the workplace or travelling.

After the secondary assessment you will have a far better understanding of your Principal and the threat he may face. You have to be satisfied that your assessment and possibly any new security review will protect the Principal from the threat that you have been assigned to protect him from.

You will have identified the vulnerable areas and must now study the Principal's professional life in more detail and how this affects the assessment.

Q: What is the Principal's line of business? - Identify all areas of business

This is not always easy to establish as a Principal's business interests are private and it is a subject that a Principal will not always be happy to discuss.

The internet can help you a great deal when searching for company information. However, whilst company information is in the public domain, private business details are not as there is a clear legal difference between the status of a company and their primary function. Business information is private information. *(This maybe subject to the country you are working in)* Individual share holdings in companies can also be difficult to identify.

When speaking to a Principal about his business interests you must ask on the basis that you really do **need to know**. That is not to say that they will tell you everything, they may not.

You may need to speak to some of the Principal's senior staff. What they say may be hearsay and not entirely accurate, but it will give you a broader outline of your Principal's business and the opinions of people around him.

Footnote: Always remember that discussing the Principal and his interests with someone else has just widened the loop of information. If you ever have to speak to staff be completely sure that you have permission for this. If not, be cautious in how you approach them and how you tackle tricky questions.

Q: Is it a competitive line of business and who are the competitors?

The internet has become a great research tool for determining the nature of the line of business as well as gathering intelligence on competitors.

Although in many fields websites can embellish their line of business or their success, the presentation, quality and text will give you some understanding of who they are, the way they approach their business and the way they trade.

Type your Principal's name into a search engine and see what comes up. This is basic research that should be undertaken, especially when working in the corporate community.
If your Principal can afford a professional CP service, the chances are there will be plenty of information about them on the net.

I recall a situation where the threat was advertising himself on the internet and making some slanderous comments against our Principal. This was legally actionable and this was all the leverage we needed to make the problem go away. When threatened with legal action he disappeared.

Some businesses can be quite ferocious in the way they trade. A common term describing this is a *"corporate assassination"* and it is a very relative threat when working in a hostile corporate community. A competitor may resort to any means, including <u>unlawful activities</u> to shame the name of another business or those involved in running it.

Q: Who are the Principal's staff and are there vetting procedures in place?

It could be a former member of staff who is behind the threat and you will need to find out who has been dismissed from employment by the Principal (or his associates) or who has been dismissed since the threat was first established or identified? *This could be a continued threat going back some years?*

There are data protection issues regarding obtaining personal information on people and you will need to discuss these matters privately with your Principal or their representative. You should always seek guidance and get clearance from someone appropriately qualified for any research in this area before proceeding.

Good threat assessors are often good detectives and you may need to discreetly review the employment process and check if the original résumés are still on record. It is surprising how many smaller businesses do not check résumé's properly or take up references. In the past I have seen fake certificates from universities that have never existed!

With an investigator's mind you should be able to establish the reliable employees from the rogue element.

Q: Could staff be responsible for the threat?

Disgruntled employees could well be behind the threat. A loss of position, failure to secure promotion or pure jealousy; the reasons can be numerous and very personal. Employees may be close to the Principal or know his routine and have access to information about him through office talk and gossip. Part of the threat assessment should be to obtain as much knowledge of the Principal as possible including staff gossip.
If new security measures are implemented this may make him less approachable but positive security is not about convenience and your recommendations should be observed.

Q: Identify new and old staff

This will be a very simple process; your Principal may know directly or can arrange for you to have a meeting with the head of Human Resources. This information should be made available to you when a threat has been made and where there is some suspicion that it may be from the workplace. Confirm that the head of the Human Resources department can be trusted to be brought into this loop of enquiry.

Q: Are there co-workers of the Principal that are trusted and with whom you can liaise?

Who do you ask? Questions hinting at some mistrust towards fellow workers will cause nothing but bad feeling. Use common sense and proceed with caution.

Always keep your eyes open, listen to gossip and trust your own perceptions and instincts.

Following on from the secondary assessment you will ultimately have to ask who would benefit from the threat being actioned and who in the workplace fits this profile?

You will need to find out what type of relationship the Principal has with his staff. Some company heads are very popular but at some point they will upset someone; it is the nature of leadership.

Q: What are the existing security arrangements for the Principal when in the workplace and who has access?

A full security review may have taken place for the Principal's home but what has been done about his workplace? You may have to recommend a whole series of procedures to secure the workplace. This may be of some inconvenience to the workforce as the whole entry and exit procedures may need to be changed. Even those who have worked there for years may now have to have photo identity or swipe cards. Such proactive and highly visual actions <u>will</u> filter back to the threat who will either look for other angles or back away completely.

"As part of your security review there will also need to be a procedure for what happens to the Close Protection team when in the work place"

Q: Does there need to be an independent review of the business security?

This may be desirable. Are you good enough to do it? Securing the business is far harder than securing the Principal's home. At work there will be many people completely unknown to you. There will be salespeople, contract and service staff and clients of your Principal. In the building there will be multiple areas for leaving baggage and other equipment. Bear in mind that the searching of people and vehicles creates an environment of mistrust and is generally a bad perception of a business. Regular searching is also expensive as it requires considerable manpower and time.

If you ever have to engage someone else to carry out a business review, ensure you are aware of their background and their qualifications and they sign a confidentiality agreement. Professional Operators in this industry will not take offence at this as it is standard business trading.

Q: How does the Principal get to work? Is the vehicle safe when parked?

If the threat is significant and determined then the mode of transport for the Principal will need to be considered. A more discreet approach may be required, including the use of multiple cars, either as follow cars that will travel with the Principal, or as decoys.

Presuming that the vehicles are made safe at the residence, you may encounter vehicle safety problems at the workplace.

Does anyone remain with the vehicle? Most corporate workplaces have multiple-use car parks and a lone security guard at the reception or gate entry point; this will not be good enough. Even if the Principal has a regular chauffeur he will often not remain sitting in the vehicle all day and will need to leave the car on regular occasions. If a chauffeur knows that he is not required he may take the vehicle away from task. Some chauffeurs will carry out personal errands during downtime. This is potentially the most dangerous time for someone to get to the car, either to plant something or even to get to the chauffeur to force entry into the vehicle. This is also an obvious time for an unprotected car to have an improvised explosive device (I.E.D.) attached to it.

There can be difficult clashes of attitude in these types of circumstances. You may have been brought in to review the security and yet the chauffeur has been doing his own thing for some years and is trusted by the Principal. If the Principal is at risk it will be up to you to be firm, remembering that the slightest incident will not rest on the shoulders of the chauffeur but with you and your career.

"Different vehicles suit different terrains. In this picture all three vehicles are exactly the same ensuring that the Principal's vehicle is not distinctive"

237

Q: Does the Principal use the same routes to work; is he a creature of habit?

There will be many choke points on the way to work. These may include having to leave the residence driveway and only being able to head in a certain direction, to having to travel across roundabouts or stopping at traffic lights.

Route planning is an essential part of a Close Protection operation and the ability to read a map is crucial.

There will always be different routes in and out of everywhere. The difficulty is explaining to a Principal why you are doing this, i.e. explaining that you will need to set off ½ hour earlier the following morning to ensure his safety.

Everyone is a creature of habit; this is why certain professions are at risk, as they do not pay sufficient attention to their own personal security. If the same routes to and from work are used, possibly involving public transport, then the Principal may become vulnerable to attack or kidnapping.

It is worth remembering that it may not be the Principal that is the target of abduction. By following him, the threat will learn everything they need to know about the Principal, his family and most importantly, where any of them are vulnerable.

"Aerial surveillance will give you another view of routes and can assist with planning. Simple programmes are available on the internet and are free to use."

Q: Are the Principal's mail and phone calls screened?

In most corporate workplaces there will be a central point for all incoming and outgoing mail. You will need to discuss the procedure for mail being marked private & confidential. Although the Principal may not open even confidential communications, you will need to establish who does, what their position is within the company and their direct relationship with the Principal.

The screening of phone calls can be dangerous ground and there is legislation regarding this. Generally you cannot record a phone line without the consent of the owner and the bill payer. If you are ever asked to monitor phone lines by attaching some form of listening/recording device or even to pick up an auxiliary receiver, you will definitely need to get it in writing to protect yourself. Never use recording devices anywhere unless you are completely sure of your legal grounds as you may be breaking the law or breaching the human rights of individuals. If you are using these recordings as part of an evidence gathering process such evidence will probably not be admissible in a Court Of Law.

When you call corporate bodies they often give warnings that *"this phone call may be recorded for quality and staff training purposes"*. This gives them some way of protecting themselves as they have directly informed the caller that they are being recorded.

Footnote: The author or publisher does <u>not</u> recommend or advise the use of listen devices at any time. You should always check whether you are allowed to do so with someone who is professionally qualified or a legal expert.

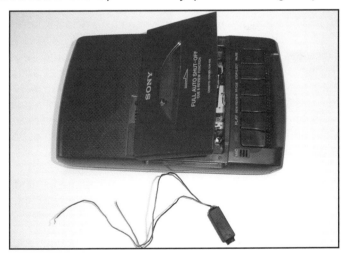

"An example of a telephone transmitter (Bug) and receiver"

Q: Does the Principal have regular meetings away from a fixed workplace?

If this is the case you will need to create a rolling assessment that is adaptable to change. It will also mean that the chauffeur or security driver must remain with the vehicle at all times. This will have to become non negotiable.

In this situation, and if the budget will allow, an advance team member should be employed. He will be of a very limited group that knows the itinerary of the Principal and all routing, transport and parking plans.

Travel

If your Principal is under threat, the location you are travelling to can bring a variety of complications in a Close Protection operation.

You will need to know whether the Principal travels regularly for business reasons or for pleasure and what locations he intends visiting.

Some threats will be localised and are only relative to the area in question. However if your Principal is of a higher status, a whole new threat can be created when travelling into different areas.

You will need to establish if the Principal owns property out of the country and whether he is due to visit there in the near future. The arrangements for visiting another country will have to be considered, as will the security arrangements of that property and how they are maintained when the Principal is not in residence.

If your Principal is in the public eye there will be the usual threat of public interaction but what if the area you are travelling to has political/religious unrest? This may not pose a problem generally but it will if your Principal has publicly passed comments that offend people. Although political comment may not make newsworthy reading in other countries from where the comment has been made, religious comments may, as will opinions on world conflicts, especially if the comments are wrong, misguided or contentious.

It is amazing how many celebrities make political comments when their only qualification for comment is that they are famous. It may be **you** that has to face the consequences of these comments.

For every worthwhile political comment made by a celebrity, there will be those that have little concept of what they are saying and more importantly the effects such comments can cause.

When you are in residence in another country you will also need to know whether it is close to areas of poverty as the threat could be the wealth of your Principal.

In your threat assessment you will also need to know who is travelling with your Principal as the security planning for them will probably fall to you as well. This can be very difficult as you may spend many hours planning an operation for it all to change at the last moment as new members are suddenly brought into the party.

Imagine protecting a famous musician or a rock/pop band who are travelling to another country; at the last moment the Principal wants some 'fans' to join them. This is a very difficult situation to plan for and work with as your focus may be distracted from protecting the Principal to dealing with these new and temporary additions.

In a properly executed operation there will be a prepared itinerary. If there is an increased risk it will be part of your threat assessment to establish who has access to the itinerary. Try to limit the knowledge of the itinerary and stress to those who prepare it *(such as a personal assistant)* not to discuss it at all with anyone else. They must also be vigilant when making phone calls in public areas to prevent eavesdropping.

If you ever have doubts of the validity or professionalism of someone who makes the itinerary you must discreetly raise these concerns. If you do so you must quantify it. If you are giving security guidance to the person who makes the itinerary and they continually ignore you this may be a genuine reason to submit your concerns to your Principal. However issues of hearsay can be dangerous in this environment. If the person who makes the itinerary is trusted by the Principal, any complaint you make will need to be justified. The Principal is not a security expert - that is what you are there for.

Part of your assessment will also have to include how the remaining travel will be planned. Are you capable of doing this?

Local knowledge is paramount when working out of country. You will need to find drivers and maybe local security to assist you. Everyone in this industry has a 'loop' and it is important to use it. A good loop can take a long time for you to establish and develop but when you have, a lot of contacts in different places will open up for you. Be sure of who you are using and recommending and ensure that they are up to the task. This includes having the right equipment, e.g. if you do not have vehicles in country, employ drivers that do and that their vehicles are of the right standard for your Principal and are they screened and vetted?

If you are compiling a threat assessment for the Principle's property you will have to make the following considerations regarding the team. If you decide to employ or recommend local security this is fine, but if the main team are also going to be working at this property and there has been an elevated threat you will also need to consider:

- **How much time has the team spent in the residence and are they fully conversant with its layout?**

- **Vulnerable weak areas of the residence?**

- **The surrounding roads?**

- **What are the danger 'hot spots' in the area?**

- **Do the team have sufficient local connections?**

- **Do they, and the Principal, have a good relationship with the local authority and law enforcement teams?**

- **What are the local residents and community's views on the Principal (if any)?**

A threat assessment is not to be taken lightly and yet can sometimes be a very difficult service to promote as a necessity to a Principal. It is the role of the professional CPO to understand and have the ability to compile a threat assessment. The drawback is the time it can take to complete and then constantly review and update. Threat assessment is a skill all of its own and some companies now offer threat assessment training where this subject is covered in even more detail.

A good threat assessor must have the ability to communicate with the Principal as well as other authorities and must handle all situations and communications with tact and absolute discretion.

Chapter Nineteen

Planning And Reconnaissance

WHERE BUDGET ALLOWS, AERIAL RECONNAISSANCE IS A GREAT AIDE FOR OPERATIONAL PLANNING

CHAPTER NINETEEN

PLANNING & RECONNAISSANCE

When planning an operation, always plan backwards from completion. By planning backwards you are less likely to miss anything. Planning backwards enables you to compile your phases of operation more easily and your overall view of the operation will be much improved.

An operation always moves in **phases.**

By adopting this method you can clearly see when one phase is completed before proceeding onto the next one.

Many Operators struggle with operational planning. Try to think of it as a drawing. If you are trying to copy something and cannot get the lines right, turn the artwork upside down and you will see the picture completely differently. Operational planning takes a long time to learn and develop in a competent, complete and workable manner; you need to see the picture in its entirety.

Whilst planning backwards always consider *"so what"* and *"what if"* for each phase of the operation; also what needs to be achieved and potentially what could go wrong.

There are seven considerations to planning a Close Protection operation

1.   AIM
2.   THREAT
3.   TYPE OF PRINCIPAL
4.   CONSTRAINTS
5.   AVAILABLE RESOURCES
6.   TIME
7.   SECURITY

Aim

Make this clear and definite. Confirm with the Principal what is required and what they need.

There must be an aim. Not just avoiding a threat, keeping the Principal alive or actions on in the event of a confrontation with the threat, but what is the aim of the mission?

"Carrying out a reconnaissance at the World Music Awards in London. Pictured along with Ian are our friends, security expert Arthur D Belovin and show producer John Martinotti"

Threat

Specific or general – Who, What, When, Why and Where?

Combine this process of thinking with 'what if' and this should give you direction when it comes to completing your reconnaissance. Remember, when providing an operational plan, it must be just that – a workable operational plan. If your plan is to be presented to the escort section then quantify your viewpoints with accurate detail. Dozens of pages of notes is not a workable plan. Keep it simple and workable but ensure you cover the most important parts and phases. Tell the escort section what they need to know to do their job effectively and efficiently.

Do not try to advise the escort section as to how they should do their job. A professional escort section will know how to protect a Principal, so telling them of obvious points such as *'watch out for the corner'* will not impress. Equally, do not tell them what formation to use, they will know. Keep the plan as workable phases but let each section do their job.

Type of Principal

Celebrity, Corporate, V.I.P?

Your Principal, their line of business and his status will determine what possible threat may exist.

When a Principal has considerable public status, this can make a plan far harder to construct –

e.g. you recommend the use of the rear doors of the venue as there has been a direct threat and you believe that the threat is determined. However, your Principal wants to be seen as they are a celebrity and the agent may demand it. Your viewpoint should be noted to cover yourself, however it may not be acted upon. Your plan will now have to detail the potential problems of using the front entrance, even though you do not recommend this. Your plan has now become a lot harder and sometimes the most obvious and safest plans have to be abandoned.

"Myself and Ian in Monaco with Danish security expert Henrik Bramsborg"

Constraints

Location, Local laws, Local Customs, Facilities, Geography.

Financial constraints and location determine how you are going to work or how difficult the operation is going be. You may be able to pre-empt the probability of success based around certain key points or events. The location from a security perspective may not be ideal but you may have no choice but to enter the area or venue because your Principal has to be there.

Your recce should detail the lie of the land to include all of the outer perimeter and routes in and out. The recce should be far more than just a land-based plan. It will also need to include friendly and enemy forces, desirable places, detailed routing, mapping co-ordinates, practiced escape routes, further security assistance details and emergency contact numbers for all available emergency services (as some examples).

There may also be local constraints that apply, e.g. by-laws, as well as certain dress and presentation codes to be observed.

Local knowledge is always very important. Try to establish trusted local liaisons on the ground.

Available Resources

Manpower, Vehicles and Equipment

Check what resources you actually have available to you. Vehicles, their maintenance, the suitability of drivers, securing the vehicles when used and not in use; operational equipment to assist with searching, security passes, access control measures. The list goes on.

Never take someone's word for it. Only trust yourself or those who are tried and tested under pressure. Operational planning is a pressured and necessary part of providing Close Protection. Try to ensure that you get what you need within any time constraints to make the operation successful.

Time

Lead in to task, Duration, Completion deadline.

Each phase will take a fixed time to complete. When your Principal has to be at a venue or event at an exact time, you need to anticipate all the possible delays. From the routes in to the venue, to other causes that can delay the Principal such as front of house hold-ups. You will need to advise the escort section what time they will need to leave the residence or hotel to ensure arrival on time. Although some celebrities may have a habit of arriving late at venues, this will not be the case for a corporate meeting or event where punctuality is paramount and extremely bad etiquette if not adhered to.

Security *(Reasons For)*

When you are constructing a plan for the first few times it is important that you do not forget what it is that you and the team are there to do. By considering this it should mean that you focus on what is really important in order to ensure the safety of the Principal.

One of the reasons for providing security is to deny any potential threat the opportunity of a physical attack on your Principal.

Another is to protect the private life of the Principal and his family from the unwanted attention of the public (especially the media).

It could be that you are employed to protect the Principal's business from industrial espionage or by other subversive actions.

Whatever the reason, when constructing a plan, ensure that it is workable and that the level of the security is relevant to the perceived threat.

"Henry and I in Toronto, Canada with our colleagues Thomas G LeClair and Nir Maman"

248

Confidentiality

Remember information can be leaked by anyone, including security staff.

Just because you and your team work in the Close Protection industry, this is not to say that from time to time things may slip out from careless conversation. Work matters should remain in the workplace and if discussed by the team should always be out of the hearing of others. This error occurs more than you would think.

- The Principal's own family and friends

The same applies with those that are closest to the Principal. This may be extremely difficult to monitor. Hopefully, the threat assessment will offer some guidance to the perceived threat and will uncover whether someone very close to the Principal could be directly responsible for the problem (or not helping it!).

- Agents and other staff

The workplace is always the centre of gossip; any Close Protection Operative that has worked in the corporate arena will tell you this. Be conscious of those around you when communicating, not just with the team, but when making private phone calls and radio communication.

Never forget 'That Loose Talk Costs Lives'

"Working at special VIP events requires detailed planning to ensure the safety of all guests"

Some Detailed Planning Considerations
(For Attending an Event/Venue)

The following list will give you a considerable amount of help when planning and conducting a Close Protection reconnaissance. Until you are confident and have had experience in planning this type of operation, use the following check list to assist you.

- Arrange a meeting prior to the event with the co-ordinator *(this should be well before an AST visit).*
- Inform venue management of Principal's identity *(if this does not cause safety or confidentiality concerns)* and size of entourage *(including probable PES).*
- Find out the appropriate dress codes.
- Ascertain if any passes are required?
- Obtain maps, timetables etc.
- Obtain list of event management.
- Confirm if possible where the Principal *(and entourage)* will sit?
- Can you have a copy of the seating plan?
  It is rare at an event for security to sit with the Principal. They are usually in a part of the room, which has an eyeball position. Confirm if this is the case.
- Recce layout of venue – exits, facilities etc.
- Establish how many guests will be attending the event?
- Research possible threats.
- Establish the condition of existing security e.g. are CCTV systems installed and are you allowed access?
- Establish how many of your own security team are needed?
- What communications systems already exist or may be required? *(Identify radio communications and dead spots).*
- Where are the drop off points for guests and parking area for vehicles?
- Where are the event media going to be?
- Order 'access all areas' passes for security team *(consider who needs them)?*
- Make contact with Police and support services/authorities *(if necessary).*
- On this visit recce as much of the route to/from the venue and consider other route selection in the event of an emergency.

"A detailed briefing pre-assignment is vitally important when a Close Protection Team will be tested"

AST will go ahead (probably on the day) to:

- Verify if there are any changes to timings, locations, entry points etc?
- Confirm number of guests in the Principal's party to event management.
- Decide method of transportation to the event.
- Confirm drop off points for cars.
- Confirm required size of PES – will they enter the event? Have 'access all areas' passes been arranged?
- Identify the specific event liaison officer.
- Complete any special security registration formalities.
- Confirm/check existing planned security arrangements.
- Arrange for PES arrival and administration.
- Inform PES of any security updates/changes.
- Liaise with event security.
- Establish positions for PES.
- Inform PES of the media arrangements.
- Check that the communications system is functioning.
- Inspect the perimeters.
- Final test of all equipment/radios.
- Confirm team positions.

MAKE SURE ALL OF THE ABOVE IS COMPLETED WELL IN ADVANCE OF THE EVENT STARTING

251

Finally check that you have covered the three areas of security

- The Outer Perimeter
- The Inner Perimeter
- The PES Positions

You can use the Military standard operating procedure to assist with the planning and also with presenting a briefing.

The Military Standard Operating Procedure
Briefing/Orders Group ('O' Group)

GROUND -	AREA OF 'EVENT', - ROUTES TO/FROM ENEMY (IN THIS CASE THE THREAT)
SITUATION -	FRIENDLY FORCES (IN THIS CASE OUR AND EVENT MANPOWER/ASSETS)
MISSION -	A CLEAR AND EASILY UNDERSTOOD AIM
EXECUTION -	IN GENERAL OUTLINE AND THEN IN DETAIL BY LOGICAL (USUALLY CHRONOLOGICAL) PHASES
COMMAND & CONTROL -	CHAIN OF COMMAND, COMMS, REPORTING ETC.
ADMIN AND LOGISTICS -	KIT AND EQUIPMENT REQUIRED, TRANSPORT, FEEDING ETC.

Failure to plan is a plan to fail.

Chapter Twenty

Bomb Threats

IF A DECISION IS MADE TO EVACUATE BECAUSE OF A
BOMB THREAT - IT MUST BE AN INFORMED ONE WHERE
REACTIONS AND ATTENTION TO DETAIL COULD SAVE LIVES

CHAPTER TWENTY

BOMB THREATS

The bomb **threat** is, and has been, a weapon of the terrorist for many years. Some terrorist organisations issue threats that are not always acted upon. Others however, use it as a standard operating procedure by issuing a warning before detonation to cause maximum damage and disruption, but with a minimal life count. This is a world apart from a suicide bomber who intends to give no warning whatsoever.

Terrorist objectives *(dependent on their beliefs or aims)* are not **always** the taking of life but to make a point or to remind us and raise awareness of their cause whilst maintaining media profile. Terrorists can be defined differently, but the saying *'one man's terrorist is another man's freedom fighter'*, is something to always keep in the back of your mind.

In recent years we have seen the rise of groups that although would not be defined as *'terrorists'* in the general perception, seek to cause as much embarrassment and disruption to Governments as possible. By causing disruption, and bringing attention to their cause, coupled with the ever present media, they are making some *'progress'* by gaining our attention.

Bomb threats and attacks however are not the sole preserve of terrorists. The procedures for how to evacuate a building and how to recognise a suspicious device is essential practise for the professional CPO.

If your Principal is in the public eye or has passed controversial political comment, they could face a threat of this nature.

There is a considerable difference between working in *'soft'* areas and working high risk assignments when a bomb threat or risk of an attack by an Improvised Explosive Device (I.E.D.) is a possibility or probability – not if, but when.

"Attention gained. Protesters outside the House of Commons in London throwing smoke bombs, causing considerable commotion in front of the world's press"

The tactics for protecting a celebrity who has made political comment or a statement that causes offence to thousands are far different from those who do the same, but resides in a volatile and unstable country where political unrest is rife. When working in high risk countries *(such as recent events in Afghanistan)* the threats are numerous – from terrorists to organised criminal cells. They all have the motivation and the availability to create explosive devices and have proven they will use them to deadly effect.

The modern terrorist or threat does not necessarily always use I.E.D.'s but may use chemical agents or gases in an attempt to kill or maim their targets.

Others may also use the mail system to send objects to scare or cause the loss of limbs or life to their victims. All CPOs should have a SOP for the arrival of post and packages to the residence.

If *(through your threat analysis)* you establish that a bomb threat has been made in the past, or if you think that the risk of a bomb threat or malicious mail object is a possibility, then you need to prepare full contingency plans for this eventuality.

How can a bomb threat be delivered?

- **Telephone call**
- **The use of a third party**
- **A written threat**
- **A Recorded threat**
- **The use of a diversion**
- **The use of email**

Telephone Call

The telephone call is the most commonly used method of threat delivery because it is easy, anonymous, and anyone can do it.

You need to draw up a plan for this type of threat and a check list of things to listen for especially if the type of threat that is being made is a bomb threat, the exact recording of details is immensely important for the preservation of life.

Never forget, if a bomb threat is made, then the person or people making the threat are doing this to preserve life so that the I.E.D. can have maximum effect without causing fatalities. You should be calm at all times if you ever receive a threat of this nature. If someone was serious about taking your Principal's life, it would be unlikely that they would ring you and tell you of this beforehand.

Things that you need to register and record:

1. Details about the bomb and reasons for attack
2. Background noises
3. The caller

Details about the bomb and reasons for attack

Although many of the following questions will not get an answer it is best to be prepared and have them to hand if you feel there is a chance you may receive a bomb threat by phone. Also bear in mind that the one who is carrying out the threat will probably hang up immediately after threat delivery. If not, try to ask the following:

- Where is the I.E.D.?
- When will it explode?
- What type of I.E.D. is it? *(Try to get an understanding of how damaging to life the device is and what their intent is)*
- What does it look like?
- Why has the I.E.D. been placed?

256

- What is your name? *(Some will volunteer names even if aliases. Terrorist organisations will sometimes inform you who they are or use a coding that can be later identified by Intelligence Agencies)*
- What is their address, where can they be found, do you need assistance? *(Highly unlikely that you will get a response to this question)*

Try to sound calm at all times. If you are taking the call you may even consider asking the threat to repeat their demands again (so you fully understand what they are saying), but it will also inform you as to how calm they are, and may give you more time to listen for background disturbance.

*Footnote: The term IED is for our use and understanding. Do not use the term IED over the phone as you need to 'humanise' the situation if communicating with a possible threat. Use the term **device** as an example. If the threat is a hoaxer or someone who is not a professional they may not even know what an IED is and therefore you have created confusion and have taken the element of control from the caller. This can lead to a loss of patience, further anger and a certain 'hang up' of the phone.*

Background Noises

Whilst keeping a threat on the phone you should listen carefully for background noise in order to assist the Police and any further investigation that you may want to make.

Listen for: *(Some examples, not a definitive list)*

- Is the phone call made from a street?
- Does the phone call sound like it is from a public phone box?
- Does the phone call sound like it is from a mobile/cell phone i.e. does the threat sound like he is walking at the time?
- Does the call sound like it is long distance, from another country?
- Background house noises?
- Is the call being made from a vehicle?
- Is there machinery or office equipment running in the background?
- Can kitchen utensils be heard, such as plates and cutlery indicating that someone else is potentially listening to the call?
- Can other voices be heard and encouraging the threat?
- Are the background voices male or female?
- Is the call being made from an airport? Can you hear a loudspeaker system or hear aircraft yourself or other forms of transport, such as a train speaker system?

The Caller: *(Some examples, not a definitive list)*

- What is the gender of the caller?
- Does the caller sound educated?
- Does the caller sound foreign?
- Does the caller sound excited?
- Is the caller angry?
- Is the caller calm?
- Does the caller use abusive and aggressive language?
- Does the caller lose his temper?
- Is the caller personal in his opinions?
- Does the caller use language associated with a political or terrorist organisation?
- Does the caller use a code word?
- Is the caller graphic, stating openly about bloodshed or the taking of life or lives?
- Is the caller sexually graphic or uses sexual language? *(usually the trait of a stalker not someone carrying out an I.E.D. attack)*
- Does the caller sound as though he is reading from a prepared note or speech?
- Does the caller sound out of breath or nervous?
- Does the caller have identifying traits such as a nervous cough or stutter?
- Does the caller speak very quietly to disguise his voice or to stop others around him from hearing?
- Does the caller sound like he is under the influence of alcohol or drugs?
- Do you have a caller ID display and is the phone number visible to you or protected?

The Use Of A Third Party

Third parties or those not directly 'involved' can be tricked, misled or coaxed into saying something that they should not. It is also possible that they are not actually aware of what it is that they have said but it will mean something to others. They may pass codes that although mean nothing to them, it may mean something to you, a Principal, or an Intelligence Agency. The third party could also be a courier who is delivering a written message or device, the contents of which are unknown to them.

Third party involvement still requires the same amount of detail to be logged whether received by a phone call message or a delivered threat.

A Written Threat

Written threats are generally the territory of stalkers. If someone issues a written threat there is no guarantee that it is going to reach the intended subject and therefore is not an effective means of threat. There is no point in issuing a bomb threat by mail if it arrives two days after supposed detonation. Written threats however, can be as personal as a phone call threat and can make reference to something very personal that has significant meaning to your Principal.

Written threats can be very upsetting and to see an actual handwritten or typed threat can be not just distressing but physiologically damaging to a Principal.

All written communications should be preserved for the Police as fingerprints and DNA can be obtained from a variety of papers and other media.

A Recorded Threat

A recorded threat is less likely to be directed to 'lower level' Principals. A group who wish to record themselves delivering some political rhetoric can make worldwide headlines, but these threats or attacks are often generalised and will not be specific to your Principal.

Recorded threats can also be used when the perpetrator wishes to conceal their voice to some degree or location and this type of threat, although in a recorded message, can still be delivered down a phone line.

The Use Of A Diversion

Be very aware that if you are working on a high risk assignment, then it is possible that the whole point of the bomb threat is to get you to move from the place you are in. With enough knowledge of the Principal the person making the threat may anticipate how you would move. If a threat of this nature is received you could walk straight into the path of a device. If threats are received on a regular basis then complacency can set in and this could be the whole point of such a diversion.

As part of your threat analysis you should consider that if a bomb threat were made, the possible source that it could come from. If the threat is close to home then this should be reflected in your plan so that you do not run into a trap.

The Use Of Email

Emailing is for amateurs. Unless in the hands of absolute experts an email can be traced back to source. Emailing is simple but not effective as there is no guarantee that the subject will receive it. Emailed threats do happen on a regular basis throughout the world and can be sent from chat rooms. If your Principal is at risk from threats like this they can be multiple as simply entering *joe.bloggs@thenameofthecompany.com* may get to your Principal. However, a Principal of the status that employs Close Protection will probably have personal assistants to open emails like this so the likelihood of it getting directly to its subject is limited. Threats generally sent by email are not threats of explosive devices but are more often personal to the Principal himself. This however, does not apply to politicians who receive very serious threats by email on a regular basis.

Proper Planning

If a bomb threat or the placement of an IED is likely, then your security plan must reflect this. This will inevitably lead to the 'hardening' of the estate and a strengthening of the presence of the security team.

Producing a workable security plan that takes into account the way a threat or device could be delivered, concealed or planted will reduce panic if something happens. If your Principal faces certain threat of this nature it is imperative that an 'actions on' plan is devised.

Rehearsing the plan with the team and, *(dependent on the level of Protection)*, the Principal and family will assist you immensely. When there is an actual threat or even a suspicion of one, the procedure should run smoothly and not cause the Principal and the team to overreact.

The use of a workable plan will minimise disruption, damage and panic.

Chapter Twenty One

Response To Bomb Threats

You Should Have SOP's For Reacting To Bomb Threats In The Residenc
But How Would You React In Other Environments?

CONCERT VENUES?

SHOPPING CENTRES?

PUBLIC RIGHTS OF WAY?

CHAPTER TWENTY ONE

RESPONSE TO BOMB THREATS

How to Prepare

Physical Security Plan

The construction of a physical plan will require the *'hardening'* of some areas. This will not always be met with the approval of the Principal as freedom to roam areas or just entering the estate by driving down the lane may have to change.

Physical (overt) security is also not attractive and may upset residents in the localised area causing friction between the Principal, local residents and possibly the Local Authority. Trying to explain to the community that your actions are due to the possibility of an explosive device or attack will not help your Principal's standing in the local community.

Footnote: ensure that any physical changes you make to buildings and grounds comply with local regulations and bylaws. Even the addition of CCTV cameras that have to be wall mounted may need approval if the building is protected by heritage laws.

You will also have to consider costs. The best surveillance equipment, sensors, alarms and Close Protection Operatives do not come cheap. Just because you recommend it doesn't mean to say that you will get it.

An elevated threat can be disturbing enough to your Principal let alone presenting him with a security improvement plan that will cost thousands. Making support statements that "we cannot guarantee your safety without" is not good business practise.

With the rare exception of some Principals that can be spoken to 'bluntly', most (irrespective of threat) will have to be approached with some diplomacy.

A scared but wealthy Principal may approve your recommendations but is likely to become incredibly nervous and understandably more difficult to work with.

The implementation of a plan that requires some 'hardening' may have to be gradual. The Principal may also be insistent on this especially where other family members are concerned.

Pulling apart someone else's work could upset the existing team if you are the new person in. Take time to review what is already in place and try to use existing equipment and systems rather than pulling everything apart.

Bomb Incident Plan

A bomb incident plan must contain all procedures for the evacuation of a premises. This will include where you evacuate to and how you get there. There should also be a back up plan where (if possible) you can use a different route if the main route has been compromised.

A bomb incident plan should also give recommendations in the event of multiple threats or devices. The plan should also state who is to be protected as a primary subject and, if you are protecting a Principal together with his family, how you deal with this.

The plan must provide a clear and defined line of command and control with individual responsibilities and their primary objectives detailed. This is to protect all those involved if actions are brought into question at a later stage.

Evacuation

The bomb incident plan will have to make it very clear who is responsible for the decision to evacuate. There should **never** be any deviation from this. It would usually be the Team Leader either from the RST team or PES team that would take responsibility for this. Do not ever take responsibility for this if you **do not need to**. Evacuating in respect of a package containing something completely harmless could cost the Team Leader or even the whole team their jobs. Such actions are not to be taken likely.

The decision will be to evacuate or not.

There is a clear difference between a phone call threat to the residence or hotel or even to the Principal's private phone compared to a physical object sitting in the mail room that you can see now!

If a threat has been received by phone you *may* take the decision to ignore it. This is a calculated risk. Not informing the Principal is one thing, as you may not want to alarm him, but being negligent or lazy is something else. Use the phone call list as detailed previously and establish if there is a pattern or reason behind this phone call and if there is any intent in the voice. When a threat cries wolf too many times it is inevitable that complacency sets in. In this business you can earn a lifetimes money in one day and must maintain vigilance at all times, no matter what.

If you feel that the threat is significant then the bomb incident plan will guide you as to how to evacuate with the minimal amount of fuss and disturbance. If you are working on an estate the plan will prioritise the Principal and family over the other staff on the estate. That is not to say the bomb incident plan ignores about the other staff, but they will probably feature as a secondary factor, not a primary.

The bomb incident plan is there to assist you, to do your job and to protect the Principal. That is what you are paid for. Everyone else is **not** expendable, but you are employed to prioritise your actions.

You may decide not to evacuate until you have undertaken a search for a possible device. The threat assessment will tell you how determined your threat actually is and how intensive the search must be. Common sense must prevail when it comes to searching for I.E.D.'s. They have to get there somehow. If a threat has been received that a device is on the estate you will need to establish through your SOPs any unfamiliar people who have entered the estate and what areas they had access to. If you have the use of a control room and the estate is covered by CCTV you should ask the operator to back track through the recorded information. The threat itself may even say where and when the device was left. Always be mindful of traps and diversionary tactics.

The threat assessment will establish if there is detailed knowledge of the Principal. If so the threat may originate from closer to home. If that is the case you will certainly have to make a clear decision to evacuate or instruct the Principal to move to a safe room or distance. You can set yourself a time limit search and decide at what point it may be necessary to perform a full evacuation. A full evacuation may mean a possible media leakage (if the media are interested in your Principal) and general staffing upset. You will need to justify your actions.

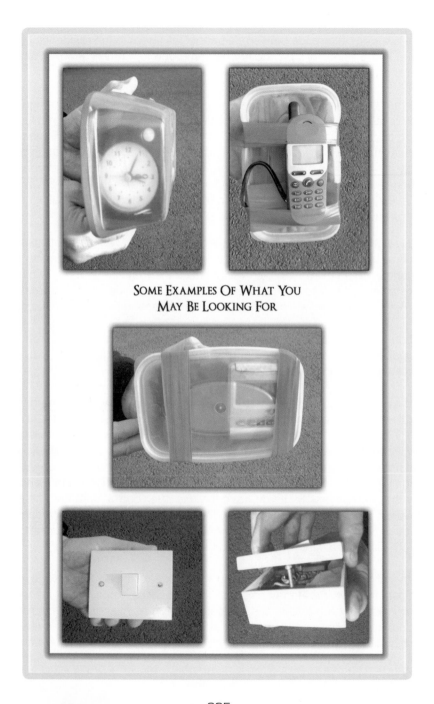

SOME EXAMPLES OF WHAT YOU
MAY BE LOOKING FOR

Search Teams

Unlike the Armed Forces and the Police Service who have extensive resources *(without wanting to start a heated debate!)*, in this business you do not.

Having a private professional bomb search and disposal team at your beck and call is unlikely. Although people who have extensive training and experience in this subject are available on the circuit, they are not in their hundreds unlike other CPOs. Having a team on standby for this does not happen and would be very expensive in any event.
Trying to justify with your Principal the need for this could just cause him to panic even further.

"These type of resources are very unlikely"

Hiring a consultant is a different matter. You can employ one to train the team in specialist bomb search procedures. He may be available on call, but unless he lives in the general area it may take some time before he can get to you if you really need his physical presence.

Plenty of reading material is available on bomb search and procedures and it is well worth studying, but if you can justify the use of a consultant then take advantage of this if you feel the threat warrants such an action.

In your bomb incident plan you will have details of how you would conduct a search.
The general principle with all searching is that more than one person searches a room or space at any time.
If time and resources allow, the use of three people to search a room is ideal, as with all search techniques. The Team Leader or a nominated responsible person will stand in the centre and will direct and check the work of the other two who are working at opposite ends to each other, working in a clockwise direction.

If your team is trained in how to search properly they should, by the very virtue of working in the residence, already know the weaker and more vulnerable areas. They should be able to identify these and confirm if they are sterile or discount them and then move on. This knowledge of the residence or place you are working from will give the team far more confidence in determining whether this is a genuine threat and will assist the Team Leader when it comes to deciding whether or not to evacuate.

This knowledge and confidence may be good enough for a Team Leader to make an immediate decision but it will never be as good or thorough as a professionally trained search team.

The Team Leader may make the decision to evacuate and then a professional team can be called in to search for a device. The weakness with a professional search team by the very nature of their job is that they are meticulously slow and decisions can be a long time coming.

Two Person Search Team

Before entering a room that needs to be searched, be completely aware of your surroundings. Look for anything that is out of place or that you do not recognise. If nothing is apparent, stand completely still and quiet in the room and close your eyes in order to attune your senses and listen for any clockwork device.

If nothing is heard, divide the room for initial areas of responsibility. In this scenario you do not have a Team Leader to watch over you so one of you will have to take control and be the decision maker.

When searching for a possible I.E.D. start at floor level and commence your search.

When you are satisfied that the room is clear, the room must be marked as 'clear'. You can purchase tape seals that are similar to those you see crime scene investigators and officials at airports use. Such seals should be put across all doors that enter the room. If you find that a seal has been broken the area is no longer sterile and another search will have to take place.

Use your commonsense when searching and do not move from room to room along a corridor if there are far more obvious places where a device could be.

IF YOU FIND A DEVICE DO NOT TOUCH IT OR MOVE IT!

Types of Improvised Explosive Devices

Letter Bombs

Letter bombs have been used by terrorists and dysfunctional individuals for many years. They can be of any shape and size and can be sent through the standard postal system. For this type of device to work there would usually be a friction or pressure release that will initiate the explosive. If a letter bomb has been sent through the postal system, it can withstand a lot of disturbance and therefore this type of device is generally *'safe'* to hold.

This type of suspicious device can be moved as long as it remains unopened.

Recognising a Potential Letter Bomb

- The envelope is (unusually) thick and stiff.
- The envelope may be oily or discoloured.
- If the envelop is an uneven texture/shape and unusual in appearance to what the Principal would usually receive.
- The envelope is 'bumpy' or is damaged and you can observe or feel a wire.
- The envelope is addressed by hand and marked private and confidential.
- The address is incorrect.
- The address is wrongly spelt.
- The address has the wrong postcode or zip code.
- The envelope is over-stamped.
- The envelope is sent from a district or country that is relative to the threat.
- The envelope has an unusual odour.
- The envelope is overweight.

Recognising a Potential Parcel Bomb

All of the above applies as well as:

- A parcel that is too neat or perfect.
- The parcel has excessive binding.
- The parcel is completely unbalanced with one end being very heavy.
- When the parcel is picked up there is no internal movement or sound (i.e. the heavy object is fixed and not moveable).
- The parcel is designed in such a way that it can only be opened in one way.

"Always be suspicious of a package that is oily or discoloured"

Bags and Cases

Recent world events have shown just how easy and devastating portable bombs can be.

To conceal a bomb in a bag/case or rucksack is easy and effective and allows the carrier to blend into almost any environment.

A carried bomb does not need to be placed in the personal residence or the workplace of the Principal in order to be effective. All that is required is some knowledge of where your Principal is going to be. The explosive device can be left there in advance or remain in the control of the one who makes the detonation. In this situation security can be out of your responsibility. You and your team cannot and should not take responsibility for areas that are public or controlled by others unless in exceptional circumstances.

One of the key areas of advance security is to stop exactly this type of situation or 'opportunity' from happening. The advance team will identify vulnerable areas and can work with other security teams to ensure that standards are 'acceptable' as well as prioritising escape routes, diversions, decoys and emergency services support.

However, advance security is very expensive and can only be effective when you know where your Principal is going and with whom they are going to meet.

If the Principal suddenly decides to take a shopping trip you will have absolutely no control of this at all. If there is a threat of an attack and the threat has surveillance skills this is exactly the type of opportunity the source behind the threat could be looking for, and if they have been surveying you, you could walk straight into it.

There is more public awareness these days of unattended baggage, but nevertheless, as history has proven, this is a very destructive and proven method.

Awareness

It is incredibly difficult to recognise a baggage bomb.

Although it has already been referred to it needs to be emphasised; when in public places this method of attack can be almost impossible to detect and there is very little that you can legally do about it.

Some bags and cases simply do not blend into areas or do not suit the carrier and your observation skills will be paramount to detection. Although you should not do it in public places, you do have the right to challenge and question someone when in private areas and grounds owned by the Principal or if you are at a venue where there are security procedures in place.

If you feel there is a threat of this severity against your Principal and you are attending a venue, obtain permission from the management and then construct a sign that random searches are in place and search everyone who is carrying baggage.

If you find an unattended bag in a public area then consider what resources are available to help you to determine who may own it. DO NOT open unattended baggage. Report it to the Police and let them handle it from there. Flag this to your Principal or Team Leader and advise them to move away from the area.

Vehicle Bombs

Similar to baggage and case bombs, the vehicle bomb or a pre-positioned vehicle bomb has been used by terrorists around the World for decades. In recent times it has been used with devastating effects where the driver is a suicide bomber allowing for a huge amount of explosives to be transported for maximum effect, destruction and loss of lives.

Where the occupants of a vehicle are the target, I.E.D.'s are sometimes fitted to the underside of the vehicle. When searching for such devices particular attention should be given to the area of the vehicle where the Principal will be sitting.

A remote detonation or timed device can be deadly but I.E.D.'s which are planted specifically for the removal of one person or a small number of people can be activated by a 'tilt' or 'trembler' initiation e.g. the starting of a car or some other movement.

Generally speaking vehicles in Close Protection should never be left unattended. If your Principal faces a threat of this nature, they should <u>never</u> be left unattended.

It is imperative that if your Principal has received a threat, or has been targeted in the past, then you must insist upon security for the vehicles. If not, then every time the vehicle is left unattended, you will have to carry out a search before your Principal can enter the vehicle. Surprisingly, many public figures, including some politicians, have been lax in this area. It is not their responsibility to carry out vehicle search procedures as they have drivers that should carry out this responsibility.

If a Principal's vehicle has to be taken into the garage for repairs or maintenance then upon its return you will have to search the vehicle <u>thoroughly</u>.

If there has been an I.E.D. threat, then make searching a habit.

Pre-Positioned Devices

A pre-positioned device can only be successful if the threat has detailed knowledge of your Principal's movements. Someone who is in the public limelight and has to make pre-planned appearances is far harder to protect. Their itinerary is often made months in advance and is generally well known, particularly when public attendance is encouraged.

To try to limit a pre-positioned device you will have to use counter surveillance skills and make your Principal a far harder target.

Vehicle checking should still take place as an SOP as well as pre-checks and recces of buildings. However, now you will need to vary your travel arrangements, use different vehicles or even resort to subterfuge.

Counter Surveillance List (not definitive)

- Vary the routes that you use and convince the Principal that different routes need to be taken, even if it takes longer to get to the destination.
- Vary the vehicles.
- Vary the way your Principal appears *(if this is at all possible)*, especially if he wears something regularly that carries a distinguishing mark, *(this will not be a popular decision with the Principal)*, or use a decoy.
- Do not park cars in the same place every day.
- Try to use different timings when you leave and re-enter the residence.
- Be aware of strange vehicles in the area.
- Use different entry and exit points at all venues.
- Be prepared to throw the occasional 'dummy' and make it look like you are leaving by a certain exit but in fact are using a completely different one.
- Carry cash as a 'slush fund' to ensure that you get maximum co-operation at venues you attend.

CHAPTER TWENTY TWO

RADIO COMMUNICATIONS

CHAPTER TWENTY-TWO

RADIO COMMUNICATIONS

Radios are an essential tool for the professional Close Protection Operator. The use of ear pieces and talking into the cuff or your jacket has become the stereotypical public image of this industry. Radios, as well as mobile phones are way and above the quickest way of getting back up, checking clearance routes and transmitting operational commands.

However, you will have seen on television those wearing earpieces that appear to have no support or assistance – who are they going to speak to then? It's true that the image can be abused. For all of the good points that radios can assist you with, there are some negatives which need to be considered.

If providing Close Protection you cannot simply hold a radio in your hand as your hands are your most important tools and they generally should be free at all times. Therefore you will need a belt attachment or a shoulder slung rig that will feed to an ear piece. Ear pieces have improved dramatically and they can be as discrete or overt as you need. Some are battery operated and are excellent for covert work as they can barely be seen. Main line ear pieces that feed directly into the radio (as in the next picture) have the PTT (Push to talk) built into the line. You will observe there is a pinch clip next to the PTT and this will clip discretely to a shirt or jacket.

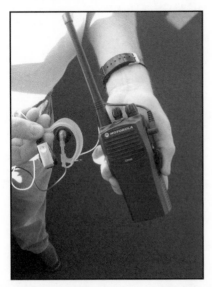

"An example of a radio rig"

Other rigs that do not have a main line directly to the radio but just sit by itself in the ear must still have a microphone. This type can have a microphone clipped into the sleeve or behind a lapel for extra discretion.

Paradoxically, radios can be time consuming to use. If you are working in a box type formation and you are providing rear cover. If a potential threat runs at number 1 or number 2, don't try to use the radio to inform 1 or 2 of what you have seen. If they have missed the oncoming threat it will certainly be too late. It may sound a little obvious but when working in such a close proximity to each other, voice commands are far quicker and effective.

In training we often observe students who are acting as Team Leader trying to communicate with the box team by radio. This is completely impractical if they are only 2 feet away.

Two Other Considerations are:

1.   The team will hear the instructions you are giving into the radio anyway *(if in a close box)* so it's unnecessary.

2.   If you are walking through a pedestrian area *(e.g. a shopping centre)* and the Principal suddenly changes direction or enters a shop that was unplanned, communicating this through the radio instead of giving an instant voice command to the box team may lead them to walk into each other, with 1 & 2 walking off into the sunset.

Another drawback of using the radio in close proximity to a Principal is that you will make a lot of noise communicating with your other team members.

*Footnote: Not so long ago I watched a television programme that showed the Team Leader in the VIP car giving navigating instructions to the lead car. An instruction was given across the radio net for every bend and approaching road and he was sitting right next to the person he was protecting! In essence not even 5 seconds would pass without him saying something. Now in fairness it was a high risk scenario, but in the real world, high risk or not, a professional CPO who is talking constantly into a piece of plastic whilst sitting next to the Principal in the car will infuriate the Principal and it will unnerve them to hear about the routes they are taking and the reasons why. A Principal **does not** need to be reminded by their Close Protection team of the risks that they face.*

"An overt ear piece"

"A more covert ear piece"

The Radio Net

Communication by radios is called 'a net' and the radios that you are using should be capable of adjusting frequencies to bring more of your Operators onto the net.

Unless you have paid for a frequency of your own, remember that others may be able to listen to you. The use of radios is prohibited in some areas and dependent on where you are working, you may require a licence.
In the past; *(prior to owning our own radio frequency)* if we were working on a large assignment where over 20 radios were needed, we hired them in. We then become covered by the licence of the company we have hired from.

The advantage of hiring radios (from a tested and trusted supplier) is that they will pre-tune your radios to the same frequency. This is helpful and they can also establish if other frequencies are being used in close proximity to ensure that you don't conflict.

On larger assignments when you have the benefit of an AST team they can check the radios in different areas as well as ensuring you are permitted to use them. They will also be able to identify radio 'black spots' where there will be no communicable transmission at all. The AST team can also check for line of sight problems where there will be communications failure or a very poor quality of transmission.

"Two different styles of radio that allow frequency changes"

Voice Procedure

If you are to use communications regularly you must learn standard voice procedures starting with the Phonetic Alphabet.

The phonetic alphabet is essential for all radio communications; it is a universal language that prevents errors being made across the net.

PHONETIC ALPHABET

A	ALPHA	N	NOVEMBER
B	BRAVO	O	OSCAR
C	CHARLIE	P	PAPA
D	DELTA	Q	QUEBEC
E	ECHO	R	ROMEO
F	FOXTROT	S	SIERRA
G	GOLF	T	TANGO
H	HOTEL	U	UNIFORM
I	INDIA	V	VICTOR
J	JULIET	W	WHISKY
K	KILO	X	X-RAY
L	LIMA	Y	YANKEE
M	MIKE	Z	ZULU

"Accuracy of radio voice procedure is essential, even more so when working and navigating in other countries"

For surveillance and counter-surveillance it is essential that your communication procedure is correct when monitoring suspicious vehicles and logging vehicle registration marks.

When communicating between units ensure that you all have unique call signs and carry out a radio check. The correct term is "radio check", not *"radio test"*.

Radio language, more commonly known as voice procedure, is a skill in itself and there is a clear distinction between the former Military Operator and someone from civilian life when using communications and voice procedure. The Armed Forces are trained and very experienced in voice procedure and are used to communicating in phonetics and transmitting clear radio instructions and operational commands.

Voice procedure needs to be practised by anyone who is new to the industry and the team need to be fluent in communicating with each other. If you need experience of this, get in touch with a private investigator and carry out a couple of urban surveillance assignments. If you have to undertake a vehicle follow your voice procedure skills will be tested to the limit.

We are very strict with voice procedure and ensure that any team that work for us communicate professionally at all times.

To study voice procedure in more detail you will need to undertake some formal training. A good specialist surveillance course will help, but examples of a few voice commands are:

Command Instruction	What It Means
CANCEL MY LAST	FORGET MY LAST INSTRUCTION
COMMITTED, COMMITTED	THE SUBJECT IS STILL HEADING IN THE SAME DIRECTION, NO DEVIATION FROM ROUTE
C.T.R.	CLOSE TARGET RECCE
EYEBALL, HAVING EYEBALL	HAVE SIGHT OF THE SUBJECT
FOXTROT, GOING FOXTROT	LEAVING A VEHICLE OR STATIC POSITION AND WALKING ON FOOT
LEFT, LEFT LEFT, RIGHT, RIGHT, RIGHT	IF FOLLOWING SOMEONE AND PROVIDING RADIO COMMENTARY TELL OTHER TEAM MEMBERS WHERE YOU ARE GOING E.G. "LEFT, LEFT, LEFT, RIGHT, RIGHT, RIGHT"
NOT 1, NOT 2	AT A ROUNDABOUT, IF SUBJECT PASSES A JUNCTION, SAY "GOING ROUND, NOT 1, NOT 2, 3RD EXIT"
OUT, OUT, OUT, GETTING OUT	IF SUBJECT IS LEAVING A VEHICLE
RADIO CHECK	COMMS CHECK AT START OF MISSION, AND THROUGHOUT
RECEIVED	INFORMING SENDER THAT YOU HAVE RECEIVED THEIR INSTRUCTION
(GOING) ROUND AGAIN, HEADING	THE SUBJECT GOES AROUND A ROUNDABOUT FOR A SECOND TIME

COMMAND INSTRUCTION	WHAT IT MEANS
TAIL END CHARLIE	THE ONE AT THE END OF THE CONVOY FORMATION
SEND	RECEIVING A CALL FROM A SENDER E.G. "ALPHA 1 RECEIVING?" "SEND"
SUBJECT (THE)	THE PERSON YOU ARE SURVEYING
STRAIGHT, STRAIGHT, (HEADING)	IF THE SUBJECT YOU ARE FOLLOWING DOES NOT DEVIATE AT JUNCTIONS AND REMAINS COMMITTED
TRIGGER (THE)	THE PERSON WHO HAS OBSERVATION IS SAID TO BE THE 'EYEBALL', THE TRIGGER
SHOWN OUT, COMPROMISED	YOU HAVE BEEN BURNT ON COVERT RECONNAISSANCE, THE SURVEILLANCE MAY BE OVER
STAND DOWN, STAND DOWN	END OF OPERATION

Many of these commands are relevant to conducting surveillance upon a person but the principles, including the use of phonetics, are very important to the Professional Close Protection Operative.

Voice procedure is necessary for the following reasons:

1. Economy of transmission time
2. To ensure that there is no misunderstandings amongst the team and that command decisions are followed
3. To speed up SOPs.

ACCURACY BREVITY SPEED

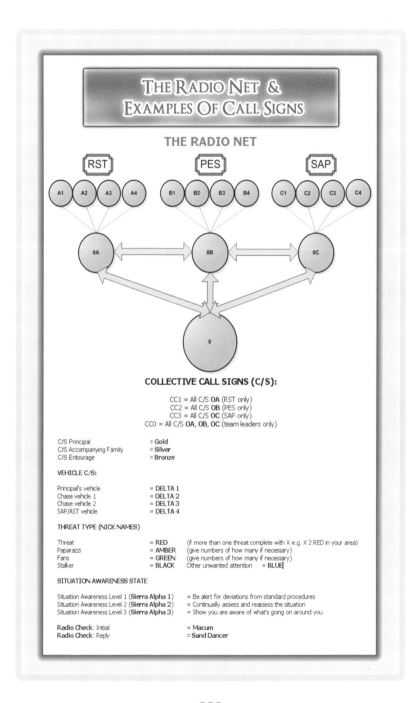

THE RADIO NET & EXAMPLES OF CALL SIGNS

THE RADIO NET

RST — A1 A2 A3 A4
PES — B1 B2 B3 B4
SAP — C1 C2 C3 C4

0A ⟷ 0B ⟷ 0C

0

COLLECTIVE CALL SIGNS (C/S):

CC1 = All C/S **0A** (RST only)
CC2 = All C/S **0B** (PES only)
CC3 = All C/S **0C** (SAP only)
CC0 = All C/S **0A, 0B, 0C** (team leaders only)

C/S Principal	= Gold
C/S Accompanying Family	= **Silver**
C/S Entourage	= Bronze

VEHICLE C/S:

Principal's vehicle	= DELTA 1
Chase vehicle 1	= DELTA 2
Chase vehicle 2	= DELTA 3
SAP/AST vehicle	= DELTA 4

THREAT TYPE (NICK NAMES)

Threat	= RED	(if more than one threat complete with X e.g. X 2 RED in your area)
Paparazzi	= AMBER	(give numbers of how many if necessary)
Fans	= GREEN	(give numbers of how many if necessary)
Stalker	= BLACK	Other unwanted attention = BLUE

SITUATION AWARENESS STATE

Situation Awareness Level 1 (**Sierra Alpha 1**)	= Be alert for deviations from standard procedures
Situation Awareness Level 2 (**Sierra Alpha 2**)	= Continually assess and reassess the situation
Situation Awareness Level 3 (**Sierra Alpha 3**)	= Show you are aware of what's going on around you

| **Radio Check**: Initial | = Macum |
| **Radio Check**: Reply | = Sand Dancer |

CHAPTER TWENTY THREE

BASIC SURVEILLANCE TECHNIQUES

CHAPTER TWENTY-THREE

BASIC SURVEILLANCE TECHNIQUES

The purpose of this chapter is to offer a very brief insight into some relevant surveillance techniques and how these can become part of a Close Protection Operation.

I strongly advocate that surveillance should be taught separately from Close Protection. Although some surveillance training takes place on Close Protection training courses, if you are interested in learning more about the subject it is worth investing in a specialist surveillance course as well as reading specific literature on the subject.

What is surveillance?

Surveillance is the systematic observation of people, places or things to obtain information. (Sometimes referred to Intelligence, Surveillance and Reconnaissance [ISR]).

Surveillance is primarily concerned with people, and is generally carried out without the knowledge of those under surveillance.

Put simply, surveillance is conducted in the hope that some form of activity will be witnessed.

Surveillance is normally conducted by one of two techniques.

Either stationary or mobile.

Stationary surveillance

The subject is not expected to move.

Mobile surveillance

The subject is on the move, either walking or in a vehicle or some other form of transport.

Mobile surveillance is undertaken either:

1. On foot (often referred to in radio procedure as "going foxtrot").
2. In a vehicle.

"Going foxtrot"

The most common techniques employed by professional CPOs are a combination of stationary and mobile surveillance.

Stationary because the **_subject_*** has not moved or has not made an appearance before mobile surveillance is required.

* Footnote: The Armed Forces and many civilian surveillance Operators often refer to "the target". Although this term is still used by many officially this has now changed.

There was a legal case some time ago involving a Police shooting. The Officer giving evidence referred to "the target" in his testimony. Under cross examination a lawyer for the defence asked the Officer what did he shoot at in firearms training? "Targets" was the response and the case was lost.

The term now used is the "subject" and not "the target".

Preparation

If you have the luxury of prior intelligence, you will need to distinguish some or all of the following:

Primary

Obtaining an accurate address and description of the Subject Person (SP). This would include any distinguishing marks or habits.

Secondary

- What vehicle will the SP possibly be using?
- What is the SP's social and professional life? *(If these things are relevant)*

There should be an objective.

You need to know why the surveillance is being conducted but you also need to know what you are looking to achieve. i.e. are you looking to obtain filmed documentary evidence or are you just looking for an 'eyeball' to see what the SP looks like? Both scenarios need to be handled completely differently.

Equipment

When you have some idea of the SP, and what is required of you in the surveillance operation, you should compile an equipment checklist.

A checklist should include:

Stills camera – This is somewhat old fashioned now as moving *(filmed)* images are preferred by Principals as well as a court of law. The quality of digital imagery has improved greatly and viewable and useable evidential stills can be taken from moving footage.

Video camera – The preferred choice. Ensure that the camera is of a quality that is up to the task and importantly the environment. It is comparable in terms of other leading manufacturers so it is easy for others to use. Its media must be compatible for current IT systems and its information stored, backed up and retrieved easily.

Map – Absolutely vital when working outside of an area of your knowledge. If you do not have the time to recce, or if the budget does not allow it, study a local map as best you can.

Flashlight – Handy in tricky situations. However, there is a time and a place for illuminating yourself when conducting surveillance.

Note book & pen – Vital for compiling evidence that may also be required at another time by the Police or the legal profession.

Toilet "facility" – In other words an empty bottle for the gentlemen. This is an absolute must when conducting trigger (eyeball) surveillance operations from motor vehicles over a long time.

Window covers – Window blinds are very useful for concealing yourself when conducting surveillance from vehicles.

"Window blinds on the rear windscreen of a vehicle can be helpful for concealment"

Binoculars – or a monocular can be useful but is rarely a necessity.

Radios/comms – Always have two types. One that is your vehicle base rig and a secondary portable one if you have to follow on foot.

Auxiliary equipment – Other specialist equipment such as NVG's (Night Vision Goggles), rural camouflage disrupted pattern material (DPM) clothing, vehicle tracking systems and covert cameras are examples of a whole variety of specialist equipment that a surveillance specialist should have at his disposal.

*Footnote: If you are pursuing work as a freelance surveillance Operator you **must** have radios and suitable filming equipment. A professional Operator should have an extensive selection of their own equipment.*

Surveillance Vehicle

Considerations

Is your vehicle right for the area and what are you trying to achieve?

Vehicle selection is very important and hopefully any prior reconnaissance will tell you what vehicle is appropriate for the area you will be conducting the surveillance from. Don't do as one freelancer did years ago on a task I was working on. He showed up at the RV (Rendezvous) in a bright yellow sports car when we were working on a very rough housing estate.

287

When conducting surveillance from a vehicle, unless working from a surveillance *'van'* you can be seen. This may sound obvious but you will need to consider the implication of being seen sitting in a vehicle for a period of time. In some areas this is not a problem at all but in others you may be only able to sit in a 'foreign' vehicle for a short time without "showing out".

You may also choose to select an old vehicle to blend in and not attract attention.

Important points when using vehicles

- There should be no obvious identification marks or additions i.e. spoilers.
- A neutral colour should be selected.
- Do not use a vehicle that a thief may consider stealing i.e. a trade person's van. You could be working inside but on the outside it may appear attractive to local thieves who think tools or other equipment may be inside. This is a very difficult situation to be in and is potentially very dangerous to both the surveillance operation and the Operator inside. For this type of assignment you must have communications and back up arranged in advance. The back up must also be briefed on how to react in the event of a compromise as well as how to implement a rapid exit.
- A purpose built surveillance vehicle may look old and worn from the outside but underneath is a well maintained vehicle.
- Do not have any window stickers that are identifiable or memorable. Be careful of car dealership stickers that say where the car was purchased, especially if it is in your local area.
- A number plate should be a 'standard' plate and not obviously memorable or personalised.
- Do not use a vehicle that is either too clean or too dirty.
- Ensure before any surveillance commences that you have a full tank of fuel and that you know what fuel that vehicle takes. This is a crucial point, as at the outset of surveillance 9 times out of 10 you will not know where the subject is going. I have often arrived at the trigger position for surveillance and have followed for over 100 miles without warning. Knowing the fuel type for your vehicle is very important as hire cars are frequently used in surveillance. You must also know where the fuel cap is and, more importantly, how to open it. These small but crucial points are fundamental to a successful operation.
- If using a *'foreign'* vehicle *(i.e. one that is not yours, such as a hire car* you should always carry out pre-checks prior to commencement of the operation. This includes the lights and indicators as you do not want defects that will cause the Police to pull your car over when on a follow.

- You must always check that you are insured to drive the surveillance vehicle, that it is taxed and roadworthy.
- Always lock all doors when in a static position.
- If you are carrying out any filming and need to film through the wind screen or rear screen make sure that you create a non-obvious clean spot to allow the camera to work properly so that it does not auto focus on a dirty piece of glass.

Climate

Climate can be an important factor as to how the surveillance is conducted. When working in the summer, the vehicle could become very hot, especially in the back of a surveillance van. This can lead to heavy perspiration and a thirst which will ultimately create a need for the toilet. As uncomfortable as vehicle surveillance is in the summer, it is much harder to work in the winter.

In the winter the glass can steam up which will cause viewing, focal and general observation problems. Filming with auto focus cameras will become difficult to the point of impossible.

When glass steams up it is also a give-away that someone is inside the vehicle. Trying to remedy this by using the vehicle heater or demister can drain a car battery in a very short time.

Some Operators like to take a flask when on task in winter. However, the steam from a flask can attract attention as well as assisting in misting up the glass. To the casual observer sitting in a vehicle with a hot flask could look suspicious and premeditated.

For a subject who is surveillance aware these are the sort of signs they will be looking for.

Always carry an ice scraper or a de-icer spray, especially if you have to return to a vehicle in winter.

Having the engine running in the winter will show from the exhaust and draw attention to yourself. An engine can be started in the summer as soon as you see the subject *(as long as he does not hear it start)* but this cannot be done discreetly in the winter.

The camera you use must suit both daylight and darkness. Particularly useful is equipment with night vision and super night vision capability.

If you are attempting to obtain documentary film evidence in the rain this can cause serious auto focus problems with cameras. Although most cameras have a manual override as well, it is much harder to maintain constant focus to provide useable evidential footage. However, a skilled Operator should be able to use a variety of equipment and the use of manual focus cameras is a must.

Most evidence gathering assignments are usually scrapped in heavy rain conditions. The reason for this is the focal problem of the lens, as a lens will always focus on the easiest point – usually rain drops on glass. If there is a chance that you could be compromised and you cannot gain useable evidence there is no point in continuing the surveillance.

In winter; especially on early mornings, you may have to have the car lights on when arriving at the point where surveillance is to be conducted from. This is a notable point. You would not want to drive past the home of the subject and have to turn so that the car lights shine straight into his windows and attract attention to yourself. Conversely, it would be very strange to enter an estate in darkness with no lights on and be seen by someone. This would bring immediate attention to you and the surveillance may be over before you have even started. Common sense must prevail.

Parking

Ensure that your vehicle is parked in a *'natural'* way i.e. if everyone else in the road parks with half of the vehicle on the kerb then you should do so as well.

In all CP operations when you are using vehicles, either mobile or static, keep a moveable distance from other cars in front and behind. This ensures that when you start the follow you do not get stuck, or if you are compromised you can escape quickly. Parking too close to other vehicles may also cause confrontation with their drivers. If you block them in you will get noticed and they will ask you to move – this may attract attention to your position and is an unnecessary disclosure.

You will have to park in such a way that allows yourself an 'eyeball' of the subject. You will then know exactly when they move. This will allow the surveillance to commence.

You can do this by either parking head on or you can park with the rear of the vehicle facing the subject where the preferred option is to use the rear view mirror or side mirrors as the visual triggers.

Concealment Techniques

The last thing you want when conducting surveillance is to be *'burnt'* i.e. identified.

Movement

When the subject initially moves, you should keep completely still in the vehicle. Quite often, if someone drives or walks past you, by keeping still, they will not notice you.

Brightly coloured clothing will also attract attention. Always dress in neutral coloured clothing. If you are bald, a hat is useful in minimising reflection and movement. Always try to give yourself as many opportunities as you can in protecting your cover when on surveillance.

Smoking when on trigger position is to be avoided as this is an obvious giveaway.

Ring the changes

If you have the luxury of a surveillance team it is important to ring the changes so that each Operator gets some time to *'rest'*. Ideally all Operators should have different vehicles. If you have sufficient team members to cover the trigger they should be regularly alternated. An urban vehicle trigger position should not last any more than two hours, irrespective of who is in position, as concentration can slip. Make full use of the people you work with. However, do not change position exactly on the hour or half hour as this will also appear unnatural.

Showing out

Showing out can be a problem when using vehicles. You will often need radio antennas to communicate with your team and these are often fixed to the roof or side of the car.

"Two examples of radio antennas. In some areas the site of either of these on top of your car will lead to certain compromise"

"Keep the radio covered"

Select a flesh coloured ear piece and wear it in the ear that is less likely to be seen. i.e. if someone walks past your vehicle on your direct right, you should have the ear piece in your left ear.

Radio comms in the vehicle should also be covered. This is easy to do by ensuring that you have a push to talk (PTT) button in line with your ear piece. By having a PTT you can put the radio in the centre well of the car and simply cover it with a map. Make sure that the radio handset is keypad locked so if any buttons are pushed accidentally you won't lose your signal.

True story

I made a considerable mistake when following a vehicle some years ago.

I was the trigger vehicle in a car follow and I was providing a running radio commentary to my two other team-mates. As I was entering an area that I did not know I picked up a map to gain my bearings. The map book was very heavily bound with a hard back. It slipped out of my hand and fell onto the radio set and completely scrambled the radio frequency. I had now lost comms with my team mates. Fortunately I had a reserve line of comms with my mobile phone. Be warned by this mistake and always lock the radio keypad.

Most triggers would usually read a newspaper *(or two)* or have a map of the area, this is important to ensure you are not continually staring at the same point. By pretending to read something your presence appears far more natural.

Dress appropriately – if arriving in a built up area during the daytime, be in *'work clothing'* so as to blend into the area.

Pretending to be asleep in the car is a common trick. Wearing glasses will assist you by enabling you to keep your eyes open but your body language would suggest that you are asleep. By pretending to be asleep you will look more natural and comfortable with the environment. I must stress however – if you are tired, pretending to be asleep is not a very wise idea.

If someone approaches your vehicle and asks you what you are doing, even if you see them approaching, you should appear to *'jump'* or act startled when they knock on the glass. That way you would seem to have been woken up by their knocking.

Have a cover story

It is no one else's business where you park *(unless on private grounds)*, where you go or what you do. However, people are very protective of their environment and if you park outside their house they can take it very personally and feel the need to investigate or complain directly to you.

When conducting surveillance more often than not there will be someone within the area who has something to hide. All too often surveillance is compromised, not by the subject you are trying to watch, but by someone else.

<u>Nosey neighbours are a serious problem in any urban or street surveillance.</u>

You must have a cover story as to why you are there. Simply saying when approached *"mind your own business"* or *"I'm here on a private matter"* will only attract more interest. If you do this, the Police may be called and the surveillance will be over.

Generally, if the Police are called they will probably arrive in a marked vehicle which will attract further attention and there is a good chance that the subject may see this.

Hiding in vehicles

The sleeping trick is one way of concealment although generally you can still be seen.

Moving into the back seat is a better concealment technique than it sounds. For some reason less attention is paid to people sitting in rear seats rather than in the front of a vehicle, this is also ideal if you wish to film from the rear windscreen as you can do it with minimum attention.

To assist your cover you can use vehicle window blinds. These of course would look completely out of place at the front of the car but not at the rear. They can be used on the rear (side) windows of the car as well as the rear windscreen. To the passer-by these look like protective baby covers and give a lot of darkness to the car helping you conceal yourself. They also assist with filming as you film between the gaps in the blinds, giving some cover to the camera.

Concealment of person

You must be able to blend and be *'grey'*, not recognisable or memorable and completely forgettable. You must be dressed according to the area you are working in. A *'tradesperson'* uniform could suit – although be careful of pretending to be someone you are not if challenged.

Footnote: In some places this could also be a criminal or civil offence.

The 'hard hat and clipboard' disguise works nearly every time. Every surveillance vehicle and Operator should come prepared with a hard hat and clipboard; it is just behind the camcorder and radio handset in order of importance.

Moving off

If you are conducting surveillance with the objective of gathering evidential photographs or film, your position will need to be closer to the subject than just gaining an *'eyeball'*. This will also have an effect on how you undertake the follow.

Footnote: Using a lens of great focal range requires a very steady hand. With long lenses it is not just the extra weight you are holding that is a consideration. As a lens stretches to its maximum range the very slightest movement can produce shaky footage or stills. Moving/shaky footage is generally not acceptable as evidence and in a legal process may not be admissible unless the subject is clearly identifiable.

When you observe the subject leaving their position, never start your engine as they approach their vehicle if you are in sound or visual range. Only ever do this if there is a significant sound distraction, such as a heavy goods vehicle passing between you and the subject *(the noise may conceal you starting the vehicle).*

In the winter, even if you have protected the sound of the engine starting, fumes from the exhaust may give you away.

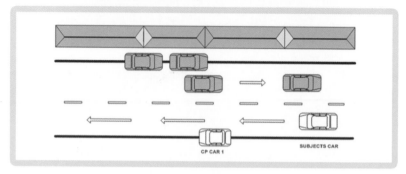

"PHASE 1, THE SUBJECT IS ABOUT TO PASS YOU"

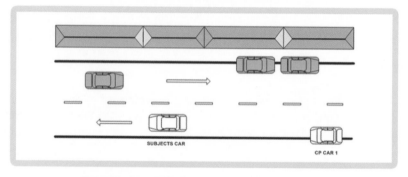

"PHASE 2, LET THE SUBJECT PASS YOU BEFORE MOVING OFF"

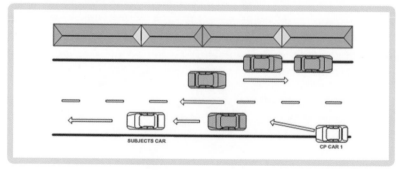

"PHASE 3, WHERE POSSIBLE, TRY TO GET COVER FROM ANOTHER
VEHICLE BEFORE MOVING OFF"

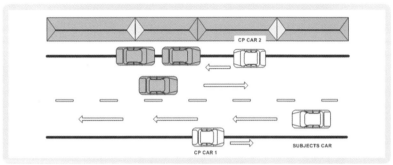

"PHASE 1, THE SUBJECT IS COMING DIRECTLY TOWARDS YOU SO CP CAR NUMBER 1
WILL NOT BE ABLE TO TAKE THE FOLLOW"

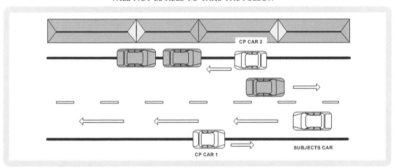

"PHASE 2, CP CAR NUMBER 2 WILL LOOK FOR COVER FROM ANOTHER
VEHICLE BEFORE PULLING OUT"

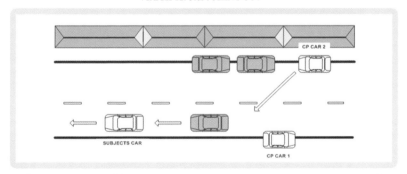

"PHASE 3, NOW THAT CP CAR NUMBER 2 HAS COVER HE WILL COMMENCE THE FOLLOW"

Footnote: These factors are <u>always</u> relevant as to how "surveillance aware" the subject is.

If you have predicted the subject's route correctly he will either pass by you or move away from you.

In terms of evidential collation and working without being compromised, there will always be positives and negatives with the way you park your car and the type of area you are working in.

A positive if the subject passes by you *(i.e. you have lain up ahead and they will drive past you from behind)* is that you can move off without having to turn the vehicle around.

A negative is that if on a quiet road you will have to wait until he is some distance away before you can move off and commence the follow. A positive on a busy road is that when a motorist goes by, you can pull behind them for cover. However, if you get caught in a line of traffic you could get stuck and therefore be unable to start the follow at all.

If you have two surveillance vehicles you should cover both directions and thereby at least one Operator can commence the follow. Always consider that if you park head-on towards a subject, although this will give you a good eyeball, equally he will also have sight of you.

If the subject moves away from you, you are facing the right direction for the follow. If the subject comes towards you, you now have to do a complete turn around in the middle of the road. This could be a major problem if the subject is surveillance aware as you may be seen in the subject's rear view mirror. If you are on a busy road you may not be able to turn at all.

Following the Subject

Whilst it is common sense when engaged on a vehicle follow that you should keep your distance from the subject's vehicle, in the real world this is impractical, especially in city centres.

In country/rural environments you can allow the subject to get quite some way ahead if you feel you have sufficient knowledge of the area to predict where he is going.

In an urban area or city this is impossible. Choke points, roundabouts and other impatient drivers will create a barrier between you and the subject and it is likely you will quickly become separated.

If performing surveillance in a busy city, (and when budget allows), it is advisable to employ a motorbike as well as despite your driving and navigation skills, losing a subject in a city centre is easily done.

Try to avoid rash and sudden moves as this may also attract attention (even if the subject drives in an abrasive manner).

If you keep tight behind a subject at a roundabout, and they go around the roundabout again this may indicate that you have been compromised. If they have made a mistake and genuinely missed their turn, they may see you in the rear view mirror as you appear to make the same mistake as well. *What are the chances of that?*

Many surveillance Operators jump red lights in order to keep up with the follow. This is not just an offence but is highly dangerous to other road users. If you speed you are also breaking the law. The penalties could lead to you losing your driving licence.

Footnote: There is a considerable difference between working in a surveillance role for a Government department and working in the private sector. You jumping a red light and colliding with another motorist and using a defence of "I was following my Principal's stalker" will serve you very little defence in a court of law. Not to mention the media implications of your actions and your Principal's standing in the media.

When the subject pulls over, do not do the same; pass by very casually avoiding any unnatural movements that may attract attention. If you have a full team, you can advise the next follow vehicle of what has happened by using your radio. They will then be able to pull over and watch the subject and they will now be the trigger vehicle. As soon as you are out of sight of the subject, you can then pull over. This can be easier said than done as sometimes there is simply no space to do so. By the time you have found a place, and then turned around the subject may be lost. If you can foresee this problem you may have no choice but to pull over as soon as possible, thus risking the subject seeing you. Do not use indicators as the repetitive flashing can catch the eye.

With all surveillance operations it will be your initiative and experience that will determine your actions. Judgements are made quickly. If you are working solo, vehicle follows are very difficult. Only experience will teach you and you <u>will</u> make mistakes at the outset of your career. A good Operator however, learns from these mistakes.

Always ensure

Carry money in a variety of denominations for car parking meters and be careful of parking in areas where wheel clamping or towing is in operation; or parking in other time restricted areas. To lose a subject because you were trying to get change for a parking meter will not be welcomed very well by a paying Principal who trusts you to provide resolutions.

Park by reversing into spaces. In any surveillance or Close Protection operation never park the car front-ways in - just in case you need to leave quickly. A professional Operator will always do this as second nature and without thinking.

A close observation of where the subject parks their vehicle is very important, just in case you lose them later when on a foot follow. If you loose them at least you will now have a place to resume the surveillance from and their car becomes the 'subject' to watch.

Foot following

Foot following (generally speaking) is far easier than vehicle surveillance because you can blend into the surrounding area whilst maintaining a distance from the subject under surveillance.

However; observation is one thing, but if you are following someone because they have made a threat against your Principal, this would need to be treated differently. You will need to be a lot closer, especially if your Principal is in the vicinity.

When undertaking any form of foot surveillance; your appearance, (as with working with vehicles), must suit the environment.

The primary objective, (*which may initially sound obvious*), is not to be seen. However, if you are a good Operator the fact that you may have been 'seen' does not mean that you are *'burnt'*. The consideration should be how and where you were seen, and could you risk being seen again?

Prior intelligence is helpful. Hopefully this will tell you if the subject is surveillance aware or not.

If you are following a subject and they continually look behind, stop for no reason, drop something on purpose or bend down to tie the shoe lace that did not need tying, then it is likely that you are following someone who is surveillance aware.

Carry out the following actions to counter this:

- Use your surroundings to the best of your ability.
- Shadow yourself behind other people.
- Do not get unnecessarily close unless you are concerned that the subject may come into contact with your Principal.

If the subject enters a shop/building and you cannot enter, either because you will be seen or you are not dressed appropriately – pass by. Use the surrounding shopfront glass to watch for movements. This is the same counter surveillance technique if you are being followed and you turn your head to the side to view the reflection, observing what or whom is behind you.

If you are 'static' and waiting for a subject to move, do something that is natural with natural movements i.e. read a newspaper or pretend to use your mobile phone. Look natural but keep visual/peripheral vision movements to a minimum so you don't attract eye contact.

Do not wear anything that conceals the face, i.e. a *'hoody'* or sunglasses *(unless the weather really allows it, and plenty of other people are wearing them)*. For someone who is surveillance aware this is exactly what they are looking for. Blend, be grey and totally forgettable.

The urban observation post (OP)

Urban operations are a mainstay of Close Protection surveillance.

The Residential Security Team should handle the estate/property surveillance through CCTV and perimeter reconnaissance, leaving the CPOs to conduct any urban surveillance requirements.

First know your objective:

- Who are you watching?
- Why are you watching?
- What are you looking to achieve?
- Where do they live?
- How can I do it?

If you are to monitor a subject, let us assume that you know where he or they live. Firstly you conduct a recce. One of the main purposes of the recce is to evaluate the ways in and out of the subject's property or area and to gain the following information:

- Where can you lie up as an OP?

  What is the visual/evidential base point of the surveillance operation where you can gather your evidence or use the OP as a trigger point? The trigger point may be for "eyes on" only, to notify your team when the subject moves (so the surveillance operation can commence).

- How many do you need in the team?
- What equipment do you need?
- What are the risks if you are compromised? – This includes not just you, but your Principal and their reputation
- Most importantly - can surveillance be done in the first place?

Lying up

If you have to lie up you must blend into the area. If you cannot blend the surveillance will not work. When lying up, (as with all surveillance gathering operations) try to select the easiest way of doing it. Far too many times over the years I have met people who make the task far harder than it needed to be. Keep it simple.

Blend into the rural or urban environment. Generalised street knowledge is helpful, especially if you are working in gang/drug related environments. At corporate level, this style of surveillance is unlikely. However, surveying an obsessive stalker may present a whole different approach. In such cases blending can make the difference between operational success or failure.

"Example of concealment in hostile areas"

301

Road surroundings

In an ideal situation you may be able to use hotels, guest houses or other premises that have a view of the subject's house or place of movement. This is a complete luxury as there is now no need for vehicles and everything can be done from a window.

Public houses (bars) can also be temporary static OP's as well as phone boxes or parking areas. Gymnasiums with big glass fronts often have great viewing positions, as do shops, flats for rent etc.

Always check your legal position if you are going to film in places that are private property. Intelligence gathering is one thing but hoping to gain lawful evidence and present it to a court is another. Laws vary in different countries and prior research is essential.

Take the picture and understand what you are photographing

If you are conducting evidence gathering surveillance it is important that you film and corroborate exactly what the assignment brief dictates. If you are working as a two person team and filming the activities of a subject. Ideally you would have one Operator filming the subject whilst the other films the overall scene. Surveillance *'evidence'* is completely useless if all you film are *'head shots'*. If the footage does not show the surroundings, who the subject is talking to, what their body language is etc. it maybe completely worthless and will antagonise a paying Principal.

Evidential surveillance can only be successful if the pictures tell the complete story. A photographic eye takes time and experience to develop. When it does you will have a natural ability to frame the shot and capture what is needed.

Conclusion

Surveillance knowledge gained from books is useful and provides helpful guidance. But there is only so much you can learn from reading. Practical experience counts for everything. Operational experience will develop your abilities and you will learn more with every assignment.

Research current surveillance equipment and select and study what you feel will promote you as a Surveillance Operator, not just a CP Operative.

Practice time and again with photographic equipment so that you can shoot film with confidence and a steady hand. If you really want to study this craft befriend

302

investigators and see if they may offer you some experience. Be prepared to work long hours in testing conditions.

Specialist surveillance courses are available and this field craft should be studied by all professional CP Operators.

"An example of rural reconnaissance in high risk environments"

"The late photographic and surveillance expert Steve Yates teaching for Clearwater......missed by all"

Chapter Twenty Four

Close Protection & The Use Of Firearms

FIREARMS TRAINING FOR HIGH RISK ASSIGNMENTS IS A WORLD APART FROM CLOSE PROTECTION CLOSE QUARTER DEFENSIVE SHOOTING

CHAPTER TWENTY-FOUR

CLOSE PROTECTION AND THE USE OF FIREARMS

This is an entry level overview only.

There is no substitute for practical training with many sectors of Close Protection. With firearms training practical assessments, testing and experience is vital.

The safe handling and tactical use of firearms cannot be learnt in a 3 day training course. Repetition and constant training is required.

The right to carry a firearm and other regulations can differ between countries and also from state to state. Private Security companies providing armed services need to be sure of the competence of the carrier and the rights and laws of carry. That the firearms, equipment and support services are sufficient to protect their Client and most importantly, the clearly defined rules of engagement.

Firearms training must be delivered in a professional environment in a professional facility where the instructors will be asking you why you wish to undertake such training?

Training with firearms for Close Protection is not something that can be taught or learnt on a weekend's shooting range. It is this sector of training that courts the most controversy within this industry and in many countries it is completely unregulated.

We receive countless calls from people who want to undertake firearms training and yet have no Close Protection training whatsoever.

In today's society it is our belief that companies that offer firearms training should only do so with complete integrity and an understanding of what they are delivering and, most importantly, to whom.

Why sniper and aircraft storming training courses are still available in the public domain is a mystery to most professionals. The companies concerned have to carry a lot of culpability for their actions.

These particular courses cater to the Walter Mitty's who will show up at the range in desert storm disrupted pattern material (DPM) looking for the respect of the tutors because they once shot a (deer/pigeon/squirrel).

Any investment you make in training must be from a company that carries credibility and has a proven safety record. What you **need** are **qualified instructors** who have a reputation for delivering an effective instructor to student ratio and are not overstretched by having to teach too many students at the same time.

The training must be relevant. A firearms safe handling course is a necessity especially for those who have never received formal training through the Armed Forces or Police service.

Before you apply for a firearms course you really need to ask yourself why you need it? If you are planning to work in a hostile country or conflicting environment and have no previous firearms experience you really should think about the reality of the conditions and type of work you will be doing.

Training should consist of weapons maintenance and safe handling, together with dry training exercises before moving onto live fire exercise and marksmanship. Before any student is proficient they must have been tested in all types of situations and in all weather conditions. Any professional CPO who works in countries where they carry firearms needs to be constantly tested on his weapon safe handling skills and marksmanship throughout their career.

There are still many concerns within the Professional Close Protection community about firearms training.

1.   Who delivers it?
2.   Who attends these courses?
3.   And ultimately where do these people end up?

True Case

A colleague of mine was at home on leave from the Middle East. He was a member of a Close Protection team working for a well known security provider. I asked him how it was going, and to my surprise he told me that although he was very happy about the money he was earning, he would not be returning at the end of his leave. The reason he gave was because more and more demands where being put on the team and more CP Operatives were required. To his surprise the majority of new Operatives had no experience whatsoever, let alone firearms training. He was detailed to spend three days with the new recruits to bring them up-to speed with firearms training. At the end of that period he was working alongside them as a team. He therefore made the decision not to return because he was concerned that these untrained new recruits were a danger to him, the Principals, and themselves.

If a Close Protection Operative is dedicated in the pursuance of this career then he will obviously benefit from firearms training. A CPO who is trained in the use of firearms will be very employable. However it is essential that the training is constantly maintained.

"2 EXAMPLES OF FIREARMS IN USE AND STRIPPED DOWN.

ABOVE IS A CLASSIC 9MM HANDGUN
BELOW IS A LARGER FORMAT RIFLE"

Which is The Right Firearms Course for the Close Protection Operative?

When looking for the right firearms course to attend, make sure that the course curriculum is **relevant** for professional CP assignments.

Here is an example of what a CP Operative's firearms course should consist of:

- All aspects of safe weapon handling
- Malfunctions
- Combat shooting techniques
- Administrative loads
- Tactical re-loads
- Shooting while moving
- Shooting at movers
- Draw
- Cover and concealment
- Target discrimination (shoot/don't shoot)
- Alternative fire positions
- Multiple threats and Principal manipulation (with and without the use of vehicles)

What to Expect After Such Courses:

After attending such a course you should expect the following:

- Proof of attending a firearms course to include:

1. Subjects covered during the course (**relevance**)
2. A recognised certificate of training and competence
3. Written references on request from the training company that provided the firearms training

Having received firearms training and qualifications, you need to consider the right firearm for you, the assignment and the country you are working in.

The following points should be considered:

- Small enough to conceal (Holster)
- Reliability
- Stopping Power
- Weight
- Calibre

- Magazine Capacity
- Range Accuracy
- Left Handed Compatibility
- Sights

Small enough to conceal (holster)

The firearm should be easily and readily accessible in the unlikely event of an attack (contact). However the firearm should be concealed at all times, any failure to do so may also be against the law - this is a primary rule.

Spare magazine clips should be carried on the belt, out of sight (x 2 extra clip's minimum).

It is quite likely that a radio will also be on the belt; therefore the belt must be capable of supporting all this weight. You may also be required to wear body armour.

"Various types of body armour are available, this vest is stab resistant only"

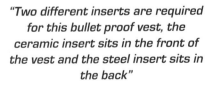

"Two different inserts are required for this bullet proof vest, the ceramic insert sits in the front of the vest and the steel insert sits in the back"

Reliability

The most reliable type of handguns are revolvers. However they have limitations:

- Short Barrel (accurate to within 30ft)
- Normally only 6 rounds capacity

Most firearms such as the pistol in this picture are reliable and field tested. However it's always best to know what to look for in the reliability of a firearm. Some considerations:

It must have a recognised high quality standard mark.
Few working parts or moving parts.

Stopping power

The firearm must be able to load ammunition that is capable of producing great stopping power. Always keep in mind that your threat may be wearing body armour.

Hollow point or lead tipped ammunition will guarantee stopping power.

Weight

The ideal weight of a handgun firearm should be no more than 1kg.

Calibre

The Calibre of a firearm is the internal size dimension of the gun barrel and will dictate what size round of ammunition to use with your firearm. Most modern hand guns are in the following calibre:

Revolvers .22, .32, .38, .44, .45
Automatic 9mm Parabellum, .45 ACP, 7.65mm ACP

Magazine capacity

Most modern automatic handguns have a large magazine capacity, which will greatly increase firepower and less reloading in a fire fight. It is important that you look for a handgun with a magazine capacity of more than 7 rounds.

Range accuracy

Range accuracy is important in your choice of firearm. Most modern automatic pistols with a 9mm calibre or above will perfectly suffice and are capable of engaging targets up to 75 meters. It is important to remember that when training, most target engagements will be within 50 meters.

Left handed capability

The majority of handguns are designed only with the right handed operator in mind.

However most weapons can be adapted to cater for left handed operators. Look for the following when choosing a handgun for left handed use:

Safety Catch on both sides of the pistol
Magazine Release Catch on both sides of the pistol

Sights

Most modern handguns have fixed blade foresights and notched back sight. For operations in poor visibility or darkness you will require sights that have Beta light capability.

Rules of Engagement

Rules of engagement (ROE) with any type of firearm must always be obeyed. You must always act within the laws of whatever country you are operating in. It is vital that you study or research that country's laws, especially with the use and carriage of firearms. Your ROE's should be clear, concise, and easily understood.

Most ROE's do have the same definitions:

Hostile Attack: *An attack or other uses of force against you the Close Protection Operative and others (your Principal/Client). Including force used directly to preclude or impede your duties.*
Hostile Intent: *The threat of imminent use of force against you the Close Protection Operative and others (your Principal/Client). Including threat to use force to preclude or impede your duties.*
Hostile Force: *Any civilian, paramilitary or Military force, or terrorist(s) with or without national designation that has committed a hostile act, or exhibited hostile intent or has been declared hostile by an appropriate authority.*
There are no fixed ROE's for the Close Protection Operative no matter where he operates. So how do we get around this problem?

In the United States a large number of the population are registered gun owners. These guns are usually kept in homes and are mainly for self defence or deterrent purposes.

The majority of these firearms owners adhere to the following rules:

1. Your firearm is for the protection of life only. Draw it solely in preparation to protect yourself or your Principal from the wrongful and life-threatening actions of others.

2. Know exactly when you can use your firearm. Your threat must have, or reasonably appear to have:

- The **ability** to inflict serious bodily injury (he is armed or reasonably appears to be armed with a deadly weapon).
- The **opportunity** to inflict serious bodily harm (he is physically positioned to harm you or your Principal with his weapon.
- His **intent** (hostile actions or words) indicates that he means to place you or your Principal in jeopardy or do you serious or fatal physical harm.
- When all of the above "attack potential" elements are in place simultaneously, then you are facing a reasonably perceived deadly threat that can justify an emergency deadly force response.

3. If you can run away - RUN! Just because you're armed doesn't mean you must confront a threat at gunpoint. Develop your situation awareness skills so you are alert to detect and avoid trouble altogether.

If you force confrontation you risk the possibility of you or your Principal being killed or suffering lifelong crippling/disfiguring physical injury, criminal liability and/or financial ruin from court actions brought against you.

RUN IF YOU CAN, FIGHT ONLY AS A LAST RESORT
(FLIGHT OR FIGHT)

4. Display your gun, go to jail. **In some Countries** you can expect to be arrested by Police at gunpoint, and charged with a crime anytime your concealed handgun is seen by another person in public, regardless of how unintentional or innocent or justified the situation might seem. Choose a method of carry that reliably keeps your gun hidden from public view at all times.

5. "Don't let your emotions get the better of you". If, despite your best efforts to the contrary, you find yourself in a heated dispute with another person while you're armed, never mention, imply or exhibit your gun for the purpose of intimidation or one-upmanship. You'll simply make a bad situation worse for yourself.

If you keep these simple rules in mind you will be a better Operator.

Commonsense, training, understanding of applicable laws and the consequences of engagement are the realities of the professional carriage of firearms.

APPENDIX 1

RELEVANT CLOSE PROTECTION ABBREVIATIONS AND TERMINOLOGY

RELEVANT CLOSE PROTECTION ABBREVIATIONS AND TERMINOLOGY

Abbreviations and Terminology used within the circuit of Close Protection is vast. The majority of abbreviations used are a direct descendant from Military and Police personnel who are involved within the Close Protection circuit.

Different Close Protection training organisations also use a mixture of their own terminology and abbreviations which can lead to some confusion.

Listed on the next pages are abbreviations and terminology which you may come across during your career as a Close Protection Operative.

CLOSE PROTECTION OPERATIVE OR CLOSE PROTECTION OFFICER?

The term officer means a President, vice President, secretary, treasurer or other senior official who performs functions with respect to any organisation whether incorporated or unincorporated. Therefore the terms Close Protection Officer or Personal Protection Officer should be avoided and the correct term is Close Protection Operative (CPO) or Personal Protection Operative (PPO).

The term Operative is a worker.

THE WALTER MITTY From Wikipedia, the free encyclopedia

"Walter is a fictional character in James Thurber's short story The Secret Life of Walter Mitty, published in 1941. Mitty is a meek, mild man with a vivid fantasy life: in a few dozen paragraphs he imagines himself a wartime pilot, an emergency-room surgeon, and a devil-may-care killer. He has become such a standard for the role that his name appears in several dictionaries".

WALTER AS A CPO

The Walter as a CPO is a person who will bluff and lie his or her way into any CP contract. They tend to boast about their fictitious Special Forces combat and Close Protection exploits. The Walter has a very bad habit of informing everyone and anyone who the person is that they are supposed to be protecting and what they are doing. This behaviour by the Walter could prove to be very dangerous for the Principal and the remainder of the CP team, if a real credible threat to the Principal gets hold of this information (especially the press).

"The secret of being tiresome is to tell everything".

The Walter is a dangerous person within any CP team and needs to be weeded out as soon as possible. They are totally un-professional and cannot be trusted.

HOW TO WEED OUT THE WALTER?
Ask him "what colour is the boat house" in Hereford?

2IC	SECOND IN COMMAND OF A CP TEAM OR NEXT IN LINE FROM TL
A&E	ACCIDENT & EMERGENCY DEPARTMENT
AAD	ANTI AMBUSH DRILL
AC	ARMOURED CAR
ACS	APPROVED CONTRACTOR SCHEME (UK SECURITY INDUSTRY AUTHORITY)
AES	ADVANCED ESCORT SECTION
AO	AREA OF OPERATIONS
APL	APPROVED PRIOR LEARNING
AS	AREA OF SAFETY (POLICE STATION, MILITARY BARRACKS ETC)
AST	ADVANCED SECURITY TEAM
AW	ADVANCED WORK
BG	BODYGUARD
BUGGS	ELECTRONIC SURVEILLANCE DEVICE PLACED IN A LOCATION TO LISTEN OR RECORD CONVERSATION (ILLEGAL)
BURNT	COMPROMISED
B-VEST	BALLISTICS PROOF VEST
CCTV	CLOSE CIRCUIT TELEVISION
CLIENT	THE PERSON WHO EMPLOYS THE SERVICES OF CP
CMP	COUNTER MEASURES AND PROCEDURES
CONTACT	STOP ALL RADIO TRAFFIC AND LISTEN (A PROBLEM) AND WAIT FOR FURTHER INSTRUCTIONS
COVOP	COVERT OPERATIONS
CP	CLOSE PROTECTION
CPO	CLOSE PROTECTION OPERATIVE
CPRR	COVERT PERSONAL ROLE RADIO (FOR USE DURING ESCORT DUTIES)
CQB	CLOSE QUARTER BATTLE
CV	CHASE VEHICLE
DOP	DROP OFF POINT

DOP's	DECEPTION OPERATIONS
DP	DANGER POINT *(OR CHOKE POINTS, LOCATION THAT WILL PLACE YOU AT A DISADVANTAGE)*
ECM	EXPLOSIVE COUNTER MEASURES
EEP	ENTRY EXIT POINT
ERV	EMERGENCY RENDEZVOUS
ES	EMERGENCY SERVICES
EX REG	SOMEONE WHO HAS BEEN A FORMER MEMBER OF SPECIAL FORCES
FA	FIRST AID
FBD	FAST BALL DEPLOYMENT
FCPO	FEMALE CLOSE PROTECTION OPERATIVE
FOXTROT	PHONETIC TERMINOLOGY FOR THE PRINCIPAL IS WALKING ABOUT
GPS	GLOBAL POSITIONING SYSTEM
HLS	HELICOPTER LANDING SITE
IA	IMMEDIATE ACTION
IAD	IMMEDIATE ACTION DRILL
IAP	IMMEDIATE ACTION PLAN
IED	IMPROVISED EXPLOSIVE DEVICE
INTREP	INTELLIGENCE REPORT
IS	INTERNAL SECURITY OR IN HOUSE SECURITY *(PERMANENT SECURITY STAFF TO THE VENUE)*
ISR	INTELLIGENCE SURVEILLANCE & RECONNAISSANCE
LIFT	STOP SURVEILLANCE ON SP
LZ	LANDING ZONE (MAINLY FOR HELICOPTERS)
MP	MILITARY POLICE
NCS	NET CONTROL STATION
OP's M	OPERATIONS MANAGER *(IN CHARGE OF AN OVERALL CP OPERATION)*
OP's ROOM	A ROOM FROM WHICH CP OPERATIONS ARE CONDUCTED

OVOP	OVERT OPERATIONS
PAPPS	PAPARAZZI (THE MEDIA)
PED	PERSONAL ESCORT DETAIL
PES	PERSONAL ESCORT SECTION
PJT	PRIVATE JET TRAVEL
POC	POINT OF CONTACT IN ORDER TO INFORM THE PRINCIPAL
POL	PETROL, OILS, LUBRICANTS (A METHOD OF CONDUCTING VEHICLE CHECKS FOR ROADWORTHINESS)
PPA	PRINCIPAL'S PERSONAL ASSISTANT
PPO	PERSONAL PROTECTION OPERATIVE
PRINCIPAL	THE PERSON THAT IS PROTECTED BY THE PPO
PRO	PUBLIC RELATIONS OFFICER
PTP	PRINCIPAL'S THREAT PROFILE
PUP	PICK UP POINT
PV	PRINCIPAL'S VEHICLE
RA	RISK ASSESSMENT
RL	REPORT LINE (FOR NAVIGATION AND LOCATION PURPOSES)
RST	RESIDENTIAL SECURITY TEAM
RV	RENDEZVOUS
SA	SITUATION AWARENESS
SAP	SECURITY ADVANCE PARTY
SF	SPECIAL FORCES (SAS/SBS/DELTA ETC)
SH	SAFE HOUSE A LOCATION OF SAFETY FOR THE PRINCIPAL (LOCATION IS SECRET)
SIA	SECURITY INDUSTRY AUTHORITY
SITREP	SITUATION REPORT
SOP	STANDARD OPERATIONAL PROCEDURES

SP	SUBJECT PERSON *(THE PERSON UNDER SURVEILLANCE)*
S-VEST	STAB PROOF VEST
TA	THREAT ASSESSMENT
TANGO	PHONETIC TERMINOLOGY FOR THE THREAT
TAPS	ELECTRONIC SURVEILLANCE DEVICE ATTACHED TO A TELEPHONE OR TELEPHONE LINE *(ILLEGAL)*
TCAT1	THREAT CATEGORY VIRTUALLY CERTAIN
TCAT2	THREAT CATEGORY HIGHLY PROBABLE
TCAT3	THREAT CATEGORY MODERATELY PROBABLE
TCAT4	THREAT CATEGORY LESS PROBABLE
TCAT5	THREAT CATEGORY PROBABILITY UNKNOWN
TL	TEAM LEADER
TOP	TYPE OF PRINCIPAL
TSCM	TECHNICAL SURVEILLANCE COUNTER MEASURES
VCP	VEHICLE CHECK POINT
VIP	VERY IMPORTANT PERSON
VOIED	VICTIM OPERATED IMPROVISED EXPLOSIVE DEVICE
VP	VULNERABLE POINT
VS	VENUE SECURITY
WALTER	A CPO THAT BOASTS OR GENERALLY LIES IN ORDER TO SUSTAIN THE STATUS OF CPO *(NO CONFIDENTIALITY)*

APPENDIX TWO

CONCLUSION

Conclusion

I started this book a long time ago as it is a struggle to get the time to sit down and write. There could have been more chapters and some parts could have contained more detail but the line had to be drawn somewhere.

During the period I spent compiling information for this book the industry has seen a great many changes. Whilst the principles of Close Protection have not altered; legislation, training and the business methods of Security Companies have progressed considerably. From regulation and quality management, to qualifications in training, the standards have improved. The employment methods of the bigger companies, including my own, have adapted to meet these changes.

Security is big business and as an industry will continue to grow.

Our society is constantly changing and security now impacts upon everyone's life to a greater or lesser degree. Throughout all this the CP industry must maintain its professional focus; that being the delivery of the highest level of training by qualified staff, and the provision of professional and suitable personnel to work within the industry.

Heed the advice about investing in training, but ensure the competence of your chosen training company and the relevance of the training to your current personal needs.

All training companies should be completely transparent. Whilst operational companies will be reluctant to discuss their business with you, this should not be the case with training companies.

To review:

Ensure the training company has a fully detailed website with original photography. The photography must demonstrate that it trains people regularly and that they are not just staged or re-constructed scenarios.

A company should always be able to send you a training brochure that demonstrates exactly what it provides (and the cost).

Establish what accreditation and standards of quality management it has.

Always be suspicious of Companies that 'guarantee work' without even having met you or trained you. If they have an operational web site that shows images of people in the public eye *(that they work with)* ensure they are the type of high level Principals you would expect to see if you are investing in them.

Most importantly, if you request a visit to the offices and training facilities this should always be allowed. Give sufficient notice and book an appointment, asking to view the facilities and meet the training team.

Undertaking multiple add-on courses with different companies is a good idea as it will demonstrate on your CV how dedicated you are in your career. This could also open potential doors with other employers and develop your personal *'loop'* of contacts.

Once qualified, you will have to turn your hand to all facets of Close Protection and may have to undertake other security related roles as your CP career develops. It can be a slow process but could lead to a new and rewarding career with a lifetime of employment at the top end of the security industry.

Over the many years that I have been involved with the CP business, I have been fortunate enough to meet many interesting people and worked and travelled to many different places.

That said, with every new person and place, the challenge is different and even today I am still learning.

Clearwater has worked with, and trained, hundreds of people since its inception in 1999. Many have remained very loyal to the company and I would like to take this opportunity to thank them for their commitment and service throughout the years.

For those reading this book who have not worked in the CP industry before, I hope that it has been an inspired read and encourages you to pursue this very rewarding career path.

Close Protection Training
from Clearwater Special Projects
A LEADING SUCCESS STORY IN THE CLOSE PROTECTION INDUSTRY

UK'S LEADING C. P. TRAINING CENTRE

INTERNATIONALLY RECOGNISED NAME

BRITISH SECURITY INDUSTRY
AUTHORITY (SIA) COMPLIANT

14 DAY RESIDENTIAL COURSE

150 HOURS OF SPECIALIST TRAINING

CLOSE PROTECTION FEDERATION
MEMBERSHIP

SPECIALIST ADVANCED COURSES
AVAILABLE

FOR FURTHER INFORMATION
PLEASE CONTACT:

TRAINING@CLEARWATERPROJECTS.COM
WWW.CLEARWATERPROJECTS.COM

PROVIDING CLOSE PROTECTION & SPECIALIST SECURITY SERVICES

CLEARWATER SPECIAL PROJECTS IS ONE OF THE HIGHEST RATED AND RESPECTED SPECIALIST CLOSE PROTECTION COMPANIES IN EUROPE

CLEARWATER SPECIAL PROJECTS IS A NAME SYNONYMOUS WITH VIP PROTECTION. FOR OVER 12 YEARS WE HAVE WORKED AN PROTECTED AN EXCLUSIVE ELEMENT OF SOCIETY. WE HAVE EARNED AN UNRIVALLED REPUTATION THAT HAS RECEIVED CRITICAL ACCLAIM. CLEARWATER HAS CONSTANTLY SET NEW BENCHMARKS AND ICONIC STANDARDS IN THE SPECIALIST SECURITY FIELD.

A FULL CLOSE PROTECTION SERVICE

WE ARE A SPECIALIST COMPANY AND WE OFFER THE FOLLOWING ADDITIONAL SUPPORT SERVICES TO OUR CLIENTS AS WELL:

- ADVANCE SECURITY PLANNING
- RESIDENTIAL SECURITY
- RISK & THREAT ANALYSIS
- SECURITY ASSESSMENTS
- PROTECTION & TRANSPORTATION OF ASSETS
- PROVISION OF EXECUTIVE VEHICLES & CHAUFFEURS
- SPECIAL BUSINESS EVENTS SECURITY MANAGEMENT
- MARITIME SECURITY & TRAINING
- SURVEILLANCE & EVIDENCE GATHERING
- CORPORATE & PRIVATE INVESTIGATION SERVICE

FOR FURTHER INFORMATION PLEASE DO NOT HESITATE TO CONTACT US.

ALL ENQUIRIES ARE IN THE STRICTEST OF CONFIDENCE.

SUPPORT@CLEARWATERPROJECTS.COM
WWW.CLEARWATERPROJECTS.COM

THE CLOSE PROTECTION FEDERATION

THE CLOSE PROTECTION FEDERATION WAS ESTABLISHED BY CLEARWATER SPECIAL PROJECTS IN 2005. WE RECOGNISED THE NEED FOR PROFESSIONAL GUIDANCE FOR EVEYONE WHO IS ENTERING THE CLOSE PROTECTION INDUSTRY.

AFTER YOU INVEST IN TRAINING, YOU NEED ON-GOING SUPPORT TO HELP YOU MAKE ACCURATE DECISIONS. WE CAN PROVIDE YOU WITH EXPERT GUIDANCE TO ASSIST YOU WITH ALL MATTERS THROUGHOUT THE DEMANDING CLOSE PROTECTION INDUSTRY.

IF YOU PASS YOUR TRAINING WITH CLEARWATER YOU WILL BE OFFERED MEMBERSHIP COMPLETELY FREE OF CHARGE - BY INVESTING IN US, WE ARE PREPARED TO INVEST BACK IN YOU.

WE CAN PROVIDE YOU WITH A 'MENTORING SERVICE' WHEN YOU NEED IT THE MOST. WE WILL PROVIDE YOU WITH YOUR OWN PRIVATE ACCESS CODE TO ENTER OUR WEBSITE AND SECURELY SUBMIT QUESTIONS TO OUR MANAGEMENT TEAM. WHEN WE RECEIVE YOUR QUESTION WE AIM TO RESPOND TO YOU WITHIN 24 HOURS (WITH EXCEPTION TO HOLIDAY PERIODS).

MEMBERSHIP OF THE FEDERATION IS SOMETHING TO BE PROUD OF AS YOU SIMPLY JUST CANNOT 'BUY IT' YOU HAVE TO EARN IT BY TRAINING WITH US. MEMBERSHIP OF THE FEDERATION IS TOTALLY UNIQUE WITH OVER 700 MEMBERS IT IS THE LARGEST OF ITS KIND.

WITH THE FEDERATION SUPPORT SERVICE, YOU WILL RECEIVE;
- CERTIFICATE OF MEMBERSHIP
- UNIQUE LOG IN ID NUMBER
- PIN BADGE
- PHOTOGRAPH OF THE CERTIFICATE BEING AWARDED TO YOU BY THE CLEARWATER MD AND HEAD OF TRAINING (SUBJECT TO AVAILABILITY)
- PROFILE WEBPAGE
- DISCOUNTS FROM OTHER CLEARWATER TRAINING COURSES

FOR FURTHER INFORMATION
PLEASE CONTACT:

ENQUIRIES@CLEARWATERPROJECTS.COM
WWW.CLEARWATERPROJECTS.COM

Covert Surveillance Training
from Clearwater Special Projects

Higher Professional Diploma (level4)

COVERT SURVEILLANCE IS AN IMPORTANT AND NECESSARY ELEMENT OF MODERN DAY SPECIALIST SECURITY AND IS AN EMERGING AND FAST GROWING SECTOR. THE SKILLS REQUIRED TO PROVIDE EFFICIENT AND EFFECTIVE COVERT SURVEILLANCE ARE SPECIALIST SKILLS IN THEIR OWN RIGHT.

THROUGHOUT OUR COURSE, YOU WILL LEARN THE ROLE AND TECHNIQUES OF A COVERT SURVEILLANCE OPERATIVE AND YOU WILL PRACTICALLY DEVELOP THE SKILLS REQUIRED TO BECOME A SUCCESSFUL OPERATIVE.

The Covert Surveillance Course Provides:

- TRAINING FOR THOSE IN THE SECURITY INDUSTRY
- OPPORTUNITIES FOR SURVEILLANCE OPERATIVES TO ACHIEVE A NATIONALLY RECOGNISED VOCATIONALLY SPECIFIC QUALIFICATION IN SPECIALIST SECURITY OPERATIONS
- OPPORTUNITIES TO ENTER EMPLOYMENT IN THE FIELD OF SPECIALIST SECURITY OR PROGRESS TO FURTHER VOCATIONAL QUALIFICATIONS AS PART OF THE PERSONAL DEVELOPMENT PROCESS

Who is the Course for?

PRIVATE INVESTIGATORS - FRAUD INVESTIGATORS - CUSTOMS & EXCISE & DEPT. - WORK & PENSIONS INVESTIGATORS - POLICE SURVEILLANCE OPERATORS & COVERT OP'S PLANNERS - CIVIL ENFORCEMENT OFFICERS - RETAIL STORE DETECTIVES - INVESTIGATION JOB ROLES WITHIN GOVERNMENT DEPARTMENTS - LICENSED OR QUALIFIED CLOSE PROTECTION OPERATIVES - ANY PERSON WHO HAS AN INTEREST IN EMBARKING ON A NEW CAREER

FOR FURTHER INFORMATION
PLEASE CONTACT:

SURVEILLANCETRAINING
@CLEARWATERPROJECTS.COM

WWW.CLEARWATERPROJECTS.COM

ncfe
Where Service Matters